THE BIRMINGHAM SIX:
AN APPALLING VISTA

COVER ILLUSTRATION: *Condemned Man,* oil painting by Louis le Brocquy, 1945.

The late Ernie O'Malley, author of *On Another Man's Wound* and *The Singing Flame,* writing in *Horizon* (London 1946) describes *Condemned Man:*

There is now no attempt to show things as what they look like, but a desire to show them as they are. This oil (painting) is a mental as distinct from a visual idea of a gaol, and it has particular interest in a country where gaol was a natural place in which to meet friends or to say goodbye. Broken interrelated planes, and the precision of all that surrounds the prisoner, make for a feeling of space. Ponderous weight of wall is indicated into which the prisoner is dovetailed; behind him a window, normally expected to give light, casts the dark shadow of oppression and hopelessness over part of his face. The prison wall is cut across to show him in stylized impersonal awkwardness as a cipher. The monotony of dull wall is brightened by a mauve book held in his hand, and by two small flowers which symbolize beauty, and, viewed in another way, an image of desire, a woman's face. A lantern-eyed cat, the only free being in the gaol, prowls beyond an iron door which leads to further cells, but yet moves carefully. High up, silhouetted against light beyond the envelopment of wall, is a beckoning figure, the sense of freedom.

THE BIRMINGHAM SIX: AN APPALLING VISTA

Editor:
OSCAR GILLIGAN

Sub Editors:
JÜRGEN SCHNEIDER
RALF SOTSCHECK

LITERÉIRE PUBLISHERS DUBLIN
DECEMBER 1990

First Published in 1990 by
LITERÉIRE
30 Sion Hill Road, Drumcondra, Dublin 9
under the auspices of

THE BIRMINGHAM SIX COMMITTEE
Usher House, 40/41 Usher Quay, Dublin 8

Hardback (limited ed. 100) ISBN 0 9517034 0 4
Paperback ISBN 0 9517034 1 2

All profits or royalties arising from the sale of this book
will go to a Trust Fund for the six men.

Set in Garamond 10 point on 11 body by
Diskon Technical Services Ltd. and
printed by the Elo Press Ltd., Dublin 8, Ireland
Book design by Patrick Funge
Cover design by The Graphiconies, Dublin

This book is dedicated to

Hugh Callaghan
Paddy Joe Hill
Gerry Hunter
Richard McIlkenny
Billy Power
John Walker

Contents

Preface

These men have served a dreadful sentence. The protests have come in thick and fast in the last few years and still, in November 1990, they lie in jail. When a range of writers and artists, journalists and intellectuals, individuals and organizations, as diverse as that represented here, can agree to speak with one voice against the conviction and imprisonment of the Birmingham Six, that in itself is a tribute to the strength of their case.

The importance of this case is no longer entirely about the fact of their innocence. That has been accepted for a very long time. It is the truly 'appalling vista' of the official subversion of justice on the pretext of protecting the national interest. Reality can be undermined by ignorance and by lies. Lord Denning would support such subversion in the name of what he is pleased to call justice, for the sake of avoiding the truth. All the contributors to this volume are bearing witness to the need to say what is truly appalling about that vista. Unless it is said, reality will be, in this instance, a fantastic assemblage of errors, lies and prejudices that will extend its bogus claims so far that the victims involved will never be able to regain their identity as persons. This volume is in honour and support of six particular persons whose lives and identities have been blighted but not erased by the nightmarish procedures of the English judicial system. Their names are Hugh Callaghan, Paddy Joe Hill, Gerry Hunter, Richard McIlkenny, Billy Power and John Walker. Long after the Birmingham Six are released, this book will serve as a powerful protest against what was done to them.

We want to know what really happened in this case, but we would also like to know that it could not happen again. Unfortunately, neither wish is likely to be granted. The higher the source of the corruption, the more effective the attempted cover-up. It is hard to forgive those who cannot be punished. The world knows that a great wrong was done and that it will not be rectified merely by releasing these men from custody and then trying to find some financial equivalent for fifteen years of their lives. There is a political and historical background to the case; in effect, relations between the United Kingdom and Ireland, as governed, then and since, by the crisis in the North. This is self-evident, both in accounting for the initial incrimination and imprisonment and for the timing and form of the eventual release. Again we have the scandal of the individual lives of these men erased at every critical juncture. They simply became victims of political decisions that were indifferent to ethical considerations.

It is to be hoped that this volume will appear after the release of these men. But it must also be said that the impressive display of support for their cause in recent times would have been more effective had it come earlier. In the days immediately after their conviction and for a long time subsequent to that, few were interested in this case except the relatives of the victims. In August 1975, Mr Justice Bridge told the six men that they stood convicted 'on the clearest and most overwhelming evidence I have ever seen of the crime of murder'. It is remarkable that such a statement went unchallenged for so long. That is another reason for the continued incarceration of these men. Protests only became vociferous when protest became safe and respectable. It is not only the whole political and judicial system that stands condemned. It is the silence of all of us who now speak and were then dumb. At least that initial silence has been broken by courageous and committed people. This volume, thanks to the generosity and commitment of its contributors, is an echo of and a tribute to their efforts. It will commemorate an injustice but it won't stop further injustices being committed. It is the early protests that are most effective in doing that. Out of them grows the melancholy need to assert again the priority of justice, the reality of the individual person and the intolerability of victimization and lies as features of any political or social system. The names of the Birmingham Six will be remembered for a long time. The names of those who had them put away will be forgotten or will remain unknown. That should not be; but then, none of this should ever have been.

Seamus Deane,
November 5, 1990.

Acknowledgements

The generosity and co-operation of many different people and organizations have made the publication of this book possible:

All those who ensured that the entire contents of *The Birmingham Six: An Appalling Vista* were given for publication completely free of charge.

Patrick Funge of Elo Press who not only did not charge for printing costs but also completed his task within a remarkably short time scale.

Margaret Doyle and Níall Funge of Diskon Technical Services who set the book with great care and attention to detail.

Charlie O'Neill of Graphiconies who designed the cover free of charge.

Anthony Farrell of Lilliput Press who gave advice on technical aspects of the publication.

Philip MacDermott of Poolbeg Press and Eugene Mallon of Cathair Books who both gave helpful advice.

Pearse Hutchinson, Maria E. Clay-Jorde, Karen Margolis, Hans-Christian Oeser, and Jutta Shannon who kindly undertook translations.

Carol Coulter who offered her summarized version of Lord Gifford's opening speech at the Appeal Hearing.

Robert Gilligan who first suggested the idea of the book and gave help at different points along the way.

Máire Gilligan and Muriel Saidléar who gave vital practical assistance.

Acknowledgement of Publications

The Editor and Publisher wish to acknowledge the services of the following contributors:

Nanni Balestrini's piece is from the English version of his book *The Unseen* translated by Liz Heron. Coypright Verso, 1989. London.

Terence Brown's *Coming from Nowhere,* the copyright of which is retained by him.

Jörg Burkhard's *Wee-Weeeee-Wee-Weeeee Nature's Nature Technical Shadows* is from his book *Live in Zombombie* published by Verlag Peter Engstler, 1990.

Gertrude Degenhardt's illustrations are reproduced from her collection of dry point etchings *Farewell to Connaught* published by Edition GD Klusterstrasse Mainz – Gonsenheim.

Peter de Rosa's excerpt from *Rebels: The Irish Rising of 1916* which appeared in the *Irish Independent* of April 13-14 1990, are reproduced by kind permission of Independent Newspapers Ltd.

Paul Durcan's poem 'Amnesty' is from his collection *Daddy Daddy* published by the Blackstaff Press, Belfast.

Terry Eagleton's *Wild Justice* concludes with an extract from his play *Saint Oscar* which was published and produced by the Field Day Theatre Company, Derry.

Brian Friel for an excerpt from his play *Dancing at Lughnasa* which was published by Faber and Faber. Copyright Brian Friel, 1990.

The excerpts from Lord Gifford's opening speech at the Appeal Hearing are reproduced by kind permission of *The Irish Times.*

Michael Hartnett's poems *Sneachta Gealaí* and *Early One Morning* have been previously published by Gallery Press, Oldcastle, Co. Meath.

Seamus Heaney for an excerpt from his play *The Cure at Troy. A version of Sophocles' Philoctetes* which was published by Faber and Faber, 1990.

Pearse Hutchinson's poem *Amhrán Bréagach* is from his new collection *The Soul that Kissed the Body* published in November 1990 by Gallery Press, Oldcastle, Co. Meath.

Elfriede Jelinek's *The Small Fall of the Damned* first appeared in the book Zeit-Museum der 100 Bilder, published by Insel Verlag (1989) Frankfurt, Main.

Klaus Jünschke's *Into the Free Part of Diez* is from his book *Spätlese* published by Verlag Neue Kritik, 1988. Frankfurt/Main.

Robert Kee's *Three Unwise Judges* first appeared in *The Times* on January 30, 1988 and is reproduced (slightly abridged) by kind permission of The Times Newspapers Ltd., London.

Ludovic Kennedy's *I Accuse* first appeared in *The Sunday Times* on February 25, 1990 and is reproduced by kind permission of The Times Newspapers Ltd. London.

Marie-Thérèse Kerschbaumer's excerpt is from her book *Der Schwimmer* published by Alfred Winter Verlag 1976 Salzburg.

Thomas Kinsella's translations into English verse of poems by Séatrún Céitinn, Padraigín Haicéad, Daibhí Ó Bruadair and Aogán Ó Rathaille were published in *An Duanaire 1600-1900: Poems of the Dispossessed* edited by Seán Ó Tuama and published by The Dolmen Press, Mountrath, Co. Laois.

Edna O'Brien's poem *When Dogs Bark* is from her recently produced first volume of poetry *On the Bone* published by The Greville Press, Emscote Lawn, Warwick, England. Copyright Edna O'Brien 1989.

Julia O'Faolain's story *Mad Marga* was first published in *Triquarterly '50* in 1981 and subsequently in her collection *Daughters of Passion* published by Penguin Books in 1982.

Nuala O'Faolain's *Can the Judges Understand Them?* which first appeared on December 10, 1987, and Liam Ó Muirthile's *Upon the Mercy of Government,* which first appeared on October 26 1989, and are reproduced by kind permission of *The Irish Times.*

Liam Ó Muirthile's poem *Ceathrar Ghuildford* first appeared in *Alpha* in December 1989.

Seán Ó Tuama's poem *Christy Ring* (Irish version) is from his collection *An Bás Tir na nÓg* published by Coiscéim, Dublin.

Gabriel Rosenstock's translations into Irish of two poems by Seamus Heaney: *Bye-Child* and *Punishment* first appeared in his collection *Conlán* published by Coiscéim, Dublin 1989.

A. J. P. Taylor's essay is from his book *How Wars End* published by Hamish Hamilton Ltd. 1985. London.

Macdara Woods's poem *Man of the Doorstep* is from his collection *The Hanged Man was not Surrendering* published by the Dedalus Press, Dublin in 1990.

KADER ASMAL

Innocence Violated

The political culture of long-established states is based on a number of myths which provide the necessary legitimation for policies which are often perceived by the victims as being arbitrary, capricious, violent and self indulgent. The impartiality of law enforcement and the even-handedness of the law are two examples of what 'superior' cultures would like to be remembered for. But when political and security considerations challenge the basis of such pretensions, the first offensive is against those values which protect the individual.

Removal of *habeas corpus*, packed juries, defence of the realm legislation and special forces have been the preferred weapons wherever there are struggles for freedom or social tension. But by and large the equilibrium is maintained on the scales of justice in the heart-lands of the metropolitan territory for fear of perverting the institutions cherished by those who live by that value system.

The case of the Birmingham Six must therefore raise serious doubts about the very nature of the judicial process in Britain and the capacity of the legal system to cherish innocence, at least as far as Irish accused are concerned. Few institutions emerge with unblemished reputations since the Six accused were arrested following the dreadful bombings in 1974 in Birmingham. The forensic scientist whose evidence was crucial was subsequently found to be discredited; the police who extracted confessions following threats and beatings were found to have been incriminated in 'fitting-up' suspects in a variety of cases; the most distinguished British judge since the war could not contemplate a successful civil action by the Six because their victory would subvert and destroy the criminal trial which resulted in their conviction; an Appeal which cavalierly and in an ill-tempered manner rejected new evidence of courageous public servants whose consciences would not allow them to remain silent and which effectively shifted the burden of proof on to the accused; a political administration more concerned to save face, confirming George Orwell's view that in certain historical contests justice gives way to expediency.

The violation of innocence in the face of overwhelming evidence pointing to the lack of involvement of these men, has destroyed confidence in the capacity of English justice to right the terrible wrongs done to the Six. Public opinion, invoking international standards of human rights, must now ensure that they are freed, not only from prison but from any imputation of guilt.

SASCHA ANDERSON

Die Erziehung des Sohnes von Hunger und Stimme

aufs ende gerichtet, der herbst die sinne das satte
fleischverfressene grün. ich, herr baron
versprach axtschlag auf axtschlag TEEZEIT AUF TEEZEIT
RETTE DIE JUNGFRAU. SO SINKE IHR PREIS
(DER FRÜHLING
DES BAUMS DES VERGESSENS) während das mobile
einsatzkommando in den himmel der ruhe vor dem sturm aufsteigt.
geiselnahme der titel. zum beispiel
das geheimnis der todesinsel
inzest voneinander entferntester uhrzeiten.

The Education of the Son by Hunger and Voice

towards the end directed, the autumn the senses the rich
flesh-gorging green. I, lord baron
promised axe-blow upon axe-blow TEATIME UPON TEATIME
SAVE THE VIRGIN. SO SINK HER PRICE (THE SPRING
OF THE TREE OF FORGETTING) while the mobile
operations commando climbs into the heaven of
the still before the storm.
hostage-taking the title. for example
the secret of the island of the dead
incest of the clock times furthest away from each other.

(Translated from the German by Karen Margolis.)

Jewish Jetset

von da hinabgesehn, wo wir uns ohne schulden treffen.
ein pferd mit sattel, doch sein reiter nicht. und ich mich
nicht mit mir und du dich mit von deiner jugend unberührten
interpreten NUR DER PAARIG GESPALTNE BERG SCHUHE.
NUR DAS
GEWALTIGE BABEL DER WEGE. NUR DIE HÖLLISCHE
FLÜGELTÜR.
EIN ELFEINHALBTAUSENDER das böse trägt von jetzt an keine
stiefel
mehr. zwar wachsen die gebete mit, doch werden sie nicht
größer. so fand den weg der ort. wo ich vieh bin
war ich fleischtransport.

Jewish Jetset

seen from up there, where we meet without debts.
a horse with saddle, but not his rider, and I
don't with myself and you do with interpreters unaffected by
your youth ONLY THE DIVIDED SHOE
MOUNTAINS. ONLY THE
MIGHTY BABEL OF THE PATHS. ONLY THE
HELLISH SWING DOOR.
AN ELEVEN-AND-A-HALF-THOUSANDER
the evil from now on wears no boots
anymore, the prayers might grow accordingly, but they won't get any
bigger. so found the spot the path. where I am cattle
was I flesh transport.

(Translated from the German by Karen Margolis.)

NANNI BALESTRINI

Excerpt from *The Unseen*

The light above the door is bright and it hurts my eyes I'll have to lie on my stomach to sleep or put the pillow over my face but I wasn't sleepy and so I started thinking about the comrades who by this time will all have mobilized around my arrest they'll all be having discussions at the centre they'll be doing things to get me out of here they'll be talking to the lawyer I can imagine how the news got round fast immediately after my arrest telephone calls appointments meetings by this time the whole movement will already know about my arrest and now they'll all be organizing for everything that has to be done when I think about the comrades I feel a bit better as soon as I'm able to write I'll bring them right up-to-date it's years since I've written a letter I try to think of everyone I must write to there are too many better to write collective letters

it comes into my mind that I'll also have to write to my parents I think of them there at home anxious worried by this business that's come so unexpectedly it was unexpected for me too even if it crossed my mind occasionally but though possible it seemed so remote and in any case it wasn't worth dwelling on it so this too is why I'm now so stunned and dumbfounded and most of all so unprepared now that it's happened but my parents couldn't even imagine that I could get mixed up with the law as far as they were concerned I was a being from another planet a crackpot a dreamer but harmless incapable of hurting anybody I hoped the comrades had gone to see them to calm them down to give them a bit of reassurance I really haven't a clue how to write I had no idea how to communicate with them

the spy-hole is opened again it's the sergeant of the guard who stares at me in silence without a word after a moment or two I jerk my head as if to enquire what's wrong he remains silent a bit longer then he asks me you wouldn't be the one who killed our warrant-officer two months ago I answer that I've never killed anyone and that I'm there through a mistake that soon it will all be cleared up the sergeant gives me a surprised look and says that all the ones like me he's ever come across so far never say they've nothing to do with it and that they've done nothing they only say they're proud to be communists struggling against the state whereas it's the non-politicals who always say they're innocent even when they've been caught red-handed

i'm put out by this I wouldn't like to have made a blunder I feel as if I've broken some kind of protocol that must exist among comrades in prison meanwhile the sergeant starts telling me that the murdered warrant-officer was a decent fellow who had children and a family that what the people who murdered him put on the leaflet wasn't true at all that he didn't have a gang that beat people up that he'd never beaten anybody up or had anybody beaten up that he was a good humane fellow and so on and he goes on to explain that they're all decent fellows that it's wrong to hold anything against them that you have to understand that they're doing that job just to get by because they have to feed their families

that it's not their fault if there's unemployment that they're the first to want to get out of there if they get a chance of anything else that they've come from the south where there's no work and they've had no education and this is why those are the only jobs they can get but they do the job with respect for others and that it's not them we should hold things against because they're only carrying out orders and they're compelled to carry them out that it's the politicians we should have it in for and not them they're in agreement that things as they are disgusting and that they need to be changed because they too realize that things can't go on like this but we shouldn't go shooting at them but at who's really in charge who's really to blame for the situation the sergeant goes on like this and there's no end to it

while he was going on like this it sounded to me just like the same reasoning the same things that the blacklegs doing overtime were saying when we went to picket in front of the factories to stop them from going in but here on top there was the naïvety with which he said those things which made it evident that they weren't his own ideas they were ideas he'd picked up talking to comrades they were crude basic propaganda clichés and all this became his justification but the point was his reason for telling me all this this was the point and clearly he was doing it because he was afraid of ending up like that colleague of his who'd been killed and he wanted to keep on the good side of anybody who directly or indirectly could be a threat to him

and the way things were at the moment I had a kind of advantage over him I knew nothing at all about prison then but I was beginning to guess that it was a different world with different rules and a different logic that I had to learn as quickly as possible because in there along with the air that smelled of shit and piss and of vomit you also got a whiff of constant fear of threat of danger so it was better to be cautious to be careful better an excess of caution than a mistake that could have consequences I couldn't even imagine I felt the danger instinctively even in what the sergeant said maybe he'd been sent there to sound me out to see what sort of guy I was and how I saw things and so the best thing to do was not to give myself away to be vague about things but then even if I'd wanted to what could I have said in reply to that speech of the sergeant

so all I did was look at him until he stopped talking because a guard was calling him I hoped I wouldn't see him come back but he'd left the spy-hole open and in fact a minute later he was back looking through it but before letting him get started again I asked him if he could give me some matches because they'd left me my cigarettes but without matches I could't light any then the sergeant of the guard tells me that the rules forbid those in isolation from having matches because there's already been a case of someone going crazy and setting light to the mattress which is foam rubber and burns in minutes and gives off smoke that suffocates you in no time and if this happens at night when the keys to the cells are up in the rotunda there's the risk of a fire that would burn everyone inside the cell

when you want a light call the guards knock on the spy-hole and they'll give you a light seeing that the sergeant was so ready to give me information I also ask him how long I have to stay there in isolation he's astonished by the question he didn't know how long I had to stay in isolation he only knew I was in judicial isolation pending interrogation and that until then I could have no contact with anyone neither inside nor outside the prison I couldn't go out into the sun nor go into the exercise yard with anyone else not even with anyone else in isolation like me and I couldn't talk to my lawyer or my parents until I'd been questioned and since I was a political isolation was even more severe these were the orders he'd received from his superiors who in their turn had received them from the magistrates

and by way of going back to the earlier conversation he gives me a wink you see it's not us who've put you in these conditions we're not the ones who make these decision do you see who's making them I ask him how long it usually is before the interrogation with the judge and he tells me that it can take up to forty days from the day of arrest I think to myself that it hasn't even been half a day and I'm already in this state I can't even imagine forty days the sergeant of the guard gives me a light and then to show him that I don't want to talk any more I turn my back on him and I go towards the bed then he closes the spy-hole and goes away I stretch out and slowly smoke the cigarette savouring every puff and I fall asleep without even noticing

I wake up again with the spy-hole suddenly being opened a fattish face taps on the door with a biro and twice says the word shopping the guard is holding a clipboard with a list of foodstuffs and other things on it I ask him what I can order and rather impatiently he says how should I know I think of cigarettes and mineral water and order that he's holding a form with my name and my registration number and he writes down cigarettes and mineral water and then shuts the door again saying he'll bring me the stuff the next day I lie down on the bed again for a bit but I can't get back to sleep then I get up and I beat on the door with the palm of my hand no one comes then I shout guard guard two or three times the spy-hole opens and a guard gives me a light with a lighter and then closes it again

when the spy-hole opens it seems for a moment that I'm not locked in that hole and for a moment it makes me feel better in the evening the prisoner who brings the food comes back some overcooked pasta with a sour red sauce one forkful with the plastic fork and I leave it all on the plate and go back to sleep now and then in the night you can hear screams from the adjoining cells you can hear people calling the guard who doesn't come the light is left on and if I'm lying on my back the glare's straight in my eyes and while I'm awake during one of the regular cell-check patrols when they open the spy-hole I ask the guard to put out the light but he says he can't that the rules say it has to stay on

a night of fitful sleep with that bright light on all the time then it's morning the first cell-check patrol comes around early and then the working prisoner with the watered down white coffee and a piece of bread half and hour later they open my door for exercise the guards outside in the corridor each carry a long truncheon and one of them uses it to point to the small door at the end of the corridor before I go outside he asks me if I want to empty the bucket but I say no the idea of lifting that stinking pail disgusts me I go through the little door followed by the guards with their truncheons we enter a kind of narrow tunnel and at the end it leads out to the open air into a kind of narrow corridor between two high walls where there's only room for one person at a time at the end it opens out into a small courtyard with an area no bigger than a few square yards surrounded by high walls

they open the last gate at the end of the left and then they lock it on me again above it there's an iron grating and through it I can see a part of one wing of the prison with the windows screened by vents broom handles with television aerials tied on to them stick out through some of the vents I think how those are the cells where I'll go after isolation I'm not clear what difference there is but at any rate there's television I don't know how many years it is since I've watched television but now I have a great desire to watch television to see anything at all with images and sounds anything at all that comes from outside anything at all with faces colours words

(Translated from the Italian by Liz Heron.)

ROBERT BALLAGH

My Earliest Experiences of London

My earliest experiences of London could be defined in terms of unbridled excitement. I used to revel in popping over to briefly immerse myself in the atmosphere that went to make what was called 'Swinging London'. I remember with nostalgia and affection, mini-skirts, hipster jeans, floral ties, denim caps, mod hair styles, the Beatles and above all the 'dedicated followers of fashion' immortalized by the Kinks. In fact my abiding memory is one of excitement, colour and friendliness. Tragically all that is indeed a memory, for if I was asked to nominate a colour for the London of today it would be grey and that greyness shot through the despairing faces of homeless young people, unfortunately many with Irish accents. However, for me, the most objectionable aspect of visiting London today is to find that, as an Irish person, I am treated differently than any other visitor. Not for me the luxury of walking straight off the airplane into the terminal building, no, instead, hail, rain or shine, I have to walk across the tarmac to a bus to be driven half way round the airport before being delivered before the scrutiny of the British special branch. Final admittance to the terminal building is permitted only after such surveillance. If for some reason I happen to arouse any suspicion I could end up spending seven days and nights in custody at Her Majesty's pleasure, all without any charge whatsoever. In order to provide this welcome for Irish visitors the British government has had to seek a derogation from Article 5 of the European Convention on Human Rights. All such harassment is made possible through the employment of the Prevention of Terrorism Act, which ostensibly, was introduced to deal with political violence, but its real purpose is, in fact, far more sinister. In my opinion the Prevention of Terrorism Act is just one weapon in a psychological armoury aimed at criminalizing the Irish people and, as a consequence, forcing them to accept a primary sense of guilt over the seemingly intractable 'troubles' in the North of Ireland.

If 30,000 Irish troops were on the streets of Lancashire underpinning, by force of arms, an aspiration by the Liverpool Irish to be part of the Irish nation and if this aspiration was sustained through the use of army raids on housing estates, the killing of children by plastic bullets and the unjust jailing of people through the use of emergency legislation, if this imagined scenario was a fact, then perhaps, we, the Irish, might be expected to feel a profound sense of guilt, but of course this fictional scenario is a nonsense, so why do we still feel guilty?

We feel guilty, because we are propagandized, day and night, by the British establishment and also tragically no effective response has been articulated by either the Irish government or the Irish media, in fact sometimes quite the opposite. I believe that the time has come for us to reject the imposition of this sense of guilt or at least to demand that the responsibility for the present tragic situation be borne fairly by all parties.

Also we must campaign actively against all measures that have been employed in Britain against the Irish, for it is only when there is true equality before the law for all citizens that there can be any real basis for a meaningful relationship between the Irish and British peoples.

MARY BENSON

A Redundant Person

This morning I rescued a small beetle,
the kind that eats the heart of a rose
and thumps against lighted window-panes at night.
It lay on its back on a smooth stone surface
and kicked and kicked. Carefully
I turned it over, set it free.

And this morning I sat sunbathing by the pool,
surrounded by wide lawns and woods and birdsong.
After swimming bare-breasted in the blue water
I basked in an illusion of youth, breathing deep, Zen-aspiring,
broke off to apply sun lotion to my skin
and in the leaf-softened light of the changing-room,
admired the reflection of my glowing face.

I returned to the pool, saw a man running toward me,
a black man with bandaged head and ragged clothes.
He loped across the immaculate green grass
toward me.
To rape? To strangle?
I kept on walking
And sat again in a reclining chair by the pool.
He stopped. Unshaven, filthy,
he sat down next to me as if an invited guest.
I said, 'You can't just sit there like that.'
He did not move, looked dazed.
'Are you all right?' I asked.
He mumbled unintelligibly. 'Work,' I thought I heard
and seized on it.
'If you go to the back of the house,' I urged,
'Right round to the back.'
He got up meekly and, clutching his tattered pants,
shambled across the lawn, heading for the opulent, ugly house.
Would he burgle? Burn?
He veered toward a slope of fresh-cut hay
and vanished beyond clipped hedges,
leaving me by the pool,
surrounded by lawns and woods and birdsong in the sunlight.
Was he ill? Drunk? Was he hungry? Hunted?

Would the staff speak harshly? Send for the police? Shoot?
Later – no, they had not seen an unwell-looking man wanting work.

He could have been Jesus. He could have been death.
Garbage, he was garbage. Our rubbish, a redundant person.
His life approached mine and left me, scorched.

TERENCE BROWN

Coming from Nowhere

Most Irish people are convinced of the significance of place. For it is one of the great Irish assumptions rarely if ever questioned that personal characteristics of great subtlety and implication are to be attributed to geographic origins. Conversations of labyrinthine complexity can be sustained on the precise differences to be observed between Corkonians and their fellow citizens from a neighbouring kingdom. Where are you from is, therefore, a question in Ireland loaded with analytic potential, one's answer as likely to provoke interpretative discussion as the revelation of an astrological sign. It can get pretty tedious, especially if like myself you don't think there's much to the whole thing. Most of us enjoy astrology in moderation. It can be flattering to have someone take enough interest in us to explain that Capricornians are depressive but ambitious. Much more than such social amusement quickly gets boring. I find the same with this Irish business about place. Recently in a kind of desperation, I've taken to telling people in answer to the inevitable question, that I'm from Co. Down. For it's damn embarrassing not really to be *from* anywhere, in that almost metaphysical way so many Irish people seem to feel they're from wherever. Much more so than having to admit you don't know your astrological sign or, very mysteriously, don't actually have one.

Co. Down has worked well for me. In company when the matter, as it almost always does, comes up at least I can pass muster. But few enough people in Dublin know much about that part of the country except that it once had a great football team and tends to figure in ghastly news reports a fair bit. I'm spared prolonged reflections on the exact constituents of the Co. Down man's psyche. Which is a relief not only because I find such speculations less than convincing but because I know my claim to be from Co. Down is pretty much unfounded.

You see in the 1950s when I grew up there, Hollywood, Co. Down wasn't really anywhere. For nobody told me about it. In that crucial period of about ten years between earliest consciousness and puberty I don't suppose I heard anything whatever about the place I was living in. My parents who had worked for over a decade as missionaries in China were full of stories about the Japanese war, adventures and catastrophes that had befallen them there, people and places they had recently known. For years after the Communist Revolution they hoped that some way could be found for them to return to a country they had loved and whose language they had so arduously acquired. The house I remember as full of visitors from abroad (one even a Chinese bishop in splendid regalia) Chinese ornaments and bric-a-brac (most of it in fact worthless for the Japanese army had appropriated almost everything my parents had possessed) and talk, talk, talk. Of Mao, Chiang Kai-shek. The long march, the Boxer Rebellion. Each year in the town, bands in orange sashes gathered to the sound of great drums. I hadn't a clue what they were at. And my parents certainly didn't enlighten me, their minds marching to a different and very distant drum. School was equally silent on the matter and on much else. My prep. school years I remember as a haze of cardboard milk-bottle tops, welfare-state orange juice, rote-learning, ink-wells and that ubiquitous map at the front of our classrooms which showed most of the world in red. I had a globe at home similarly coloured and I remember gazing at it in wonder that as tiny a spot as Northern Ireland belonged to so all-encompassing an Empire. And China where I had been born was huge. Neither map nor globe showed my birthplace. One day the Minister for Education from Stormont visited us and we waited in the rain for two hours – nobody told us why we had to endure the soaking. On another, we waved paper Union Jacks as the new Queen of England (was it really she?) sped by our school gate. Again nobody explained a thing. But we'd all got a silver spoon when she had been crowned. For years I kept it in a tin box along with a Chinese million dollar note that the Nationalist government had issued in the inflationary months before its collapse. Each was as exotic and inexplicable as the other.

So I lived in an environment that was for me bereft of codes – for no one was decoding those that lay all about and you can't do that yourself. So my imagination has as a primary possession a place about which I knew nothing. I don't know if this accounts for the intensity with which it's still present to me, or whether everyone is so affected by the place in which they first came to consciousness. But what I recall is a line of hills, a lough with lights twinkling on the farther shore, a pigeon-filled wood that in Spring was almost painfully green, a rookery that sent me to sleep and woke me, the sound all through my childhood of a steam-train puffing out of a station and on foggy winter nights the eerie sirens of the ships heading out into the Irish sea. Much later I was to read Louis MacNeice's poem 'Carrickfergus' with its recollection:

> Our lights looked over the lough to the lights of Bangor
> Under the peacock aura of a drowning moon

and I who had looked across the same lough at the lights of the poet's home town felt a flood of nostalgia and a rare sense of belonging. But any sense of belonging I may have developed in adult life, as distinct from loyalties, duties, personal involvements, commitments, hasn't really anything to do with the place I have inadequately evoked here. The moment's community of feeling MacNeice's poem gave me was, I think, simply due to the realization that the place I so intensely remembered had also affected another person similarly. For what my own place, known with such intimate ignorance, with such exacting purity, does for me is to remind me of what the Czech novelist Milan Kundera calls 'The Unbearable Lightness of Being'. By this he means that since everything happens only once 'We can never know what to want, because living only one life, we can neither compare it with our previous lives nor perfect it in our lives to come'. So my primal place speaks of absolute transience. I can't go back. For of course in secondary school, at last, a devoted and unusual (for that time in the North) teacher told us Hollywood had once been Ard-mac-Nasca, a centre of Druid worship, that in Christian times an abbey was founded there to enshrine a copy of the Bible given to an Irish saint by Pope Gregory, that one of the founders of Oxford, John de Sacro Bosco was from our Holy Wood and that the Maypole in the town centre probably dated from the seventeenth century. So names that had simply rested like stones in the bottom of the mind – My Lady's Mile, Nun's Walk, the Palace Barracks – were raised to the surface of rational understanding and an interest was generated that would take me to other 'places', Derry, Dublin and to the study of Irish literature and history.

But that coastline, that lough, garden, those childhood sounds challenge the mind to a fundamental recognition. Mythologies of place are a kind of emotional kitsch by which we try to stabilise the flux of our lives into consolatory patterns. But none of us come from anywhere really, for the places from which we believe we derive have long ago vanished. Now is where we come from.

JÖRG BURKHARD

Wee-Weeeee-Wee-Weeeee
Nature's Nature Technical Shadows

Like the hare hedgehog is already there out he gets 't beats me on German soil no/ TV should never ever be switched off brown mown lawn sods villages outskirts autist's/ bahnen tronic colourisation WILLIAMDAVIDCHARLIE weeksdaysclouds passing/ WILLIAMDAVIDCHARLIE WilliamDavidCharlie andsoon diguiding out of the/ world it never as beautiful again beyond recollection the dazzle nothing never no/ FUCKING WAY 2 from the tape recorder run-down batteries DEUTSCHLAND, EISIG KATERLAND hififi/ from the auto bahn white noise traffic rush speedbeach/ from loudspeakers or windows auto bahn sea roaring buy and/ sell endlessly AND WHAT ABOUT THE DIRECTION OF FLOW NATURALLY ENERGY FLOWS FROM SURPLUS TO SCARCITY nature's/ nature nature's Mister Scarcity: '. . . eh, is it afterall an ex expr expression of the in/ ina inability to com comprehend the su su surroundings an' explain 'em pro properly eh' DRIVE/ EAT SEE TEE VEE FUCK ff ff fast forward;/ '. . . studying the noise quite oftenly reduced a simple root/ -mean-square the ruleless temporal/ independence a noise ratio for example in the following expression . . . eh. givit to me missus/ Schramm. . .' Mister Scarcity hypertonically: 'an and the noise is prima-/rily prima linea eh seen as being unwanted one should never forget that/ speakin about noise reality separates from its laws, doesn't it?' cutting Denise Schramm short ANDITISTHEREFOREIMPOSSIBLE all in Chorus COMETH A BIRD FLOWN SITS DOWN TO EXPERIENCE SOMETHING FROM NOISE ON TRANSMISSION TECHNIQUE he she it DRIVES TRAM DRIVE rain DRIVE MerzedeSS onehundredandninety SS 'the same procedure with Beethoven an exact tinnitus blue noise green noise golden noise orange noise field-grey noise. . .' drive eat see tee vee fuck ff ff fast forward BREAK then there is nothing for a long time Hallo Mister Dust cometh loan and bulding association's warden Mister Dust soul and semtex of your party making things go knocking down the residential area FRG building site researched bananareality binary mini-loud-/ speaker-voice from Japanese dictator: 'Shall I tell you something?'/ 'YYess!' 'You talk too much!' Fifth of May Fifty-Five not/ forgotten to the second Muss O'Lini's delivery the new railway-station special/ opening ceremony ten tracks passengers with bulky luggage rolling material NO EXIT/ railroad police officer Manfred BeiSSman with

Alsatian police dog 'Pansy' shortly/ shows himself NOBODY ELSE outside the first snow is falling to comit suicide/ is visually in brackets QUALITY urged upon socially undesirable manpower by General Public Design G P D the chimney/ smokes syph do it yourself isolation ward stand down march, march! watch the Doc/ of the ex-medical orderly: 'do U lie on the button/ the rest of your buddy is terribly sore HALLOH MISTER DUST!'/ Hallo Mister Dust!' 'Halloh MisMistMister Dust/ Emergency call nineninenine/ divisional-officer of the incendiary-brigade Mike Spritzle: 'Adolf one pleeease, comin, pleease in Ballymun/ a lamp-post is burnin' o'er Roger Crack' Addoff wuuunn/ got it over Roger crackcack. . .' periphery. people's/ set ROGER OVER ROGER weeeee-weee-weeeee-weee welding/ changes to merges with is superimposed by low-flying aircraft-frequency multicoloured noise simultaneously heli-/ copter do it youself drilling-plant continuous sine waves tinnitus 17kHZ O'ER CRAACK K K k k k

(Translated from the German by Jürgen Schneider.)

ANTHONY W. CLARE

The Courage to Admit to Being in the Wrong

The ability to forgive, a wise old psychiatrist once observed to me, is a cardinal feature of mental stability. The ability to admit to being in the wrong is another. We all make mistakes. As Bernard Shaw remarked, 'A life spent in making mistakes is not only more honourable but more useful than a life spent doing nothing'. Yet many of us manifest a remarkable unwillingness to acknowledge we have made a mistake. It is as if our very identity is threatened by such an admission of mortality. Faced with incontestable evidence that we are in the wrong, we wriggle, evade, insist on advancing an elaborate rationalisation that rewrites the facts so as to establish that somehow or other we have been right all along. Acknowledging error becomes akin to acknowledging a dreadful personal defect. An inability to confess error reflects an infantile need to be omnipotent. The individual who is never in the wrong, were he to exist, would not be human at all but Godlike in his infallibility. Yet the proud, unbending never-wrong person invariably insists that he is indeed dedicated to the truth and would readily admit to error if error could indeed indisputably be demonstrated to have occurred. It is this particular example of our human propensity for self-delusion that provoked Jonathan Swift to inquire caustically 'Who can deny that all men are violent lovers of truth, when we see them so positive in their errors, which they will maintain out of their zeal to truth, although they contradict themselves every day of their lives?'

Institutions are no better. Institutional status, power and prestige depend upon a reputation for justice and truth. The admission of error exposes the core of an institution, be it the courts, the medical profession, the Church, a major broadcasting authority or a department of state. In addition, however, to the psychological challenge involved, other factors operate. The medical profession, for example, points to the problem of litigation. Individual doctors would readily concede to having made errors but the lawyers at their elbow insist they say nothing lest they subsequently suffer in the courts. The courts often appear reluctant to admit to error for fear that public confidence will be shaken. Lord Denning's 'appalling vista' touched on just that fear. How can anyone continue to have reasonable confidence in the British police, judiciary and penal system if intimidation, perjury and conspiracy can enmesh them so horribly? The Church operates similarly. Truths are handed down with a solemn certainty of immutability despite a history of u-turn and revisionism worthy of Machiavelli. By maintaining a discretionary silence about such spectacular turn-abouts as the moral status of money-lending (once a dreadful abomination, now one of the main planks underpinning the Vatican's power) and the spiritual health of the newly-delivered mother (once dubbed unclean and in need of 'churching', now as befits a response to the new feminism an object of devotion and purity), the Church hopes to continue to convince the faithful that its current position on birth-control and divorce are immutable. Past errors cannot be too closely examined if today's 'truths' are to exert their potency.

Secular politics is no better. Despite the fact that being wrong in politics is no bar to progress and success, few politicians see the need to confess to past mistakes and misjudgements. There is, anyway, the adage that says that people do not expect their political representatives to admit to being wrong. Those politicians who find themselves seized by an irresistible urge to tell the truth and admit to faults often live to rue the day. Better to brazen things out than engage in any displays of humility. Politicians can afford to be wrong as long as they do not draw unnecessary attention to the fact and never ever admit that error has occurred (unless of course it can be blamed on somebody else). It is only when they have retired that politicians can reveal that they were often economical with the truth, did not know precisely (nor indeed imprecisely) what was going on and made not one but a veritable series of misjudgements. In retired politicians, such candour is readily interpreted as evidence of statesmanship. In active politicians, it is regarded as a sign of incipient dementia.

A major factor influencing our inability to confess to error is the belief that people need to be able to believe in truth, certainty, competence and justice and admitting to mistakes shakes belief. Confidence once shaken cannot easily be restored. There is of course much truth in this. But should we not face it? Why do we seem to demand such commitment to the security, the purity, the perfection of institutions such as the courts, the professions, the police, the armed forces? To so much as suggest that they can and do fall short of their ideals is like spitting on one's mother. The analogy is apt. Our adult faith in the major institutions of church and state does echo that childish belief in the infallibility and power of our parents. We believe because we need to and not necessarily because it is wise to believe. So intense can such a desire for belief be that it moves us to reject those who confess to mortality and error. The doctor who reveals he got the diagnosis wrong, the politician who acknowledges an erroneous judgement, the churchman who so much as admits he does not have all the answers far from being praised for their humanity can find themselves pilloried for their seeming inadequacies. Children become adults not in proportion to their willingness to believe but in proportion to their readiness to doubt. It is surely the sign of a child-like society that it has an intense need to believe in institutions and individuals who are never wrong and who never make mistakes.

Such thoughts are provoked by the arguments over the Birmingham Six. It is not so much a question of their guilt or innocence as the impact of an admission that a dreadful error has been made that seems likely to determine what happens next. Of course admitting error shakes confidence. The Guildford Four has been a shattering experience for British confidence in their system of justice. Releasing the Birmingham Six will be a further body blow. But there is no alternative. To conceal an error and to pretend no error has been made postpones but never prevents the ultimate reckoning. Worse, people thus deceived are even more bitter about the deception. For a while, such refusal to acknowledge error bolsters up the child-like and hungry belief that there are indeed institutions which rise above human flaws. For a further brief moment, those potent fantasies of perfection, the impartial policeman, the objective judge, the impassive surgeon, the detached psychiatrist, the unworldly churchman exercise their awesome hold on our imaginations and emotions. But error inevitably and ultimately is exposed and with it our true humanity emerges kicking and screaming into the sunlight. 'A man should never be ashamed to own he has been in the wrong,' declared Jonathan Swift, 'which is but saying in other words that he is wiser today than he was yesterday.' Being wiser today than yesterday – one of the noblest aspirations of them all – is what is at the heart of the tragedy of the Birmingham Six.

SÉAMUS DEANE

A State of Injustice

It is wrong to use the coercive apparatus of the state to maintain unjust institutions. That is a form of force which it is right to resist. The question of the Birmingham Six is not simply a question of a particular injustice done to the victims. It has been shown beyond any shadow of doubt that they were imprisoned for something they did not do and that their imprisonment involved corrupt police practices and a process of judgement that was as ruthless as it was scandalous. The effort to have the convictions overturned and the men freed should, by any rational standard, have been successful long ago.

But we are not dealing, in this case, with rational principles. We are dealing with deep-seated prejudices that have their roots both in the long conflict between Britain and Ireland and in a fear of what time and again has been exposed by it. The history of that conflict is heavily punctuated by instances of the corruption of the legal system for political purposes. The exposure that is a result of such practices is the more difficult for the British people to bear because their public faith has for so long rested on the conviction that they have the 'best' system of public justice in the world. If a case like that of the Birmingham Six shows that this is not true – that it is, in fact, an absurd belief – then the fault, it has been argued, lies with the Irish themselves. For they are so irrational, so far below the threshold of what is acceptable, that they corrupt the legal system just as they also poison the political system and the reputation of Britain in the world beyond. In a profound sense, it doesn't matter which Irish people you imprison, just so long as you imprison some Irish people for what has been done.

There is, indeed, the question. What has been done? The people killed in the Birmingham explosions and all of those others killed or injured in IRA attacks in Britain are even more innocent, in public perception, than the large group of innocent civilians killed in Northern Ireland. Because they do not live there, because very few have been there as soldiers or as civilians, and because they know little or nothing about the conflict, their victimization by a random bomb or bullet seems the more outrageous. They are 'soft targets', as the saying goes, harmless people wickedly murdered by ruthless terrorists who have no respect for life or law. Even when the victims are political – as the Brighton bombings of the Conservative Party Conference – the outrage is equivalent since such an action is visibly directed at the very institutions of the state itself and reveals how much the terrorist is against the idea of democracy, representation and political discourse. All killings by the IRA (and, to a lesser extent, by Protestant paramilitaries), are inexcusable since they are ultimately directed against the notion of a fair and decent society in which democratically elected representatives can argue the case for their respective communities.

No terrorist killing, even of armed soldiers, is justifiable. The killing of terrorists, by armed soldiers or police, is justifiable. The killing of innocent civilians, by soldiers or police, may be regrettable but is not punishable since it is a consequence of the general situation for which the terrorist is responsible. Torture, perjury, special courts, the bending or the abolition of the rules of evidence, the employment of special units or death squads, collusion between the security forces and protestant paramilitaries, special legislation, black propaganda and censorship are all employed in the war against the terrorist in defence of democracy. Policemen and soldiers do not go to jail for these offences even when they are investigated, as in the Stalker affair, the result is negligible. The system cannot incriminate itself; increasingly, it cannot even bear to investigate itself.

This would be even more tragic than it is were it the case that we are watching a democratic system becoming increasingly infected by the virus of terrorism and counter-terrorism. But that is not the case. The political entity called the United Kingdom of Great Britain and Northern Ireland was corrupt from the beginning because from the outset it was founded on injustice, violence, discrimination. All of these features were integral to the State, not later diseased derivatives from it. In the twenties and the thirties the RUC and B Specials (now the UDR), murdered catholics with impunity as a means of establishing the power of the state. They still do. That is terrorism. That is the foundation of the British State as at present constituted. It is not an Irish problem, it is a British problem from the consequences of which the Irish suffer much more than anyone else. Above all, it is a problem in which democratic procedures are erased initially so that they may be established later under the guise of and in accord with the principle of majority rule.

It is impossible, in such a situation, to make a moral distinction between different kinds of killing. The only distinction available is a political one. To attempt a moral distinction – a worthy aim – is to go beyond the conditions that make the existence of the United Kingdom of Great Britain and Northern Ireland legitimate. The British legal and political system makes the claim that there are, at its source, foundational principles of moral justice. The history of that system in Ireland reveals this to be untrue as such. It is not untrue within Britain in the same way, whatever the integral defects of the system may be. But it is, in fact, the contrast between what we may call British justice within the geography and history of Britain and British justice transposed to other circumstances that matters. The history of British justice within the British Empire is a gory tale, but it is especially gory and especially important in Ireland because it is a territory incorporated directly within the British system. If British justice could not, as an ostensibly moral system, be extended to Ireland, then it must be a system peculiar to, even exclusive to British circumstances. It is not an argument to say that the Irish are different, for that is the whole point – the absorption of difference within a universal system. If the difference cannot be absorbed, the system is not universal. It is mere prejudice to say that it is the malign difference of the Irish that prevents its being universal. If you have to suspend your laws to deal with the Irish that's because there is something either defective in the laws or something about the laws that prohibits their extension. The laws are culture-bound, but Britain's imperial experience has led the British to believe that they have universal applicability. They do not have that. When they are shown not to have that, the response has been violent in the extreme. The victims of this violence are people like the Birmingham Six who become scapegoats for the rage of the populace, the police and judiciary. The rage is directed against those who killed the people in Birmingham – and those who did so are not the actual bombers themselves but the whole constituency of people from whom the bombers come. As well those six as any other. This is precisely the rationale behind the bombings themselves. The British are killers, as their record shows in Northern Ireland now and in Ireland as such. Therefore, British people should be killed – as well those in the pub as anyone else. It doesn't matter that they are not in the SAS or among those who actually planted bombs or fired guns in Northern Ireland. They are from that constituency. Show them what political violence is like at home, since they are so good at exporting it to others and still are sufficiently hypocritical to regard themselves as peaceful or justice-loving people.

Killings, even those of innocent civilians, either by the IRA or the security forces, are political actions. This is not to deny moral atrocity; it is to deny the interpretation of some and not others as morally atrocious. The political element derives from claims to legitimacy and the legitimacy of the moral claim needs, if it has any chance of survival, to be free of coercive action as its rationale. Legal systems, although they are inescapably punitive, like to parade themselves as moral systems in action. In an ideal world they might be so; but they are not in the world of British-Irish relations. Ireland robs Britain of any claim to universal status for its legal system to the extent to which it has been victimized by it for political reasons. In the case of the Birmingham Six, the political reason overrode even the most rudimentary need to present a case that would at least have a façade of coherence. The police involved were profoundly stupid as well as corrupt. The judiciary was merely corrupt. The rules did not apply, because the people concerned were outside the rules. They were Irish, not British. That was guilt enough.

But it is not guilt at all, never mind guilt enough. The legal system separated itself from the principles of justice to defend a political system that had never been conjoined to them in the first place. That is the crux of the matter. The Birmingham Six have been punished in such a manner as to expose this fact. Given the various instances of legal corruption – the Guildford Four, the Winchester Three, the Maguires – and adding to those the history of investigations and inquiries – the Stalker affair, the Kincora investigation, the early investigation of the RUC by Sir Arthur Young, the Widgery Tribunal, the Compton report and the various internal police and army investigations into killings by the security forces, it is painfully obvious that justice is simply not in the running when the political stability of the state is in question. But in Northern Ireland, it has always been in question. Therefore justice within that frame, is inconceivable.

Still the Birmingham Six were convicted on what is quaintly called 'the mainland'. It is not only the crisis in Northern Ireland that has produced the climate in which they were victimized. That has also been created by Thatcher's Britain. More specifically, it has been created by the alliance between the executive, the judiciary and the police that has been such a marked feature of the Thatcher regime. The police, in the broadest sense, includes the security services. Their role has been to link the police with the army. In total, all these forces converge in their practice in a manner that is unprecedented within Britain – although not within Northern Ireland or any other territory that is not of the insular 'mainland'. As Britain has undergone economic privatization, it has become more and more a State-controlled political system. Privacy is the one condition that has been nationalized.

The Interception of Communications Act of 1985, the Security Service Act and the Official Secrets Act of 1989 and the interlinked furores over the *Spycatcher* affair, the Tisdall and Ponting trials, the miners' strike, the race riots, the investigation of CND members, all point in the same direction. Police powers are extended, the security services act more and more outside the law, but always 'in the national interest', the judiciary clings parasitically to the government's patronage and regurgitates its propaganda. As power becomes more concentrated, its operations become less visible. Any action can be defended or damned in relation to the 'national interest', something which is, it seems, the prerogative of the government to define. Emergency powers, so often used in Ireland that they scarcely deserve the epithet any longer, have been smuggled into the internal British system. It is hard to determine to what extent the Northern troubles have been the cause or the excuse for this process. But central to it are the men in jail for the Birmingham atrocity.

They are the victims of an Irish and of a British crisis. It is not a legal matter as such; it is a political matter. One test of any political system is the safety of the citizens who live under it. The British system fails such a test, not only for Irish people – but for them more than most. From the Irish point of view it seems incredible that in these circumstances the Irish government should be doing all it can to co-operate with the Thatcher government in the realm of what we must ironically call 'law and order'. It is right that Dublin should argue for the release of the Birmingham Six; it is contradictory that it should, at the same time, show every sign of exposing its own fragile system to the infection that has made such deep inroads into the British system of justice. It is long past the time for the release of these innocent men. But it is still timely to state publicly that the failure to release them is in itself a cruel indication of the *political* corruption of a system that should be isolated rather than embraced. If when they are released it is perfectly possible that they will be replaced by other, equally innocent, victims whose lives will be ruined for the sake of a political system that sees the law as nothing more than a weapon in the hands of the executive. In the end, it was not the police or the judges that put the Birmingham Six away. It was Her Majesty's government. The same government keeps them in jail. Their release is a political issue; their lives have been destroyed by a calculated choice, not by a freakish accident.

GERTRUDE DEGENHARDT

GERTRUDE DEGENHARDT

PETER DE ROSA

Excerpts from *Rebels: The Irish Rising of 1916*

Most men seem to die as they have lived. Awaiting execution in Kilmainham Jail over a period of two weeks, the leaders of the Easter Rising showed the kind of men they were. Some cut buttons off their tunics for their friends. Others scratched their names on coins. Others wrote letters to their families which, in poignancy, match any ever written.

Patrick Pearse was his usual mixture of the mundane and the mystical. What most vexed his conscience was his unpaid bills. But to his mother he wrote with great tenderness:

> I have just received Holy Communion. I am happy except for the grief of parting from you. This is the death I should have asked for if God had given me the choice of all deaths – to die a soldier's death for Ireland and for freedom.
>
> We have done right. People will say hard things about us now, but later on they will praise us. Do not grieve for all this, but think of it as a sacrifice which God asked of me and of you.
>
> Goodbye again, dear, dear, Mother. May God bless you for your great love for me and for your great faith, and may He remember all that you have so bravely suffered. I hope soon to see Papa, and in a little while we shall all be together again. I will call to you in my heart at the last moment.
>
> Your son, Pat

With the time of execution near, a young Capuchin, Fr. Aloysius, gave him a ten-inch crucifix of brass and black wood. Pearse took it reverently. When the priest left and the cell door was locked, he took a last look through the peep-hole. He saw Pearse in silhouette on his knees, with that crucifix, now in Kilmainham Museum, in his hands.

Prosaic, elderly Tom Clarke gave a typical message to the Irish People to his wife Kattie. It was short and uncompromising.

> I and my fellow-signatories believe we have struck the first successful blow for Freedom. The next blow, which we have no doubt Ireland will strike, will win through. In this belief, we die happy.

Thomas MacDonagh, Brigadier of the Dublin Volunteers, kept gazing in wonder at pictures of his infant children, Donagh and Barbara. To his wife Muriel, he wrote:

> To my son Don. My darling little boy, remember me kindly. Take my hope and purpose with my deed.

> To my darling daughter Barbara. God bless you. I loved you more than ever a child has been loved.
> My dearest love, Muriel, thank you a million times for all you have been to me. I have only one trouble in leaving life – leaving you so. Be brave, darling, God will assist and bless you.
> Goodbye, kiss my darlings for me. Goodbye, my love, till we meet again in Heaven. I have a sure faith of our union there. I kiss this paper that goes to you – he touched it with his lips. But for your suffering this would be all joy and glory. Goodbye.
> Your loving husband, Thomas MacDonagh.

Michael Mallin had been in charge in Stephen's Green. On his way from Richmond Barracks to Kilmainham Jail, he passed his own house.

'My precious darling wife,' he prayed fervently, 'come out and show yourself with little Joseph.' She never did.

He felt he had lost his last chance of ever seeing them again. He was wrong. He did see his wife and four children in cell 18 just before his execution in the Stonebreakers' Yard. He was able to hold in his arms his son Joseph, aged two-and-a-half.

Sean Heuston, a young man who had fought magnificently in the Mendicity Institute, wrote to his teacher-sister, a Dominican nun:

> My dearest Mary,
> Before this note reaches you, I shall have fallen as a soldier in the cause of Irish freedom. I write to bid you a last farewell in this world.
>
> If you really love me, teach the children in your class the history of their own land, and teach them that the cause of Caitlín ní hUalacháin never dies. Ireland shall be free from the centre to the sea as soon as the people of Ireland believe in the necessity for Ireland's Freedom and are prepared to make the necessary sacrifices to obtain it.

Eamonn Kent had been in charge in the South Dublin Union. In the condemned cell, he took out his watch, the one thing he wanted his son, Ronan, to have. It showed 2.30. The seconds, the last of his life, ticked audibly away as he wrote to his wife:

> My dearest wife, Aine,
> Not wife but widow before these lines reach you. I am here without hope of this world and without fear, calmly awaiting the end.

He had for some while adopted a veneer of cynicism to stop his weakness overwhelming him. Now, at the end, he seemed to become what his friend Stephen MacKenna once called him, a kind of remote, tranquil harvest moon. He recalled the sweet days of his courtship when he had a pet name for Aine:

> Dearest 'silly little Fanny'. My poor little sweetheart of – how many – years ago? Ever my comforter, God comfort you now.
>
> What can I say? I die a noble death, for Ireland's freedom. Men and women will vie with one another to shake your dear hand. Be proud of me as I am and ever was of you. My cold exterior was but a mask. It has saved me in these last days.
>
> You have a duty to me and to Ronan, that is, to live. You will be – you are, the wife of one of the Leaders of the Revolution. Sweeter still you are my little child, my dearest pet, my sweetheart of the hawthorn bushes and summer's eves.
>
> I remember all and I banish all that I may be strong and die bravely. I have one hour to live, then God's judgement.
>
> Adieu, Eamonn.

Sean MacDermott had been the great organizer of the rebellion. With James Connolly, he was the last of the leaders to be shot. Immensely calm in his death cell, he wrote to his brothers and sisters:

> By the time this reaches you, I will, with God's mercy, have joined in Heaven, my poor father and mother as well as my dear friends who have been shot during the week. They died like heroes and with God's help I will act throughout as heroic as they did.

He assured his family he had had priest friends constantly with him over the last 24 hours.

> I feel a happiness the like of which I never experienced in my life before. You ought to envy me. The cause for which I die has been re-baptized during the past week by blood of as good men as ever trod God's earth.

He asked them to contact his friends.

> Tell then that in my last hours, I am the same Sean they always knew and that even now I can enjoy a laugh as good as ever.
>
> Goodbye, dear Brothers and Sisters, make no lament for me. Pray for my soul and feel a lasting pride in my death. I die that the Irish nation may live.
>
> God bless and guard you all and may He have mercy on my soul.
>
> Yours as ever, Sean.

PAUL DURCAN

'Amnesty' (from *Daddy, Daddy)*

I
The perimeter wall of a prison presents a problem
To a small boy,
Particularly if he is nine and a half
And he does not know, and nobody is ever going to tell him,
That when he was born, he was born in prison,
A confinement within a confinement.
Pardon? Pardon.

II
As he drives past the prison, Daddy does not explain –
'That's the prison.' If it was any place else
He'd spin around from the driving wheel and explain –
'That's the Rotunda Maternity Hospital'
Or 'That's the Wellington Monument'
Or 'That's the Four Courts.'

I swivel about in the back seat of the car,
A pair of small boy's eyes splattered all over the prison walls.
The prison is a blocked-up keyhole.
Its gates do not deign to speak to me.
They despise me.
Its barred cells to not deign to speak to me.
They despise me.
A grey, granite, waistcoated pile of sarcasm –
Like my arrogant, alcoholic big brother
The day he vomited into the fireplace.
Pardon? Pardon.

Each time we drive past the prison
– Which is four times a day –
I can see through its walls.
The prisoners' faces are decked out in vomit.
I am dejected that Daddy does not name it.

He who is the great namer of things;
For whom the names of places and people
Are the signs by which he teaches me
That they are holy and precious;
That the plankton of all human life is mercy.

Perhaps it is that a prison is not a holy and precious place –
A place that does not have a name.
Perhaps it is that prisoners are not holy and precious people –
People without names;
That the plankton of all human life is mercilessness.

III
I lie awake in bed at night fretting about the prison.
The headlights of passing cars toss shadows on the ceiling
That are cell bars. There are no faces.
But then the face of the Pope is projected on to the ceiling,
The Supreme Pontiff is appearing on the balcony of St. Peter's.
I ask myself: when the Vicar of Christ's
Standing out there, explaining things to the world,
What does he make of the bars across his eyes?
How is it that I've never seen him put out his hands
And, falling to his knees,
Clench those bars fiercely, helplessly?
Yet Jesus is the patron saint of all prisoners
Because he was a prisoner himself,
Not a special category prisoner
But prisoner like the rest of us,
One of three.
Today you will be with me in paradise.
Pardon? Pardon.
Daddy puts his head around the bedroom door and whispers
'Are you alright?'
I tell a lie and answer him
'Yes, Daddy, I am alright.'
But I am not alright. The prison is all over the ceiling
And I am hiding from it down under the sheets.
The pink vomit of my big brother's sarcasm is all over my face.

IV
Against Daddy's wishes I courted a black girl,
A medical student from Cape Town.
'The most beautiful city in the world,' Daddy groaned,
Sobs of fury in his throat.
He put me out of the house and told me never to come home.
He loved me as no man ever loved his son
But he said to me – crisply, glassily, over the breakfast table,
Over the cornflakes and the marmalade – 'Don't ever come home again.'
Pardon? Pardon.

I went to another country and to a far place,
A mining village in northern Ontario,
A dark new habitat in oblivion,
And I freed myself from the dream of being his favourite son
And I found peace of mind in the company of my wife,
In the loving kindness of her bed.
We have four boys and a girl, the youngest,
Whom we named Amnesty – after a radio programme
We'd heard, about people who write letters to prisoners.
It was the word, and the acoustic of the word:
Amnesty.
The etymology of the word:
Amnesty.
All participle, all verb;
Oblivion;
Like holding hands behind a waterfall;
Like a lake dwelling on stilts in deciduous forests;
Like a nest caught up in a weir in a river in spate;
Like traffic lights at red when there's no traffic at night.

V
On winter nights when she's playing ice hockey on Main Street
I like to put my head out the door and call out her name –
Amnesty.
It's so fortified, yet vulnerable, and it falls away
Or gathers itself to itself
Like a yard of deer bunching
In an open space at the treeline
Or between telegraph poles on a wet day.
'It's getting late, Amnesty, it's getting late.'
When I behold her racing back down the street to greet me
What I feel is a sense of zero:
Amenesty.
It is such a swift and shedding spectacle to see her face
Peering out at me from its fur hood,
Its nimbus of expectancy with serrated edges,
All frills,
Oblivion,
And to hear myself reiterating her name –
Amnesty.

Pardon? Pardon
It is such a delight to reiterate her name –
Amnesty –

That I cannot pronounce it often enough –
Amnesty –
And after we've made love
My wife puts me back down into sleep,
Oblivion,
By seashelling into my ear the lullaby of our daughter's name:
Amnesty
In the key of A minor

Into the seashell of my ear, the lullaby of my fate –
Amnesty.

TERRY EAGLETON

Wild Justice

Anyone who confronted the British police on a picket line or at a demonstration during the miners' strike some years ago would have noticed a significant change in their customary behaviour. Normally, the police on such occasions put up a feeble show of neutrality, holding the ring (as they say) between conflicting interest groups. As far as the mineworkers were concerned, the police made no bones about the fact that they regarded them as their enemy and were out to belabour and imprison as many of them as they conveniently could.

The traditional appearance of neutrality of the British police or judiciary is not just a fine old instance of English hypocrisy, though it is doubtless that too. On the contrary, there is a real material basis for such apparent disinterestedness, one built into the very structures of the capitalist state. In previous social orders, legal, political and economic functions in society were often united in the same individuals: the lord of the manor policed and protected his subordinates, as well as economically exploiting them. Under capitalism, however, these functions become relatively independent of one another. The capitalist does not need himself to be an agent of the law or arm of religious ideology in order to induce his workers into the factories. What Marx once called the 'dull compulsion' of economic necessity is enough to ensure that. The political and juridical functions can then, as it were, be delegated elsewhere, to specialised bodies of men and women who really are relatively independent of the economic order. In the long run, to be sure, they help to secure its interests; but in the meanwhile they are able to present themselves as sublimely disinterested, thus furthering those interests even more effectively. The 'neutrality' of the state is, of course, a pathetic illusion; but it is not *just* an illusion. It has a real ground in the material workings of our kind of societies – as opposed, for instance, to the societies of Stalinism, where nobody was ever lunatic enough to suppose that the state even *pretended* to neutrality. The state in our kind of society may well be the instrument of the ruling order, dedicated to securing the conditions under which capital may be untroubledly reproduced; but this is true only in the last analysis. In the shorter term, the capitalist state, simply to achieve this ultimate goal, may be forced to work against its own immediate interest – as, for example, when it needs to sacrifice some direct promotion of its own aims to the end of achieving social consensus.

The 'relative autonomy' of the capitalist state is, of course, one immensely powerful way in which its subjects are mystified into viewing it as dispassionate; and nowhere has such a delusion been more marked than in the oldest capitalist nation in the world. The lengthy, well-entrenched history of middle-class rule in Britain, relatively unscathed by the political convulsions which have rocked other European nations, means that power in such a society can afford to diffuse itself into the very textures of daily culture, operating by custom, habit and taken-for-granted piety rather than by brutal coercion. Hence the notoriously devious, oblique, understated nature of English ruling-class culture; and hence also the traditional importance in English society of 'manners' – that meticulous self-disciplining and self-policing whereby each of us, as it were, becomes our own local seat of self-government, without apparent need for some authoritarian supervision on the part of the state. What threatens to discredit this tacit, routine mode of self-repression is any too embarrassingly brutal display of the state's coercive powers – anything that shows it up for the viciously prejudiced institution it actually is. Edmund Burke knew well enough that the law works best when it is invisible – when it figures in our lives as spontaneous impulse and customary practice, rather than as the sledgehammer on the door in the early hours of the morning. The law, so Burke appreciated, is 'male' in its authoritarian force, but cloaks this rude strength, most of the time at least, in female drapery, persuading us to love and admire it by the apparent sweet reasonableness of its yoke. The law for Burke is transvestite; and if he detested the French revolutionaries, it was because they were offering to strip the law of all its seductive drapery and expose its phallus, reveal the unlovely barbarism beneath the beguiling exterior.

In Britain today, the whole of this traditional ruling-class strategy is breaking apart, and the Birmingham Six are among its most notable victims. When the capitalist system moves into crisis, it will be forced more and more to reveal its arbitrarily coercive hand, and thus risk stripping the decent drapery of delusion from the eyes of its admiring subjects. If the police were able to run riot during the miners' strike, it was surely because they knew – in their political bones, if not by explicit instruction from their Inspectors – that the political sensibility of contemporary Britain was in process of shifting from consensus to cynicism. And it is exactly this cynicism which is one of the more appalling features of the Birmingham Six case. For there is surely no doubt that the British state is quite aware of their innocence, as it may not have been, for example, of the innocence of a James Hanratty. What does it matter which six Paddies languish behind bars, as long as political credibility is maintained? The state may – indeed often does – behave with flagrant injustice and brutality; but for it tacitly to abandon ethical criteria altogether signals a decisive new phase of British repressiveness.

With Thatcherism, in other words, we have begun to move into what one might call the postmodernist phase of late capitalism, in which – as in the work of various postmodernist theorists – truth as a concept is now discardable. Of course truth, justice, freedom have often enough been flouted over the centuries by this kind of political system; but there was a time, even so, when it could be proclaimed that whitewash, cover-up and lying through your teeth were regrettable accidents of the regime, untypical of its daily operations. In the kind of social order where lying through your teeth has now become a daily, structural necessity, it would seem that truth and justice are well on their way to being abandoned in *theory*, not just violated in practice.

This is not, however, a policy without severe dangers for the state itself. In seeking to bring low its political opponents by forgery, suppression and psychical terror, that state is in danger of undoing itself. For though the great bourgeois ideals of truth, freedom and equality are of course quite unworkable in social practice, they are nonetheless indispensable ways in which the state seeks to legitimate itself in the eyes of its underlings. The more it tramples them underfoot, and the less it *cares* about appearing the bigoted, deceitful, self-interested body it actually is, the more ruthlessly it strips the decent drapery of credibility from its own figure. The bourgeois state is less and less able to tolerate the truth, and as reliant as it ever was on maintaining some shred of appearance of it. If this is a dilemma, it is not one we should be particularly eager to help it out of.

If the Birmingham Six are victims of British political cynicism, so was that earlier Irish scapegoat of the English Establishment, Oscar Wilde. Wilde, it would appear, was not tried and imprisoned simply because he was a homosexual; he was prosecuted as part of a political conspiracy to save the skin of the then English Prime Minister, Lord Rosebery. It is likely that Rosebery had himself been conducting a homosexual affair with his private secretary Lord Drumlanrig, elder son of the Marquess of Queensberry. The Marquess was baying for blood; but the blood which pacified him was not Rosebery's but Wilde's, who was having a relationship with his younger son, and thus, as it were, stood trial in the Prime Minister's place.

The trial of Oscar Wilde forms the centrepiece of my play *Saint Oscar*, produced by the Field Day theatre company; and in writing Wilde's final speech from the dock it was inevitable that I should have in mind Hugh Callaghan, Patrick Hill, Gerard Hunter, Noel McIlkenny, William Power and John Walker. Hegel says somewhere that all historical events happen twice: the first time as tragedy, the second time as farce. He forgot to qualify: for the Irish under British rule, the first time as tragedy, the second time as tragedy too.

Judge: Mr. Carson, would you like to sum up?

Carson: Thank you, my lord. It is clear, I believe, how the accused would wish to present himself to the world. He is enlightened, we are benighted; he has thrown off the chains of common morality, whereas we are still its helpless dupes. He has been known to declare that there is no such thing as a moral or an immoral book, only a well-written or badly written one. This is the kind of maxim which trips easily from his tongue, and for which he is fêted throughout fashionable society. His life is one facetious witticism after another; he is so avid of applause that he is heedless of what reckless, insulting remarks cross his lips. He spins one vacuous paradox after another and calls it genius; and those who fawn on him affect to find such flippancy profound because they are terrified of being thought conventionally minded. Does Mr. Wilde then believe that a book which, shall we say, advocated the massacre of an entire race, or one which gloated over the systematic mutilation of a human being, is not immoral? Or is he so enraptured by his own glib tongue that he will say anything whatsoever for the infantile pleasure of creating an effect?

Mr. Wilde urges us to reject the idea of truth – another dreary shibboleth of the so-called Establishment. Very well, let us take him at his word. Let us inform him here and now that we are not concerned to weigh the evidence in this case, but are intent on sentencing him to imprisonment with hard labour whether he is guilty or not. Let us decide that it is of no consequence whether he is in truth the father of his own children, and remove them forever from his sight. Would not this wipe something of the smugness from his lips? Would he then be so eager to instruct us that truth is nothing but mood, impression, opinion?

Mr. Wilde is a professional mocker, who has the knack of making us lesser mortals feel commonplace and gauche. His life has been one long gesture of contempt for those ordinary men and women who, lacking his leisure and privilege, must work for their living, nurture their children, exercise responsibility for one another – men and women who have neither the time nor the education to appreciate the doctrines of Mr. Walter Pater. Mr. Wilde thinks of these anonymous individuals as nothing – as inferior, obtuse, fodder for his wit, foils to his own flamboyance. They are the lesser breeds who exists to cook his food, tailor his clothes, fill his bed. And all this from a man who has the impudence to call himself a socialist. He is an iconoclast who lives off the fat of the land, a bohemian who will frequent only the very best restaurants, a born rebel who cannot pull a shirt over his head without the help of a servant. He bestows the high-sounding name of aesthete on his own congenital sloth, and turns his own squalid self-interest into a lofty spiritual doctrine. He indulges his crudest appetites and calls it artistic self-expression; he wanders aimlessly from one fashionable watering-place to another and calls it the cultivation of personality. He is vain, arrogant and self-deluded; he believes himself impregnable, beyond the reach of common human judgement, contemptuous of the opinions of others, heedless of the warnings of his friends, convinced that he is so godlike that nothing can harm him. He is so besotted with himself that he would sell his own mother for the sake of a smart quip. He is a spoilt brat who has never done a decent day's work in his life, and who at the ripe age of forty presents the grotesque spectacle of one striving to perpetuate his undergraduate years. He has done nothing in his life for others, ruthlessly dedicated as he is to his own supremely trivial pleasures.

My lord, it is time that Mr. Wilde had a little seriousness introduced into his futile existence. It might indeed prove to be the making of him. I therefore ask that he be sentenced to the fullest term of imprisonment with hard labour which the law sees fit to prescribe for the offences in question.

Judge: Mr. Wilde, have you anything to say?

Wilde: I have, my lord. My lord, I can say only this in my defence. The only power which has ever enthralled me is the power of words. I know nothing of law and politics but the rhetoric of them. I have a wife called language, to whom I am faithfully wedded, and with whom I occasionally play fast and loose – it's known as poetry. I speak of course metaphorically, but there's no other way of speaking. I thrill exquisitely to Shelley but can find nothing but tedium in Hansard or the penny catechism. I have never understood the meaning of the term morality, other than as a ploy for oppressing others. I am, in short, a decadent. But I fear that your health may be more diseased than my decadence. Better a sensationalist than an imperialist. I fear for the moral health of an entire nation obsessed with which hole to put it in. You subjugate whole races, you condemn the mass of your own people to wretched toil you have reduced my own nation to misery and despair, and all you can think about is which sexual organ goes in where. You prate of liberty and crush anything that differs from you as soon as it stirs. You look about you and can tolerate no image but your own; the very sight of otherness is intolerable to you. You bow your knee to art and give not a fart in your corduroys for it. You preach of the family and abandon your children as soon as they can crawl to nursemaid and prep school. You worship God and would crucify his daughter along with his son were they rash enough to appear next time in tandem. You crucify your own women and dub it marital duty. I am the son of Lady Wilde of Dublin, who is proud to bear the name of feminist, along with that of republican.

You disgust me. You disgust me most of all because you tempt me into seriousness, a temptation to which I refuse to yield because to do so would be to play your own game. My lord, I object to this trial on the grounds of a fundamental incompatibility between the English and the Irish notions of truth. Truth for you means whatever is the case; I am afraid that we Irish have very little idea any longer of what is the case, if indeed we ever knew. I object to this trial on the grounds that no Irishman can receive a fair hearing in an English court because the Irish are figments of the English imagination. I am not really here; I am just one of your racial fantasies. You cannot manacle a fantasy. I do not believe in your morality and I do not believe in your truth. I have my own truth and morality, which I call art. I am not on trial here because I am a pervert but because I am an artist, which in your book comes to much the same thing. You hold that a man is a man and a woman is a woman. I hold that nothing is ever purely itself, and that the point where it becomes so is known as death. I therefore demand to be defended by metaphysicians rather than by lawyers, and that my jury should be composed of my peers – namely, poets, perverts, vagrants and geniuses.

(Pause)

Judge: Have you anything to add, Mr. Wilde?

Wilde: Yes. Have I got off?

(Blackout)

BRIAN FRIEL

Epilogue to *Dancing at Lughnasa*

Michael
And so, when I cast my mind back to that summer of 1936, different kinds of memories offer themselves to me.

But there is one memory of that Lughnasa time that visits me most often; and what fascinates me about that memory is that it owes nothing to fact. In that memory atmosphere is more real than incident and everything is simultaneously actual and illusory. In that memory, too, the air is nostalgic with the music of the thirties. It drifts in from somewhere far away – a mirage of sound – a dream music that is both heard and imagined; that seems to be both itself and its own echo; a sound so alluring and so mesmeric that the afternoon is bewitched maybe haunted, by it. And what is so strange about that memory is that everybody seems to be floating on those sweet sounds, moving rhythmically, languorously, in complete isolation; responding more to the mood of the music than to its beat. When I remember it, I think of it as dancing. Dancing with eyes half closed because to open them would break the spell. Dancing as if language had surrendered to movement – as if this ritual, this wordless ceremony, was now the way to speak, to whisper private and sacred things, to be in touch with some otherness. Dancing as if the very heart of life and all its hopes might be found in those assuaging notes and those hushed rhythms and in those silent and hypnotic movements Dancing as if language no longer existed because words were no longer necessary. . .

(Slowly bring up the music. Slowly bring down the lights.)

THE END

PATRICK GALVIN

The Uniform
(For the Birmingham Six)

In this place
Beyond stone walls
Behind steel bars
The day bleeds us
The night binds us
The cell door closes our eyes
And then buries us.
Listen:

We are still alive.

After
The dark years
After
The beatings and the lies
After
You have turned away
And tried to forget who we are –
Listen:

We are still alive.

We shall not be forgotten
We shall not be moved aside
We are not blind
We will rise up
And with our eyes open
We will stare you out
And accuse.
Listen:

We are still alive.

I
The room is prepared for one person.
There is a table and a chair
And a blue lamp
Brightly burning.

In the centre of the table
There is a blank sheet of paper
And a Parker pen containing
Green ink.

When I am questioned
In this room
The answers are never
Satisfactory.

The uniform says:
We must try again.

II

It begins
By knocking my head against the wall.
I expected that.
Then it kicks me on both shins.
I expected that.
It says that all this
Is for my own good.
I hadn't expected that.

I try to please
The uniform.
I try to dream up
A satisfactory answer.
Perhaps, I've forgotten
Something?
I'm concerned
For its happiness.

But the uniform says:
We must try again.

III

The wall, it says,
Is a very special wall.
It is made of concrete
And when knocked hard
By the human head
It bleeds profusely
And changes colour
But it does not bear grudges.

I am grateful to the wall
I promise to remember it
In my prayers

And when my head begins to swell
And my shins begin to change colour
I tell the uniform
That they will not bear grudges
Either.

The uniform is fascinated by colour.
It says it has artistic tendencies
And, sometimes, it paints the wall
Red
But at Christmas it paints the wall
Green
Because it once saw the Infant Jesus
In an emerald crib.

I say
Ireland is full of artists
I say
We are always painting pictures on the walls
And digging holes in the ground.
I invite the uniform to come alive with us
And wear a silk smile under a black hat
And change its name to O'Flynn

And the uniform says:
We must try again.

IV
The table, I notice,
Is painted white.
It has iron legs
Embedded in the floor.
The uniform says
They can withstand anything
Including explosives and blarney
From murdering Irish bastards.

It asks me to sign a confession.
It says that the guilt clings to me
Like vomit
And it can smell the remains
Of the dead and the dying
Still lying in the streets of Birmingham.
It says that if some had their way
They would blow my fucking brains out.

I say that I am sorry for the dead
I say I am sorry for all those
Who were mangled and destroyed
I say that their pain crucifies me
And their tears anoint me
But I was not there
I am not responsible
I know nothing about it.

And the uniform says:
We must try again.

V

Only
The dead live here.
Their names scratched on the wall
Their confessions written in blood
Their wounds exposed
By the excrement of authority.
I tell the uniform I'm innocent
And the uniform shatters my mouth.

It says
The Irish are full of mouth
It says
They have an inbuilt cancer
Breathing terrorism and murder.
It presses a revolver to my head
And speaks of Russian Roulette
And the need for capital punishment.

Then
It changes tactics.
It places the Parker pen in my hand
And says
The green ink is for my benefit.
It says
The Irish are like children
And offers me tea and a chocolate biscuit.

Only
The Gods are brave
Only
The walls shed tears
For the lost and friendless.

I say
My tongue is on fire
And my lips bleed colour

And the uniform says:
We must try again.

VI
In a corner of the room
There is an electric cable.
It has a live wire painted
Brown
And a neutral wire painted
Blue.
I tell the uniform I'm neutral
And the uniform turns out the lamp.

It says
The light is only for show
It says
The two wires sparking in the dark
Are only for show
It says
Britain is a Democracy
And raises the revolver in the air.

I believe in democracy
I believe that the dog
Barking in the yard
Is only for show
I believe that the gun is loaded,
The uniform is wonderful
And the innocent have everything
To fear.

I confess to my life
I confess my nationality
I confess to being in the wrong place
At the wrong time
Wearing the wrong clothes
And having the wrong accent.
I confess my innocence
And sign accordingly

And the uniform
Buries us.

We are still alive.

Our mouths
Silenced in stone
Our eyes
Mirrored in grief
Our lives disfigured
Beyond pardon
Or release.
Listen:

We are still alive.

We are not dead
We are not afraid
We shall upheave the earth
Turn on the light
Unbend the lies
Open the gates
And walk free.
Listen:

I give you our names.
Callaghan
McIllkenny
And Hill.
Walker
Hunter
And Power,
Listen:

We are still alive
We are still here
We shall outlive the night.

CHRISTIAN GEISSLER

greetings of solidarity to the birmingham six!

i am citizen of a state in which anyone who has preserved a keen memory knows that the ruling class employs any means to retain its bloody might and cut down any self-assured radical fighter.

being a citizen of the city of hamburg who in 1945, as a young man, was liberated by the british soldiers from hitler's fascism, i, for years, loved great britain as the land of freedom and democracy. freedom then was for me an individual possession rather than a hard-to-achieve objective in the struggle between irreconcilable class interests.

today i know from experience – and today anyone is in a position to know from experience – that the ruling class of great britain is no better than its german counterpart or any of those power groups so destructive of human beings.

looked at from this point of view the injustice found in british jails, police stations and courtrooms, the sixteen year torture of the birmingham six is but normal: he who belongs – and be it only for reasons of history or language – to those that defend themselves against repression is literally in permanent danger of his life. he who loves life – a life in freedom – is meant to perish. for it is the living person – the person who loves a life in freedom – who poses the only real threat to the ruling class.

what is to be done.

i find it nonsensical to approach the ruling class and its base justice on moral grounds. killers are not moved by moral pleas and appeals. their morality defines as 'right' whatever serves the interests of capital. their proprietorial justice, their proprietorial morality does not want to take note of the living person, it is not able to; its only aim is to oppress the self-assured so as to exploit them. should they refuse to be exploited they will have to be done in and destroyed. therefore the prisoners have to be freed. today in particular, considering the worldwide victory of proprietors, we are all prisoners. we, who love life in freedom. hence we will have to learn to fight hard for our liberation. otherwise we shall perish.

socialism or barbarism.
it is that simple. and so difficult.
we'll go on.
we shall not give up.
we greet all struggling prisoners!

(Translated from the German by Hans-Christian Oeser.)

DAVOREN HANNA

Sweet Dreams, Your Honour!

Will you sleep the sleep of the just
When you reach the end of the trial?
The long denial of evidence
Has probably tired you out.
Real felons need not fear
When you decide to wake
Because Libra has not only lost
Her sight but her heart also.
What will you tell those men
Who stand dejectedly
At the gates of Britain's Chancery –
That they've failed the test of truth?

MICHAEL HARTNETT

Sneachta Gealaí '77

Mé féin faoin aer san oíche,
ag speachadh seoda sneachta i bpáirc,
gach teach reoite, gach nead préacháin
mar ghealach dhubh ag snámh le hais na fíor-ré.
Mé féin ag damhsa faoin ngealach,
seanrince gan cheol leis ach ceol cuisle:
is mé féin go huaigneach – an seanuaigneas.

Thar imeall na spéire tá céasadh is goin
is an bás go fonóideach
a lámha ina phóca
ag feadaíl sa tsráid;
mé féin sa sneachta gealaí
ag moladh nead préacháin –
an file go sotalach, foclach, slán.

Moonsnow '77

Myself outside at night,
kicking snow-jewels in a field,
each house frozen, each rook's nest
a black moon swimming by the real moon.
Myself dancing under the moon,
an old dance with no music
but pulse-music:
and myself lonely – the ancient loneliness.

Over the border, torture and wounds
and death sneers
hands in pockets
whistles at street corners:
and myself in the moonsnow
praising a rook's nest –
the poet, arrogant, verbose, safe.

Early One Morning

There was nothing there
but the darkness and myself:
then slowly out of sleep
my eyes pulled me,
needled by a speck of lead dust.
No one else had thrust
a limb out of the headless
shadows of themselves:
I could see them stacked
on their beds.
At last I was the first.
A grey fingerprint
embossed my eye.
I knew I had something to say.
I began my cry.
A slow bubble of grey spread:
every shadow grew a head,
every shadow began to shout.
Then a film of blood
seemed to coat all things
and I was loudest of all beings
though my cry had lost its meaning.
A fan of silver
underglowed the blood:
we stared at each other,
none being understood
and grey and red and silver
washed the world
louder and more clear
than all our noise.

SEAMUS HEANEY

Excerpt from *The Cure at Troy.*
A Version of Sophocles' Philoctetes

Chorus

Human beings suffer,
They torture one another,
They get hurt and get hard.
No poem or play or song
Can fully right a wrong
Inflicted and endured.

The innocent in gaols
Beat on their bars together.
A hunger-striker's father
Stands in the graveyard dumb.
The police widow in veils
Faints at the funeral home.

History says, *Don't hope*
On this side of the grave.
But then, once in a life-time
The longed-for tidal wave
Of justice can rise up,
And hope and history rhyme.

So hope for a great sea-change
On the far side of revenge.
Believe that a further shore
Is reachable from here.
Believe in miracles
And cures and healing wells.

Call miracles self-healing:
The utter, self-revealing
Double-take of feeling.
If there's fire on the mountain
Or lightning and storm
And a god speaks from the sky

That means someone is hearing
The outcry and the birth-cry
Of new life at its term.

The full thunderclap and eruption-effects occur. Then a lingering, wavering aftermath of half-light. Brilliant spots find Philoctetes *and* Chorus.

Philoctetes
(Crying out)
Hercules:
I saw him in the fire.
Hercules
was shining in the air.
I heard the voice of Hercules in my head.

Chorus
(Ritually clamant, as Hercules)
I have opened the closed road
Between the living and the dead
To make the right road clear to you.
I am the voice of Hercules now.

Here on earth my labours were
The stepping-stones to upper air.
Lives that suffer and come right
Are backlit by immortal light.

Go, Philoctetes, with this boy,
Go and be cured and capture Troy.
Asclepius will make you whole,
Relieve your body and your soul.

Go, with your bow. Conclude the sore
And cruel stalemate of our war.
Win by fair combat. But know to shun
Reprisal killings when that's done.

Then take just spoils and sail at last
Out of the bad dream of your past.
Make sacrifice. Burn spoils to me.
Shoot arrows in my memory.

And, Neoptolemus, you must be
His twin in arms and archery.
Marauding lions on that shore,
Troy's nemesis and last nightmare.

But when the city's being sacked
Preserve the shrines. Show gods respect.
Reverence for the gods survives
Our individual mortal lives.

Philoctetes

Something told me this was going to happen.
Something told me the channels were going to open.
It's as if a thing I knew and had forgotten
Came back completely clear.
All that you say
Is like a dream to me and I obey.

Neoptolemus

And so will I.

Chorus

Then go, immediately.
The winds are blowing and the tides are high.

Philoctetes

(In a sort of daze, on all fours perhaps, or clasping an upright support: knocked out, flattened)

But I can't believe I'm going. My head's light at the thought of a different ground and a different sky. I'll never get over Lemnos; this island's going to be the keel under me and the ballast inside me. I'm like a fossil that's being carried away, I'm nothing but cave stones and damp walls and an old mush of dead leaves. The sound of waves in draughty passages. A cliff that's wet with spray on a winter's morning. I feel like the sixth sense of the world. I feel I'm a part of what was always meant to happen, and is happening now at last. Come on, my friends.

Chorus

Now it's high watermark
And floodtide in the heart
And time to go.
The sea-nymphs in the spray
Will be the chorus now.
What's left to say?

Suspect too much sweet talk
But never close your mind.
It was a fortunate wind
That blew me here. I leave
Half ready to believe
That a crippled trust might walk

And the half-true rhyme is love.

(Curtain.)

DESMOND HOGAN

A monologue from *Wars*, a stage-play in progress

'And the limp word 'search' clearly does not apply to a triumph over a muteness that demands unrelieved superhuman effort.'

Andrei Tarkovsky.

Last year I lived in a small town in the Southern States. There was a colour on the main street called Persian watermelon. A kind of mauve-pink. The yard of a store on the street was thronged with terracotta dalmatians. Towards the end of the street, farthest from where I lived, old men slouched interminably over apple dumplings and cinnamon sauce in Woolworths. Off the main street was Johnny Ray's Two Dollar Perm and Curls shop and Sheik Beauty Parlour – a hut with maroon writing outside.

Years ago I wrote a story called 'The Man from Korea'. It was about a young Korean war veteran who visits a small Irish town in the mid-fifties. The town is that story merged with the town I was living in now and out of this meeting came a film script.

My story 'The Man from Korea' begins:

> Afterwards it had the awkward grace of a legend; a silence when his name was mentioned, an implied understanding of what had happened. Few know what actually happened though, so to make it easier for you to understand I will make my own version.

I updated the story to 1960. Karl is the war veteran. When I was a child young Americans frequently stayed in the guest houses of our town, guinea gold crew cuts, red check shirts. I associated them with the words of a song of that time:

> The wayward wind is a restless wind.
> He was born the next of kin, the next of kin to the wayward wind.

Karl comes to stay in the guesthouse of Roseanne and Nonie, two orphaned girls. He first arrives when Gregory, a little boy from up the road whose mother is in hospital, is performing the apparition of Our Lady of Fatima for Roseanne and Nonie, dressed up in towels, sheets. This image I got from a story of mine called 'By the River'. I wrote 'By the River' one Christmas in Lewisham. I spoke to an Irish traveller outside the church of Saint John the Baptist and Saint John the Evangelist in Lewisham that Christmas about an ancestor of his who'd fought in the Crimean War. There are many travellers in this script. Karl is a kind of traveller. In many ways Karl is me as an adult, Gergory me as a child, two parts meeting. While I was teaching in the Southern States I showed Andrei Tarkovsksy's film *Mirror*. I ordered it from New York. First time it was stolen from the train. Second time it arrived. It sees life as a collage. It gave shape to what I was doing with my script – a collage like the colours of the main street in that Southern town were a collage, demarcations of cranberry, russet, mulberry, the colours which haunt Karl's mind, the colours of home.

'I've made a long voyage and been to a strange country, and I've seen the dark man very close,' wrote Thomas Wolfe from Ashville, North Carolina. Karl too has done all these things.

These are the scenes of Karl's arrival, October 1960.

1. Interior. Drawing room of Duane's
Bed and Breakfast House. Day.

Gregory, a boy of nine, is dressed as Our Lady of Fatima, bathtowels, sheets, scarves, on the ledge of the street window. Yellow curtains by the side, lace behind.

Roseanne and Nonie are seated, watching the performance, Roseanne a tall, thin, marigold-haired girl, Nonie small, dark, distortedly cherubic.

Gregory:
I am Our Lady of Fatima (His hands are piously joined.) I have come to warn you of a terrible darkness that will cover the world if you do not repent and say the rosary. This is your last chance. Get on your knees or there'll be a war the like no one has ever seen.

(Knock on door. Nonie answers it. A jumble of voices. Roseanne waits eagerly for the next instalment while Our Lady of Fatima is frozen. Enter Nonie with Karl, a young American, dark suit on him, white, open-necked shirt. His fair hair is cropped. He carries one bag.)

Nonie (to Roseanne):
This is an American. He wants accommodation.

Karl (to Roseanne):
I want a quiet room. I'm not going to be here for long.

(Silence. Partly because there's something stunning about Karl.)

Roseanne:
We have one at the back of the house.

Karl:
I'll look it over. (He looks quizzically at Gregory.)

Roseanne:
This is Our Lady of Fatima. She's very fashionable in these parts.

2. Int. Croffey's Pub. Night.

Two men chat by the counter. We see a sign advertising Guinness on the drinks shelf, a French couple of the Fifties having Guinness under the Arc de Triomphe. 'The world and his wife drink Guinness.' A woman hovers attendance. Onion, a small, intent, slightly greasy man, drinks distantly on counter – alone.

Man nearest camera:
It's about these fallas who race cars on cliffs. And one of them goes over the cliff. And the fellow he was racing is blamed for telling the police about the lot of them. Arah it goes on like that. Nothing worse than a bad picture. And a heap of them looking at you if you walk out.

(Karl enters. There's a sudden tacit silence all around.
Karl goes to an unoccupied part of the counter, sits on a stool and waits for service.)

3. Int. Pub. Night.
Onion has sidled up to Karl.

Onion:
Call me the shy sort.

4. Int. Pub. Night.
Onion (exclaiming):
I met an American here once and do you know what he said to me?

Onion (conversationally):
'We may never meet again but let's be friends when we meet.'

5. Int. Pub. Night.
Onion:
I used to break stones in Kilmainham in Dublin for six shillings a day. Then I got a job on the railway here. It's good money. (His voice goes very quiet.) I get magazines easily. Magazines from England. Would you like to look at some?

6. Ext. Open roofed urinal. Night.
Onion shines a torch downwards as Karl and a number of other drinkers urinate.

Onion (to Karl):
I use this so I won't get my feet wet.

(The reason he uses it should be surreptitiously obvious.)

7. Int. Duane's kitchen. Night.
Gregory, Nonie, Roseanne converse around a table. They're all having tea. There's a picture of Tennessee Ernie Ford on the wall, Buddy Holly and the Crickets; Anita Bryant's record sleeve 'Suddenly there's a Valley'. There's a stuffed owl over a cupboard. An egg timer with a faded picture of skyscrapers on it and the word 'Chicago' underneath, a snowball with the round towers of Glendalough inside – these two items on a smaller cupboard. It's quite a cramped kitchen.
The teapot between the three people is steel.

Roseanne:
He's a very quiet. Stays in his room all the time.

Gregory:
Maybe he's working for the government.

Nonie:
Why?

Gregory:
He looks like someone from the government.

(Noise in the drawing room. Porch door opening.)

Roseanne (almost panicking):
O God. He was out all the time.

8. Int. Drawing room. Night.
Roseanne pokes out from the entrance to kitchen to greet Karl on his way in. She just gets him as he's about to enter that door to go upstairs.

Karl:
Been to Croffey's for a drink.

Roseanne:
Won't you come in and join us for a cup of tea?

9. Int. Kitchen. Night.
All four around table.

Roseanne (explaining Gregory):
Gregory's mother is in hospital. She'll be there for a few weeks longer poor soul.

Gregory:
What part of America are you from?

Karl:
Alabama.

(Roseanne, Nonie, Gregory look quizzical.)

Karl (quietly singing):
Oh Suzanna won't you cry for me
I'm going to Louisiana with my banjo on my knee
It rained all night the day I left
The weather it was dry
The sun so hot I froze to death
Suzanna don't you cry
I'm going to Alabama my true love for to see.

(Roseanne, Nonie, Gregory nod in sudden understanding. There's a pause.)

Gregory:
Were you a soldier?

Karl:
I was in the war zone.

10. Int. Karl's room. Night.
It's a small room.
Karl is undressing, taking off his shirt. From the pub nearby we hear amplified words of a song, sung by a man.

Song:
I close me eyes and picture
the emerald of the sea.

(Karl, in grief, in remembrance, suddenly covers his face in his hands.)

11. Int. Drawing room. Day.
Karl is seated reading a newspaper.
Two little girls enter – front door open – they're giggling. They go up to Karl. One of them rubs the side of Karl's crew cut. Then they both run away – giggling.

12. Int. Drawing room. Night.
Karl is in the same position as last scene. Gregory lets himself in. For a moment he stands watching Karl scratch the naked end of his left leg.

Karl is an apparition in this scene – the light of the spacious drawing room on him – as indeed he was in the last scene.

13. Int. Snug. Night.
Gregory, Karl, Roseanne, Nonie sit around a blazing fire in the snug which is separated by partition from drawing room, a door into the drawing room and subsequently to door leading to kitchen. Sofa in front of fire, armchairs to side, all of brownish hue.

On the wall is a framed message from 'His Majesty King George VI'. 'Help to make the world a better place and life a worthier thing.'

There is also a framed poem:

'Have you had a kindness shown?
Pass it on.
'Twas not given to you alone.
Pass it on. Anon.'

There is a ceramic of what could be Queen Victoria in a dress splattered with fuchsia. On the mantelpiece is a photograph of Mrs. Duane as a young woman – black thirties dress – she has almost an identical appearance to Nonie.

Gregory:
Tell us about the war.
(Karl takes out a tobacco tin.)

Karl:
Prince Albert tobacco.
(He puts the tin to his mouth and makes harmonica sounds on it.)

Karl:
There was this Chinese guy who'd fly over each night at the same time in a little plane made of canvas and sticks. We called him Bedtime Charlie.

Gregory (wide-eyed):
And wasn't he ever shot down?

Karl:
We liked him too much.

14. Int. Kitchen of Gregory's home. Day.
Gregory addresses a grandfather who is seated under a calendar with a picture of a Chinese cardinal on it, underneath the picture these words: 'Cardinal Tien – exiled primate of China and archbishop of Peking.'

Gregory:
Karl doesn't believe in war.

(Grandfather who has been reading the *Irish Independent* just looks at him.)

15. Ext. Street. Day.
Gregory addresses a man intensifying the claret colour of the cinema, a ladder beside him, behind him in a window a poster of Doris Day and Rock Hudson in *Pillow Talk*. We don't see the name of the cinema in this scene.

Gregory:
Karl doesn't believe in war.

(The man continues painting.)

16. Int. Kitchen of Gregory's home. Day.
Gregory addresses a sleeping ginger dog that could be just about of any breed but he's big and fat.

Gregory:
Karl doesn't believe in war.

17. Ext. Street. Day.
Karl walks along with camera.
He passes two girls, around nine.

Girl (to other):
What did I tell you? What did I say just now?

(Further down the street a blonde girl, also around nine, stands against a wall.)

Blonde girl:
What's your name?

Karl:
Karl. What's yours?

Blonde girl:
Edel. Are you Australian?

(Karl takes her photograph.
Karl speaks in voice-over over this episode and the next. At first there's a mystery and disjointedness about these voice-overs. Is he speaking to someone in Duane's or in the pub?)

Karl (voice-over):
In Korea a camera was a way of shooting yourself. You didn't exist anymore. You hitched a lift at the motorpool and went into Seoul and shot the dark green trams or the lepers outside the cathedral or the threadbare prostitutes and afterwards sent the photos home. Or you walked with your ansco camera into the wide plateaux, away from the combat zone, if that's where you were, and shot river deer or turtle doves or swan geese, rhododendrons, azalea or skeleton firs and you

sent back pretty pictures to Alabama as news of you. The pictures took away the responsibility.

18. Ext. Street. Day.
Karl photographs war veterans at the end of the street, afterwards shaking hands with them, chatting with them under the voice-over. These men fought in the Great War. Some have legs missing. Some are very fat, one or two tiny and thin. They are a customary sight at the street corner, recounting over and over again, for all to hear, anecdotes of war. Abused, drink-ruddy, remembering faces.

One man (about Jumble Breetches, a large fat man with a leg missing):
And sure didn't that one-legged eegit go back to war. Off with O'Duffy's men from Dungarvan in 1936. And then he couldn't find the war.

Yet another:
But he found the ribero wine.

(The man who's just spoken starts doing a mock flamenco dance, hands above his head, the music coming from his throat. Karl photographs him. Then we see the still, in black and white.)

PEARSE HUTCHINSON

Amhrán Bréagach do Phaidí Ned Mhóir

Dúradh léi gur manach búdach í
i mbeatha eile dá cuid fadó;
's gur fhág fós gan críochnú
dealbh mhór shuaimhneach an bhúda.
Gheall an cailín go gcríochnódh
sí féin an dealbh naofa.

Dá mb'fhíor athbhreith
cá bhfios nach dtiocfadh ar an saol arís
ambasadóir ina rúnaí óg,
ina chailín? iarla ríoga
ina bhádóir óg, ina bhuachaill
cúig bliana déag d'aois
ar loch geal na síochána?
clúmh-agus-tarradóir ina bhean óg
i ngrá le saighdiúr gallda?
nó saighdiúr marfach aineolach
ina stailc ocrais,
ina bhró feamainne?

Nó gach duine mór-le-rá
ina dhuine?

Nó, ina fheithid –

Agus an bádóir óg
cá bhfios nach dtiocfadh ar ais
ina dhealbhadóir an áthais?

Amhrán Bréagach
for Phaidí Ned Mhóir

She was a Buddhist monk, they told her,
in another life of hers, long past;
she'd left unfinished then a big
serene statue of the Buddha.
The girl promised to finish, now,
that holy likeness.

Who knows, if reincarnation
is true, an ambassador won't
get re-born as a young
woman secretary? a royal earl
as a young boatman, a boy
fifteen years old
on a bright lake of peace?
tar-and-featherer a girl
in love with a foreign soldier?
a murderous ignorant soldier
as a hunger-strike,
or a kelp quern?

Or every VIP
a human being

Or, as an insect –

And the young boatman:
who knows he won't come back
a sculptor of happiness?

Author's Note:
Amhrán Bréagach: Literally, 'lying song'. Generic name for a not uncommon kind of Gaelic folksong, also known as Amhrán na mBréag ('song of lies'). Such songs, often used as lullabies, gave admirable scope to the imagination, often resulting in what might be called folk-surrealism.

ELFRIEDE JELINEK

The Fall of the Bodies

Peter Paul Rubens: The small 'Fall of the Damned'. (Alte Pinakothek, Munich.)

From the kisses and the coasts, from their shores, they are falling. God knows, through their own fault. At some time or other they chose the wrong exit, even though it would have been easy to reach Heaven if only they had chosen the straight and narrow path of Roman Catholicism. The counter-Reformation unrolls its placards. The large 'Fall of the Damned' shows the compact configuration formed by the blessed and the damned in a vertically dominating and looping composition. On the left, giant naked bodies are pushing upwards, on the right they are dragged, shoved, kicked downwards. They are like thoughts incarnate from the Father's head, thrust down by him. The small 'Fall of the Damned' then, when turned on its compositional axis, merely leaves a vertical cascade of bodies and is, strictly speaking, a genuine downfall into the inferno. The idyll in the lunette above, having probably been added later by one of Rubens' scholars in his workshop, is no more than a sketch making slight suggestions. In a morose way the blessed ones are pushing their lives along the ropes of an earthly boxing ring, dimming and thinning at the edges – pure light to which God lets himself down in good time.

Yet do they know it is their own fault or do they know nothing? Are they acting, even though fallen, trodden upon by angels? Could it really be that Rubens, an enlightened, educated man of the world, a philosopher with a preference for Antiquity, and a brother of a philosopher, wished to express, without the slightest hint of irony, that these monstrous heaps of flesh have fallen into the hands of God, wished to depict the Celestials' zeal, Mother Church's claim of sole representation? Or is this painting not, as it seems to me in the enormous nude beings with angelic heads, a last triumph of the flesh which caused such a scandal that it had to be removed from the Jesuit Church of Neuburg on the Danube for which it had been painted? These bodies are oversized toys for a hero shooting arrows. With whom do the Gods play and what does the indivisible God say, whom does He harness to His cart? Rubens never needed any excuse to exhibit nakedness but the nakedness has its history written in its flesh. And there is nakedness of two kinds, woman and man, and there is God who created both and shows us so.

In the classical theme of 'The Battle of the Amazons' (Alte Pinakothek) the bodies are of a classical symmetry, a thing-for-itself.

The women are active, and although they fall like grass when hit by an arrow, they remain standing, alone, struck down in battle, yet in nobody's power but their own – honourable opponents of their enemies. In the religious painting, however, the bodies are cast by God becoming completely resigned to their fate. Those, who on earth were robed in sin and lived in it, are thrown down by Him with the help of His angels. The central part of the painting: a carpet of interwoven bodies leaving no space between darker masculine and lighter feminine flesh. Human floods, God's material, the souls are one with Him, having been captured and fallen into His hands, and on the last day they slip out of the packing, a glomerate mass of flesh on canvas. God has formed these lumps of clay and throws them about. God holds their strings and only in this way do those beings become visible as subject to God and as conquered by God. It is only in this contortion of bodies that their flesh proves to be real and refers to itself and nothing else, and becomes its own habitation after their souls have returned to God. The falling men, entangled in their mountainous masses of flesh, even when being thrown, keep their shape, and remain independent like the one in the centre of the painting with an angel pushing on his head and a demon of hell already pulling on his foot because he, who is condemned by God has to become his victim. Yet the soft bodies of the women: in their fall, their sinking seems to be even more unavoidable and it seems as if their surrendering to God becomes more deeply engraved on the female body, as if woman did not sin as an autonomous being, but even in her sin was still dependent, seduced, and persuaded to evil. The body of the woman in its softness is more exposed to gravity. She is no captured eagle, her sin is stuck to her flesh. Her tumbling down is no autonomous submission to punishment.

The most fascinating couple for me in this painting has always been the demon on the bottom left who exposes the naked female sinner. In a parasitic motion, being induced by the other, in the utmost twist of the body, the nakedness of the woman manifests itself as a metaphor for nakedness itself. The woman is not only displayed by her conqueror, she is laid bare. While the men stand for themselves and even receive punishment to their genitals (in the central bottom part of the painting a snake bites a naked man on the penis), each motion of the twisted woman's body is triggered by the male demon. For a long time I wanted to believe that this contortion of a female body which is induced by the male devil who stands straddle-legged on the ground in search of balance because his trunk gets dragged by the man (but at the same time the woman seems to be pulling the devil's ear looking for a last hold, and the devil, though not a human being and certainly insensitive to pain, pulls his face with indignation, and even evades her hand!) – that this contortion was an excuse to make a quasi-pornographic presentation which should draw or force the viewer's attention to the physical details of the woman, I do not believe this any longer, because, as I have said before, Rubens never needed any excuse for the presentation of female flesh. (Or did he perhaps need excuses to stretch it to the extremities, to distort and deform it?)

In the foreground of 'The Feast of Venus' (Kunsthistorisches Museum, Vienna) there are similar if very earthly couplings of nymphs and satyrs. The bodies of the satyrs seem to turn the women's bodies 'to the camera' so that the women's glances appear to fix the viewer, yet at the same time banishing him back to his position, eternally distant and without male companionship. Rubens' great artistic ingenuity does not exist in the fraternization between the male viewer and the male inducer (Creator!) of the female motion, who first unveils the woman down to her nakedness. Yet the history of the flesh is written in the female smoothness of the skin and also in the muscular structure of the male, and his history is not hidden but exhibited. The apparent innocence of the painting gets its history back, it turns political, becomes a history of differences.

The texture of both paintings (the small 'Fall of the Damned' and also 'The Feast of Venus') is an intricate web in which all values are equal; the flesh does not stand out obtrusively. The viewer seeing the 'Fall of the Damned' is unmasked as a voyeur who sees a thing he-must-not-see, but at the same time is kept at a distance where he is meant to see a thing he-must-see for as long as he rambles through life and has sufficient time to change his ways. One figure, however, this time in the large 'Fall of the Damned', seems to break out of the uniformity of the texture. In the bottom right of the painting there is a devil who holds a naked woman, grasping her from behind and lifting her breasts with his left arm, pushing them up, so that the extraordinary shine and firmness of the flesh in all its materiality leaves the viewer with no other option than to bring it into focus. The woman reflects a double vision. Two creators, Father and Man, see her in her physical entity, and at the same time can perceive in her body the history of her sex. Rubens suspends motion for a moment before the imminent impact of the mass of flesh seen in the middle of the painting, in order to set off the narrative level in the bottom part (as opposed to the one full of aestheticism seen in the middle) with its body pairings of devils who expose the women's sinful bodies taking possession of the sin itself, thus drawing visual attention directly to it. Here, the history is re-told over and over again. The women appear to be glued to the men's armoured bodies, like the couple in the middle shown in profile. It seems as though the man gave birth to the woman

– in a strange form of partheno-genesis, as though he split her off from himself. She is a secondary being who is nothing without him, in contrast to which he remains the Other. One is missing the Other, and this must remain so forever. It is only in their sinfulness, when cast away by God, that they complete each other.

(Translated from the German by Jutta Shannon.)

JENNIFER JOHNSTON

Excerpt from *The Invisible Worm,* a novel in progress.

Such scenes stay with me.
The feel of his fingers pressing through my coat and the black woollie will stay with me for ever . . . not, of course, in the front regions of my mind; but I will be able to recall the feel of those fingers, the faint smell of Eau Sauvage, the sound of his steps, confident on the polished parquet as we walk across the hall.
Such scenes reverberate and conjure up other similar scenes from the past: my father's soft white fingers imprinting their marks on my bare arm, as he shook me and my feet clattered on the floor and a dog barked at nothing outside in the sunshine.
Some memories are so joyful that you could bask for ever in them; others you long to shove back, away back, into the darkness out of which they have sprung uninvited.
As we drive in the car towards the church, I try to exorcise that picture of my father and myself by calling into my mind happier, more tranquil recollections.
Maurice talks, but I don't hear him; his words patter round me like a summer shower.
The streets around the church are lined with cars.
The car park is full.
Women with nothing better to do stand around the church gate waiting to catch a glimpse of something or someone out of the ordinary; a Cabinet Minister, a Bishop, the diminished red rimmed eyes, the tears, even better, of the bereaved. I intend to disappoint them.
It is a huge ornate church.
We walk past the waiting hearse and the watching women.
My mother never put foot inside this church.
I wonder to myself if, had she lived, she would have been with us now, walking beside Maurice and myself.
'A vulgarity,' she once said to me. 'Built on the backs and out of the pockets of people who could hardly afford to feed their children. Or buy shoes for their children. They, those people, paid more for it than your father ever did, or his brothers and sisters, because they felt what they gave; those few pounds impinged on their lives.'
My father always hoped that she would turn.
I once heard her laugh at him.
'Devil a bit of it,' she said. 'Haven't you got my house and my land and my beautiful body? What makes you think you should have my soul as well?'

He hated such irony.
She was the only person in the world who didn't jump when he snapped his fingers; who didn't succumb to his enormous charm: perhaps I shouldn't say that, perhaps she had indeed succumbed and thereafter had to protect herself from it.
The organ is playing; something sonorous and unrecognisable. Our feet clatter on the tiles as we walk to the front of the church.
Tall windows: red, blue swathes of light, patterns of haloed heads, hands extended in prayer or blessing; red, green blue, shadowing the faces of the living, patterning also the walls and floor.
Of course we have to sit in the front.
I do not look to left or right as I follow the little fellow who leads us along the aisle. I don't know who he is.
He is dressed in sober black, black tie, sombre face. . . a professional I would think; his walk is that of a professional, unobtrusive, adapted to my pace, consoling almost in its smoothness.
He turns and inclines his head slightly towards me as we reach the front pew.
I move past him and kneel down.
Our Father which art in Heaven. . .
The only prayer which trips from my tongue.
Hallowed be Thy name. . .
A poem.
Thy kingdom come. . .
Maurice settles to his knees beside me, dipping his head down towards his hands.
Thy will be done on earth. . .
My mother's voice whispered the words.
As it is in heaven.
Every evening, her hands folded over mine.
Give us this day our daily bread. . .
It also came trippingly from her tongue.
And forgive us our trespasses, as we forgive them. . .
'Laura.'
that trespass against us.
I can't.
I cannot forgive.
Forget it God.
Forget I ever said those words.
I cannot. . .
'Laura.'
His elbow nudged me.
'Laura.'
I get up from my knees, angry with myself.

'What?'
'The President's ADC has just arrived.'
Across the aisle from us, he is being settled into the front pew, with all due obsequiousness.
My flowers are the only ones on the coffin, I notice.
Spring flowers, yellow and green and white; a smile stiffens my mouth for a moment. I had never intended such a patriotic statement, but I'm sure that the President's ADC has made a pleasant mental note. I'm sure that the Ministers and other dignitaries present will commend me in their hearts.
Along the aisle the flowers are heaped, wreaths, crosses, cushions, sprays, a great sheaf of wax-like lilies lies to the right of the coffin.
There is a rustling at the back of the church; the sound of the organ swells; we all stand up.
The ceremony will take it course.
Oration, peroration, homily, sermon, valediction, obsequy, exequy.
If I got up and spoke the words I have inside me, what a shock they'd get.
The hole they dig for you won't be deep enough, dear father.
How petty to think such a thought in the middle of all this formality.
They dance: the words, like music, punctuate their movements.
With each amen the tempo changes.
They dance to the glory of whatever God may be: advance, retreat, turn, bow; men dance, boys dance.
They dance in celebration of my father's life.
I feel cold.
A wind has penetrated the stone walls and numbs my body; or maybe the cold is spreading out from me, maybe it will embrace the whole church, the whole town, the whole island. I will infect the race with my hatred.
Maurice is praying; his hands placed together like some saint in an Italian painting. His eyes are closed. His face still is tinted with brown from his two weeks in January spent in Mustique.
Will you come dote?
How can I come? Isn't my father dying?
There's nothing you can do about that.
I must be here.
Suit yourself.
He'd have got a rare shock if I'd said yes; if I'd rushed up to town and bought the bikinis, the silk shirts, the Ambre Solaire.
Forgive me. Forgive me. Forgive me.
I had to stoop right down almost to the bed to catch the words, so frail was his voice.
Forgive me.

The nurse read a novel in a chair by the window.
Will you?
Last week. That was last week. The spring sun hurt his eyes and we had to keep the blinds half drawn.
Yes.
I said yes.
I had to say yes.
I touched his cold fingers; for a moment they were still, then as I lifted my hand, the restless plucking and tearing started again.
Yes.
That's all now, said the nurse putting her book on the table and getting up from the basket chair that crackled as she moved and her starched apron crackled as she came over to the bed.
He's tired, Aren't you pet?
'Laura.'
The procession is forming: the dancers move slowly from the altar towards the aisle.
Without much grace the coffin is lifted onto the shoulders of my four cousins, my father's nephews; their feet clatter as they move down the church.
Maurice takes my arm and together we walk between the watching people as we had done on the day of our wedding.

KLAUS JÜNSCHKE

Into the Free Part of Diez
Excerpt from *Spätlese*

'Temporary release' surely is such an impossible phrase because it still contains the very idea of jail. For a few hours you are allowed outside those walls, yet every single minute of it you remain a prisoner. All the same, my temporary release was a beautiful experience. Not only because at long last it meant the beginning of the end of all those years in the clink. It was simply terrific to be able to move beyond those walls.

I was taken out by Bundschuh, the psychologist who was in charge of Manfred and myself and who had written our reports. As is obligatory with TR, there was also a prison officer who normally works as a warder in the wing which houses me. I had asked him would he be willing to join Bundschuh and myself on this doggy-walk.

When it became plain that my outing was finally to take place, I quickly found peace of mind again. Over the past months I had been in turmoil like I hadn't been for a long time. I noticed it most clearly when I was studying (I could hardly concentrate) and when I was writing letters (if I wrote any at all, they got shorter and shorter). I had withdrawn from prison life and had only gone to watch TV when we had free time.

Now then, Tuesday, January 14th, 1986:

Around 11.30 a.m. the aforementioned officer, Herr Reichardt, arrived and took me from my cell to the store. There I changed clothes, swapping my prison trousers and jumper for jeans and jersey from my clothes bag. And there was my old parka dating from the times of the Extra-Parliamentary Opposition. Somebody, probably Elisabeth, had sent it to Zweibrücken when I was in custody there awaiting trial. There we had been permitted to wear our own clothes. Anyway, the only thing that made me feel awkward about the outing, was this old US Army parka. Of course, once we were outside, it didn't even attract any attention at all, especially as there was a drizzle for most of the time. This kind of olive-green could be seen quite a bit in the streets. Diez is a Bundeswehr garrison with several thousand troops. But I find it very hard to look at myself in such a get-up. It's just that a parka might be practical but it also has a military look, it's a uniform. At any rate, this is how I explained to myself why I would have preferred to roll up this rag and tuck it under my arm.

The last time I got TR to see the doctor (handcuffed, accompanied by three prison officers and with police cars in front and behind the prison mini-bus), I had to undress at the store and was kitted out with completely new prison gear. But, as I said, this time I could keep my underwear and my sturdy winter boots on. It meant that in future I would be treated the same when I was going to see the doctor: no handcuffs, less humiliating clothes. The doggy-walks lying ahead of us are also called 'relaxation outings' because they are designed to prepare us for a relaxation of prison regulations such as parole and open prison.

From the store we went on to the cashier's office where I received 50 deutschmarks. This is only done when someone goes on an outing or on parole. Otherwise the possession of cash is strictly prohibited and punished accordingly. For example, if someone is caught smuggling cash into the clink, he is immediately taken out of the open prison and transferred back to the closed institution for at least three months. The opening hours of the cashier's office served as an argument as to why we had to be back in jail by 4 p.m. – so that I could hand back the remainder of my money.

Thus for the first time in 13½ years I walked through the prison gates on foot, in my own clothes and without handcuffs. After all those years in Zweibrücken jail, where I was forever walled in, I would certainly have freaked out emotionally, my pulse would have quickend and my heart would have been in my mouth, as had been the case with my first yard exercise in Diez. Now, in the street in front of the clink I was moved by what I saw in the poky gate lodge: There hung the latest wanted posters. Posters with so many photographs as I had never seen before.

I had had this feeling of the walls coming down in 1980 and 1981 in the jail's open-air enclosure where the football pitch is (it's only now that we may use it again). At that time we were allowed to do some long-distance running (the 900 metre track along the internal wall gives you an impression of the size of the grounds). When we ran out the first few times, I had the feeling as though to my left and to my right there were no longer any walls surrounding me. It had always been right inside my body, this sense of near and unsurmountable walls (since we were constantly subjected to additional checks by the prison personnel).

Once outside, we straight away turned into the road on the right. I had been allowed to choose for myself where we should go and what we should do. The only condition was that we had to go into Diez. My TR had been sanctioned as early as Autumn, so it had long been known what I fancied doing. When I looked through the window of my high security cell, in which I had been for years, I could see the old folks' home on top of the mountain and beyond the Diezer Hain, a little wood which was a protected nature reserve. I had always entertained the idea of looking down at the clink from up there, right into my empty cell, so to speak. That's why we went up there first. A few months before, something else had been more important for me. The wood on the hill had been in radiant autumn colours, red and orange and yellow, and I really had wanted to see that close up. Also I had pictured myself walking on paths covered with colourful leaves as I used to know them from walks and hikes in the woods. Now all of it looked somewhat more sober. It was cold and wet, the colours long gone.

On our way up to the old folks' home (the last stretch of the road is called 'Zur Ruhestatt' – resting-place – to my mind it's really bad taste) we passed through a street lined with villas which had been built over the past few years. Bundschuh had never been there, either. Some of those hovels were so peculiar that we couldn't control ourselves and burst out laughing. Incidentally, this residential area built for some members of the high society in Diez seemed to me like one of those streets which Derrick turns into on a Friday night to have a look at one of the corpses that will keep him on the go for the rest of the night. In the clink you naturally get square eyes. Like the people outside who spend their lives in front of the goggle-box.

When we reached the little wood, a jogger came running along the path that we were going to take. Had I been on my own, I would of course have started running myself, at the latest up there where there were no more houses. And I would have screamed. And jumped into the air. Just as I would have climbed one of those old trees to extend my view of the valley and the jail and the city of Limburg beyond.

But I couldn't expect my escorts to let me make off just like that. So we stood quietly next to the old folks' home at the edge of the forest and gazed down into the valley: the small prison, the river Lahn, Limburg hospital on the mountain behind and Limburg cathedral.

It is quite mean not to be allowed to be reunited with your relatives or your best friends to share with them the joy of such a gratifying moment. Other prisoners are permitted such arrangements. All the same, I was determined to be delighted and to take my first steps in freedom without a grim face.

On the forest path I admired the old trees and stared again and again fascinated at the undergrowth. As it was without leaves, it didn't look much on a day in January, but there was something unspoilt and original about the twigs and branches criss-crossing. It gave you an idea that in summer it would be a realm all of its own, inaccessible and so dense you wouldn't be able to see in. Now I understood why in jail I could sometimes see a herd of deer running at the crack of dawn from the river Lahn across the fields towards the little wood. In spite of all those tracks, the thicket provides them with a safe habitat. Yet there are any number of tracks. And at every turn there is a keep-fit sign. We passed a frame with rings for pull-ups and I tried to pull myself up, but very gently. I had grown more cautious over the past years after all the experience with my body, physical exercise and the weather. I am not keen on pulled ligaments any more. When we walked slowly downhill and came out of the little wood (having walked less than 500 metres in it), there was yet another sign pointing to the keep-fit trail. I would have loved to lie down on my back and stretch my arms and legs. Too much smartness is fatal. Unfortunately I can't remember what it was called. 'Vita Parcour' – something like that. Health in a crystal glass with a Portuguese cork stop. At any rate something so posh that the whole forest would have shaken with laughter if it could read.

At the edge of the wood there was again a proper street. With a modern phone box. No dial but press-buttons instead. Those I only knew from TV. At least the tattered directory was a familiar sight.

Behind the phone box there was a small cemetery. A forest cemetery. Looking over the hedge I saw three graves so tiny that they must have been children's graves. Afterwards I thought to myself that it wouldn't have been a bad idea to walk around that cemetery.

The street that led down the fairly steep hill into the old part of Diez, typically enough, wasn't called 'Zur Ruhestatt' but something like 'Schöne Aussicht' – Bellevue. As opposed to the old folks' home, however, the vista wasn't particularly beautiful. To the right below the cemetery there was an impressive old quarry: a view of the uninhabitable bowels of the earth. The detached houses which lined the street were all older than those on the other side of the hill but none of them were done in such bad taste as some of the modern ones.

There was a dog compound next to one of the houses. Two red-haired Lassies barked at us loudly. Bundschuh and the officer tried in vain to think of the proper name given to that breed. The street became more winding. And still we were walking downhill. We passed the hospital of Diez and the district court. This is the seat of the 'Strafvollstreckungskammer' – the chamber of court which decides on our appeals against being remanded in custody, and on remission after 15 years in accordance with article 57a of the penal code. The judge presiding over this court, which is not very popular with anyone, is called Korn, and the inmates only speak of the court as the 'Kornkammer' – the granary.

A little further along a school had just finished for the day. Children stood about on the pavement. Bundschuh greeted the daughter of a family he knew. It's a small world in Diez. A few minutes later a car pulled in on the main street and we could once more see the children, who in the meantime had been collected from school. The driver was one of the women assistants who work in jail in an honorary capacity.

We said a big hello. In spite of the persistent drizzle we were in high spirits, and encounters such as this only helped lift them. By the way, back in the clink I didn't meet a single prisoner who was annoyed about my getting TR. Everyone whom I know a bit better was glad for me.

After the car with its load of little children had hit the road to get them to their dinner-tables, we decided to go for lunch ourselves. In a restaurant on the main street. Studying the menu displayed outside I could make up my mind whether or not it would appeal to me. It did. I can't, however, remember the name. Molinos? Anyway, there was a grill, a big kitchen and about forty square tables, all laid with table-cloths, napkins, knives and forks and candles. Festive.

We hung up our coats at the door, and Bundschuh put down his old umbrella, asking us to remind him of it when we were leaving.

We sat down at a table at the back wall. When I picked up this enormous menu, I felt flustered. The choice was simply too much. German, Italian, French, even Chinese – more than 150 dishes and beverages. I decided in favour of a French dish. I have forgotten its name, too. Even though I do have some French. The last word was 'Tahiti'. I suppose it stood for the pineapple and the other tropical fruits which had been placed on top of the fried veal stuffed with ham and cheese. Sweet and hot. With some rice. But the meat alone was plentiful. My palate was jubilant. Before that I had orange juice. It took a while before the meal was served. enough time to have a look around and take in our surroundings. Everything still felt quite unreal. Snippets of conversation wafted over from the adjacent tables where some businessmen were having their meals. This is what I felt like: as if in a shop. Quite alien. Even though the atmosphere was friendly and fairly warm. This was partly due to my escorts. When I had to be excused, I went to the toilet all on my own without anybody following me. There was never any tension between us.

When we left the restaurant, it was half past two. Already more than half of my outing gone. I felt more and more at ease.

In keeping with our programme, we now went to the river Lahn. This was something else I had asked for: a view of the river from the bridge. The river was in flood and had burst both its banks. We walked across the new bridge and gazed at the face of the town which was familiar to me from all those picture postcards of Diez. I knew the castle from the prison history. Before they built the prison in Freiendiez (Free Diez) in 1912, the prisoners had been incarcerated in the castle. Today it houses a youth hostel.

Herr Reichardt could tell us a lot about the Lahn, its navigability and the pleasure boat which we can spot from the clink sometimes. He used to be a bargeman before he got 'jailed' himself.

I took note of the wild ducks and the swans searching for food at the bank but, as I became aware afterwards, I did so without much interest. Some years ago it had been quite different. I had been fascinated by a pair of wild ducks which for a while used to fly past my window into the prison yard and so quickly scoffed the slices of bread thrown at them out of our windows that they were a joy to watch.

We went back to Diez across the old bridge over the Lahn. A sightseeing tour around the old city. A brother and sister, both about fourteen, were the only people to be seen in these few alleyways. I had a look around so as to have seen it. There isn't a lot more to be seen in Diez. In all probability I would have preferred to climb about a heap of metal in a car dump to traipsing around all this masonry. After such a long time in the clink you are fed up with walls. Haus Eberhard, known to me through reading the local pages of the Lahnzeitung newspaper, was the only ray of hope. It's the exhibition centre for the artists of Diez and all the works of art coming to Diez. When we went past it peeping in from front and back, it was completely empty, but at least you could tell that it was a place for people to meet.

Where would I like to go when I shall be in the pre-release section having a pass till 9.30 p.m. three times a week?

4 o'clock was drawing near. At a kiosk (a little cabin draped with the products of the West German press – 30 to 40 magazines of all descriptions, a concentration of feeble-mindedness in colour) I bought some picture postcards. Afterwards I went to the post office for some stamps. At the post office I wrote greetings to my family and my friends and posted the cards on the spot.

From there we went down the Limburger Straße towards the clink. I felt as if I was slightly tipsy. It had been a marvellous feeling to be free or at least outside those prison walls. Next to the prison there is the leisure centre of Diez with its indoor swimming pool, ice rink and tennis court. Through the glass panes which reach from the floor to the ceiling one can glimpse the pool from the street. I would love to go there on my last outing.

It didn't pain me to have to go back to jail. Maybe because I had well prepared myself for it. Why, I have to get the knack of walking regularly in and out of prison or of going on holidays over the next few years, while at the same time finding the inner peace which allows me to prepare and pass my master's degree.

January 19th, 1988
(From letters dating from 1986)

(Translated from the German by Hans-Christian Oeser.)

RICHARD KEARNEY

Protest

Cordon of batons circle the night
barring access to Saint Germain;
Paris students march in line,
to chants of *police assassin*!

The two ranks touch in concave sweeps –
Seigneur to virgin in unwilled embrace:
helmetted, he lays flowers at her feet
and bloodies her shy face.

But victims of militia rape
march again in double time:
orphans in hobby-horse parade
they think they steer the wooden steeds

which, by some pre-established text,
are nailed by hoof and belly to the ground –
the more they struggle with the reins
the more they circle round and round.

Finger Prints

The print of fingers
bled onto a prison wall:
vermillion scar to seal
a breeze-block envelope.

The print of fingers
extended from the tortured
to the torturer:
cruel braille of hope.

The print of fingers
unable to bequeath
carbon-copy handouts
for funeral tropes.

Here is a morse-code of alarms –
blind epigraphs of touch.
But where are the readers of palms?

ROBERT KEE

Three Unwise Judges

A disturbing aspect of Thursday's decision against the Birmingham Six by three Lord Justices of Appeal – posterity might want to know their names, Lord Lane, Lord Justice O'Connor and Lord Justice Stephen Brown – is that few people expected anything else.

From the first days of the hearing it was widely assumed that the judges would use the referral procedure to protect the name and past performance of British justice rather than to uphold it by seeing that justice was done. It was assumed that their judgment would echo that of Lord Denning in an earlier phase of the case when he said that if the six were found to be innocent it would open a vista of police wrong-doing and perjury so appalling to contemplate that it could not be contemplated.

The only surprising thing about Thursday's decision is that Lord Lane, Lord Justice O'Connor and Lord Justice Stephen Brown should have shown so little concern to make their own approach sound different. It is a bad day for British justice when such assumptions, whether correct or not, can seem so easily to be confirmed.

It is an important principle of our system of justice that while judges are there to expound, direct and administer the law, the guilt or innocence of the accused is decided by juries.

Thirteen years ago a jury decided in the light of the evidence it heard at the Birmingham trial that these six men were guilty. In the interval since then not only have new considerations of substance appeared to cast lurking doubt on the scientific evidence, but quite new evidence has appeared allegedly to cast more than a lurking doubt on the evidence of the men's confessions.

No jury has been called upon to decide the men's guilt or innocence in the light of these new considerations and this new evidence. Lord Bridge tied his own reputation to the correctness of the verdict thirteen years ago, and this week Lord Lane, Lord Justice O'Connor and Lord Justice Stephen Brown have decided it for themselves.

They could have ordered a new trial. Would a jury have come to the same decision in the new circumstances? Would it have 'had no doubt that the original convictions were safe and satisfactory'? Can it be right that we do not know?

I attended the hearing on the day on which the most important new evidence of this referral procedure was heard by the court – that of Mrs. Joyce Lynas, a former police cadet in Birmingham who, expanding evidence she had given a few days before, said that she had seen one of the men physically maltreated at the police station at the time when their confessions were made. In this second appearance her credibility was particularly on trial since she had to explain why she had not told the full story originally.

The manner in which she did this over a period of half-an-hour or more was so totally convincing to me that had I been a member of a jury asked to judge her credibility there would have been no question in my mind that she was speaking anything but the truth, or that in consequence very considerable doubt attached to the validity of the men's confessions. I cannot believe that any fair-minded British jury man or woman would have thought otherwise.

Lord Lane and Lord Justice Stephen Brown barely looked at Mrs. Lynas throughout her whole time in the witness box, being busily engaged – as the antiquated procedure of the court seems to require – in writing down in longhand what she was saying. Lord Justice O'Connor looked at her occasionally as if to assess how much trouble she was going to cause. Millions of people have since been able to judge her credibility on television news programmes. But not a British jury. The decision of the three Lord Justices of Appeal was that Mrs. Lynas was 'a witness not worthy of belief'.

THOMAS KENEALLY

Excerpt from *Flying Hero Class*

Pauline's father Dr. Cross had in her early childhood run a fashionable dental clinic on Sydney's North Shore. He engineered and repaired the teeth of many knights, military, industrial, conservatively political. He fixed the mouths which spoke in boardrooms, and in those days this gave him cachet. On the North Shore of Sydney there were always ambitions towards fashion. Though these were under siege from the sun and from the sad fact that in Australia nearly all the *riches* were *nouveaux,* they were persistent enough to make Dr. Cross what could be called a *society* dentist.

One day in Pauline's childhood and McCloud's, he was filling the teeth of some heavy-engineering knight's second, younger wife when she gave what he would tell the coroner was *a small gurgle or moan* and collapsed in the chair. He did all the right things, even using compressed oxygen to try to revive her. His nurse had already called for doctors and ambulances. They were some twenty minutes arriving, and it was apparent to him long before that the woman could not be revived.

This young woman had grown up in the country, and her fillings had been done by old-school dentists. As he would later tell Pauline in explanation of the new course he would set his life on, he became aware, as he watched the woman's open mouth, of what he'd already known in an off-hand, notional way. Like those of a lot of country girls, her teeth had suffered considerable decay early in life. Each of her fillings had been marked on her dental chart, certainly. But he had never before paid full attention to the extent of the work which had been done. And most of the holes had been filled with gold. It must have cost her parents a large proportion of their wool cheques to go on repairing their daughter's mouth.

Waiting for the ambulance therefore, he spent a long time gazing into her golden mouth. He accepted the idea that there was something wrong with his gazing, though he acted with reverence and knew that – unlike the alcoholic carelessnesses of his father-in-law – his behaviour would not attract the censure of the Dental Association.

McCloud, who had grown up in one of the less preferred but still affluent reaches of the North Shore, heard of this tragedy by eavesdropped adult rumour, and because the Sunday papers loved the tale of the young woman's death in the dental chair. In what the papers and adults muttered about the case there was the suggestion that Dr. Cross had known the woman as more than a patient. A photograph appeared in the tabloids of a New Year's Eve party at some golf club where Dr. Cross sat next to the knight's wife. Mrs. Cross had been sitting on Dr. Cross's right hand side in the original, harmless photograph, but the press had cropped her out for fear she marred the story and the imputation.

Had Dr. Cross gassed or poisoned his mistress? That was the question which hung over all the suburban rumours and the circumstantial press reports. The earlier and startling Clark case had set people up, if they needed setting up, to ask such a question.

At the time of the scandal Pauline was twelve and attending a Presbyterian ladies' college on the North Shore. McCloud did not know her then. In fact, when he first saw her she was twenty-four; it was at some party, and she was pointed out to him by someone who remembered the Dr. Cross story. Given that a great whisper had altered or perhaps ended his own childhood, he looked at her and wondered how the even juicier rumour which flared for a time in her life had been absorbed into her tidy beauty, her competent, square-shouldered, smallish frame.

The coroner had found that the knight's young wife died of a cerebral haemorrhage, and had called the innuendos attaching to Dr. Cross unfounded and shameful. (Again, there was a parallel with the Clark trial, which to the young McCloud was the McCloud case.) The judge uttered the devout hope that Dr. Cross's patients would stand by him, for his professional reputation was intact. But there was never a chance that they would.

Dr. Cross himself forestalled them. He closed his surgery and sold the practice to the first comer. He took to going to the bush and living, first for weeks at a time and then for months, in a tent on a friend's farm on the old goldfield at Sofala. After the absences became all but permanent, Mrs. Cross told him – for his daughter's sake – to keep away. Life in a tent had by then made him a different man, an inadvertent one. He spent his time re-panning old gravel beds and taking to the flanks of hills with a pick. It may have struck Mrs Cross that he was looking for some image of *her* mouth, the mouth of the knight's young wife. In McCloud's novel anyhow, the fictional Mrs. Cross would accuse her husband of that.

Reworking the nineteenth century mullock-heaps and gravel beds, Dr. Cross grew old and uncomfortable to be with and became a brief ghost at the wedding of those two orphans of rumour, McCloud and Pauline. He had built a shack amongst old diggings and left-over cyanide treatment tanks used by prospectors who had earned a small living there during the Depression. Here he died of some respiratory illness; though of course to Pauline he had died first when he went to the bush, looking a century too late for all that Sheba bounty of Sofala.

It was the twelve-year-old Pauline, the spruce child in an early stage of her ultimate bereavement, clearing away her homework books, who was a reproach to the novelist McCloud in his brief, random sleep.

LUDOVIC KENNEDY

I Accuse

On a November night 16 years ago, a group of Irish drinking companions sat playing cards on a train out of Birmingham as two IRA bombs caused dreadful carnage in the city centre. Within hours, accused of being the killers, they were gripped by a nightmare from which they have still not been released.

These men, the Birmingham Six, should not be in prison. The British legal system is keeping them there, having corrupted both the police and the judiciary into incarcerating them against common justice.

The six have maintained in court that false confessions were beaten out of them by the police, and witnesses have come forward to give evidence of their treatment. Yet the judiciary has refused to accept this.

Eminent counsel, who have fought in court on behalf of the prisoners, are known to have been left greatly shocked and angered by the rude and dismissive attitude of the bench towards their case, to the point where the reputation of justice came into question.

Now, at last, it can only be a matter of time before the Home Secretary decides the ordeal of the Birmingham Six must end (I understand he is considering fresh evidence on police violence) and for them to receive proper compensation for their years inside.

When that has happened, the three judges who had the evidence and the power to open the prison gates for them on appeal and yet failed to do so, and in whose integrity not only the public, but some members of their own profession, have now lost faith, might care to consider their positions. For, by their perverse findings, they have seriously undermined confidence in British justice.

Just over two years ago the Court of Appeal in the shape of Lord Lane, lord chief justice, Lord Justice O'Connor and Lord Justice Stephen Brown heard fresh evidence in the case of these six Irishmen: Patrick Hill, Hugh Callaghan, John Walker, Dick McIlkenny, Gerry Hunter and Billy Power, who had been serving life sentences for murder since 1975.

The evidence was led on the two main points that had resulted in the men's convictions: that it could no longer be concluded that any of them had been in contact with explosives, and that their alleged 'confession' had been obtained by threats and violence (as in the case of the Guildford Four, released last year from long prison sentences for IRA bombings).

The court rejected both submissions. 'The longer this case has gone on,' the judges said, 'the more convinced this court has become that the verdict of the jury was correct.' The appeals were dismissed.

So were the judges right in their judgment or wrong? In many murder cases where justice is later found to have miscarried, it often happens that quite early in their investigations the police light on some small but seemingly convincing piece of evidence that leads them to draw the wrong conclusions; and which, if pursued tenaciously, leads in turn to wrongful prosecution, conviction and sentence.

In the case of the Birmingham Six, their undoing was their association with an IRA bomber named James McDade who, on November 14, 1974, blew himself up while planting a bomb in the Coventry Telephone Exchange. Three of the six had been schoolfriends of McDade in the small Roman Catholic enclave of the Ardoyne in north Belfast, while McIlkenny and Callaghan, who were older, had been close friends of the McDade family.

All had come to Birmingham to seek work, mostly in the 1960s. Until McDade blew himself up, none of the six (with the possible exception of Walker) suspected that McDade was an IRA activist.

They were not members of the IRA or even of Sinn Féin. But they were staunch supporters of the republican cause. Several helped to raise money to send to dependants of Ulster fellow Catholics who had been imprisoned or interned.

On November 21, 1974, the body of James McDade was to be flown from Birmingham to Belfast, and five of the six agreed to combine attendance at his funeral with a visit to their families. Their friend Hughie Callaghan saw them off at Birmingham's New Street Station on the 7.55 p.m. train which would connect with the night boat from Heysham.

At 8.17 p.m. the first bomb went off in the Mulberry Bush pub and a few minutes later the second exploded in the Tavern in the Town, both near the station. There were horrific casualties of 21 dead and 162 injured. Ports and airports were alerted, and when the booking clerk at New Street reported that he had sold tickets to a group of Irishmen travelling to Belfast, the Lancashire police were asked to interview them at Heysham.

The five reached Heysham at 10.45 p.m., having spent most of the journey smoking and playing cards and having been observed by a British Rail guard as being in good humour. Paddy Hill was out first and, after showing his luggage to the waiting police, was allowed through to the boat. There he settled in the bar to wait for the others. They were interrogated and had their luggage examined.

In Walker's coat were found Roman Catholic mass cards for the funeral of McDade. The local police called up the head of Lancashire CID, who ordered the men to be taken to Morecambe police station for further interrogation, and for Dr. Frank Skuse to be there with his equipment for detecting traces of explosive. As the four men were being taken away, they asked what had happened to Paddy Hill. He was then taken off the ferry to join them.

If the six were guilty, there are already two things wrong with this scenario. First, as Lord Scarman has pointed out to me, as trained IRA men they would not have set the bombs to explode at a time which would give the police 2½ hours to await their arrival at Heysham. Second, they would not have called the police's attention to the missing Paddy Hill.

On arrival at Morecambe they were put in different cells. In the small hours of the morning Skuse arrived, also Supt. George Reade from Birmingham and detectives from the West Midlands Serious Crime Squad (now disbanded during investigation of many of its officers).

One by one the five men were escorted to Skuse to have their hands swabbed in the Greiss test. This was regarded as a reliable method of detecting nitro-glycerine, but now, like Skuse himself, is considered unreliable. McIlkenny's, Hunter's and Walker's hands proved negative. But the right hands of Power and Hill proved positive. This, said Skuse, made him 99% certain that both Power and Hill had recently been in contact with explosives.

Before considering the 'confession' that followed, and the ruthless beatings the six say they received, let us follow the forensic evidence (which began with Skuse's findings at Morecambe) through to the final verdict at the Court of Appeal.

At the trial of the six in Lancaster, Mr. Justice Bridge said the forensic tests were one of two 'absolutely critical' chapters in the prosecution's case. Yet Skuse, in evidence, had to admit that when he subjected the traces of Power's and Hill's right hands to two further tests (one of which, a gas chromotography mass spectometry, known as GCMS, was said to be far more sensitive than Greiss), both registered negative. But he stuck to his 99% certainly of the Morecambe tests.

Dr. Hugh Black, for the defence, said the Greiss test by itself was not adequate to detect the presence of nitro-glycerine.

In May 1985, the Granada Television programme World in Action invited David Baldock and Dr. Brian Caddy to carry out the Greiss test on a variety of common substances. They found that items such as lacquer, aerosol sprays, cigarette packets and old playing cards all gave positive results. (The men were smoking and playing cards on their journey to Heysham.) Asked later if he was surprised that Skuse had been so certain of his findings at Morecambe, Baldock said he was amazed.

On appeal, the evidence of Baldock, Black and Caddy again clashed head-on with that of Skuse. The result was that the judges found themselves obliged to admit that, 'in our judgment the Greiss test at Morecambe should not be regarded as specific for nitro-glycerine'. But, like shipwrecked sailors on a spar, the judges clung to Skuse's positive finding on Hill's right hand in the GCMS test, and found another spar in the evidence of Dr. Janet Drayton who would go no further than to say of Hill's left hand, 'possible NG present, very small increase'.

On this flimsy edifice the court announced: 'So far from creating any doubt, the fresh evidence on this topic (Dr. Drayton's) makes us sure that Hill's left hand is proven to have nitro-glycerine upon it, for which there is, and can be, no innocent explanation. That conclusion is fatal to the appellants.'

Let us now turn to the 'confessions'. First it is necessary to look at the background circumstances in which the 'confessions' were obtained.

When news became known of the pub bombings, with their appalling casualties, there was hardly a man in Birmingham (as well as a vast number outside it), who would not have been ready and willing personally to lynch any of those responsible. When the six arrived at Winson Green Prison on remand, only three days later, they were beaten up mercilessly. A number of prison officers were subsequently tried and acquitted of assault.

The question at the heart of this whole case is what happened to them while they were in police custody before being passed on to prison. They maintained at their trial that they were assaulted ferociously by detectives. They gave evidence of sustained police brutality and callousness designed to break them down and make them confess.

Callaghan testified: 'I was in a state of shock. I do not know what I said. They said things to me. I agreed. At the end one of the officers put a pen in my right hand, placed it over the paper and guided my hand as I signed.' Similar assertions were made by the Guildford Four.

The 'confessions' themselves were a mass of contradictions and untruths. Three of the four referred to the bombs being carried in plastic bags. In fact they had no plastic bags with them, and forensic examination of the remains showed that the bombs had been carried in holdalls or briefcases.

Callaghan said he put his bomb outside the Mulberry Bush public house on one side and that Hunter had put his outside on the other. Forensic evidence showed the bomb, or bombs, had been placed inside the pub. Despite Callaghan's claim that he and Hunter had bombed the Mulberry Bush, Walker claimed Hunter had been with him bombing the Tavern. Callaghan said there were six bombs. Walker and McIlkenny said three.

At their trial neither judge nor jury believed the allegations of beatings or disbelieved the 'confessions'. Mr. Justice Bridge spoke of the allegations against the police as being 'of the most bizarre and grotesque character'. If the defendants were telling the truth, he said 'I would have to suppose that a team of 15 officers had conspired among themselves to use violence on the prisoners and to fabricate evidence.'

Poor innocent, he discounted how desperate the police can become for confessions.

The judge concluded: 'All the police officers, who gave their evidence of the circumstances in which the statements were taken, impressed me as being straightforward and honest witnesses.' But this is how police officers are trained to appear; that is why some lie and lie and know they will be believed.

In November 1977, the six men brought a civil action against the police and the Home Office for injuries they had received while in police custody. For fresh evidence they were relying on the findings of Dr. David Paul, a former police surgeon and City of London coroner and a specialist in the interpretation of injuries from photographs. Shown enlarged photographs of the six, taken while they were in custody at Queen's Road, he found signs of injuries on all.

The action was allowed and application made for legal aid. But the police appealed and, in an uncharacteristic judgment, Lord Denning upheld them. If the action were to succeed, he said, it would show evidence of police perjury and violence, and the six might have to be pardoned. This was such an appalling vista that the action could not be allowed to proceed. In other words, from the layman's point of view, better that the six rot in jail than to find there had been police wrongdoing.

But the supporters of the six, including some of the media, continued to press their case. In December 1986 a retired police officer by name of Tom Clarke, who had been at Queen's Road at the material time, appeared on Granada Television to say what he had seen and heard. Seven weeks later, the Home Secretary announced he was sending the case back to the Court of Appeal and was ordering an inquiry by the Devon and Cornwall Police.

At the appeal hearing, Clarke confirmed the prisoners' claims of police intimidation and ill-treatment, even admitting that he himself had joined in verbal abuse of the prisoners ('I was thrilled to know we had got the right people').

He described one prisoner as having on his stomach a red weal turning bluish and measuring about 6 in. by 4 in. 'He had been hit so badly that, although I wanted to see him dead, I was worried about him.' When he went off duty, he said the prisoners were 'scared out of their wits'; and when he came back he observed puffiness over and under their eyes and red faces. 'They had,' he told the court, 'been hammered.' By the time he left again, the prisoners were 'all in a petrified state and physical wrecks'.

Tom Clarke knew when he came to give evidence that he would be discredited as a witness for having been dismissed from the police force for stealing £5 from a prisoner. He contests that verdict and, having read his papers on the case and spoken to him, I would say there could be a doubt in the matter. But he was supported in his Appeal Court evidence by a former member of his first-aid team, Sergeant Brierley, who said Clarke had told him within weeks or months of the bombings that cell doors had been banged, the prisoners had been kept standing up and police dogs had been let into the cell block to bark at them.

Another former policeman, Paul Berry, told the court of having called in at Queen's Road at this time on a routine matter and seeing a prisoner 'whose left eye and lip were puffed and swollen'.

The most impressive witness for the appellants was Joyce Lynas, who was on duty at Queen's road as a police cadet. She gave evidence to the court on two occasions. On the first she said that the prisoners had been intimidated but she denied having witnessed any prisoners being assaulted.

But a few days later she was back in court to say she had witnessed a prisoner being assaulted. Asked why she had not said so at her first appearance, she said she had been frightened off by two telephone conversations. The first had been in the summer when she rang Queen's road and was told by an officer: 'You know what you saw and heard, but remember we have families.' The second had been an anonymous call to her home before the hearing began, with the message: 'Don't forget you have children.'

On the Saturday after her first appearance, she had seen a television programme about bullying in the army and people not reporting it. After talking to her husband and her church minister, she volunteered to return to court, even though it meant having to admit to perjury.

What new evidence did Joyce Lynas have to offer? Simply that when she took tea to officers who were interviewing the prisoners, she saw two officers holding one by the arms while a third kneed him in the groin. As she entered she heard the third man say: 'This is what we do to murdering bastards,' and what she called 'other vile words'.

There was other confirmatory evidence of the prisoners having been beaten up. Prison officer Brian Sharp of Winson Green was on duty when they arrived at the prison, on the Monday morning. He said that when Walker undressed, 'his torso from the neck to the middle had numerous amounts of bruising, purple, blackish, some had tinges of yellow'.

How did the three Appeal Court judges respond to the overwhelming evidence that, over a period of three days, the appellants had been assaulted and intimidated by the police and their 'confessions' were therefore no longer tenable?

Although most people who attended the court, particularly the appellants' counsel, believed the judges had decided early on to reject the appeal, they had not bargained for the manner in which their witnesses would be rubbished. This is what the judges said of them:

Tom Clarke: 'A most unconvincing witness and an embittered man. His motive was . . . at first at least to make money and secondly to blacken the reputation of the West Midlands police force.' (A year later the reputation of the West Midlands Serious Crime Squad had become so blackened that it had to be disbanded.)

Paul Berry, who had glimpsed a prisoner with a puffed and swollen face, was 'mistaken'. But how could he have been mistaken? All the cells were occupied by the appellants. There were no other prisoners.

Brian Sharp, who had said that Walker's body was covered with bruises on his arrival at Winson Green, was, the judges said, trying to conceal or minimise the violence that prison staff and inmates had inflicted on the prisoners. But Sharp had no motive to conceal anything. He had been tried for assaulting the appellants and been acquitted.

Joyce Lynas: the judges described her as 'a witness not worthy of belief' and her reasons for changing her story were 'not acceptable'. Lynas is a committed Christian whose character, while in the police force, was assessed as 'exemplary' and she was angered and distressed by these attacks on her integrity. 'I did not have to go back,' she told me. 'I went because I felt I ought to, and I told the absolute truth.'

For the judges to declare, in the light of all they had heard, that the original verdicts were safe and satisfactory (which is the criteria the law sets) seems to me an abuse of the English language as well as an insult to anyone's intelligence. How could they possibly have come to believe, as they must have done, that the appellants' graphically detailed accounts of assaults by the police were a total invention? Why did they come to their conclusions?

I fear the harsh truth is that, just as some policemen corrupt themselves by their readiness to fabricate evidence against those who they have convinced themselves are guilty, so there are judges, otherwise honourable men, who corrupt themselves by refusing to recognize police fabrication, even when it is staring them in the face.

'British justice is in ruins,' said Lord Denning after the release of the Guildford Four. But it had been in ruins for a long time. Judges at trials of first instance as well as judges in the Appeal Court have consistently refused to entertain the ideas of police fabrication unless it is so clear-cut that they have no alternative.

Every judicial inquiry into miscarriages of justice in recent years preferred to accept dubious police evidence rather than give the people concerned a clean bill of health. In so doing they have done both themselves and British justice a grave disservice.

Yet, to be fair, it is less that the police and the judges have corrupted themselves as that the system has corrupted both of them. The adversary system, a comparatively late development in English criminal law, and which turns a trial into a kind of phoney sporting contest which each side feels it has to win, is no way to dispense justice. It invites corruption and the concealment of the truth.

What we need is a change to the inquisitorial system. In all serious criminal cases we need a judicial figure to oversee the police in their inquiries, interrogate suspects himself or herself and thus pre-empt 'confessions' to murder by such as the Birmingham Six.

BRUCE KENT

Beyond Reasonable Doubt

I really don't know how to express what I feel about the Birmingham Six. These men cannot possibly have been found guilty 'beyond reasonable doubt'. The reasonable doubt is overwhelming. Discredited scientific tests, discredited policemen, discredited judgements. Yet they are still in prison now, as I write this New Year's Day. I don't know if disgust or rage or fury or despair best describes how I feel. I feel a mixture of them all.

Why doesn't someone with the authority and the power just do what was done for the Guildford Four and turn the key? These men still have lives to lead, families to live with, children to care for. What is going on? Does it always need a Cardinal or an Archbishop to get justice done?

Prisons are horrible places. I've visited too many. Keys and slamming and busy cheery chaplains and impersonal Prison Officers who have to work the system, and too many forgotten people.

It's easy to forget what goes on inside. I live within a couple of miles of two major prisons: Holloway and Pentonville. Buses go past, children play, women carry shopping as if a normal life was going on. Within thirty feet of them over a high wall normal life is not going on. There is another world and for many it is a world of hopelessness. A Prison Governor very honestly once called Wormwood Scrubs a human dustbin. That is exactly what prisons are. Into such dustbins the Birmingham Six were put and the lid was slammed firmly on top. But it can't stay there. Even for the great majority of guilty people prison is not an intelligent answer to their crimes. For the innocent (and we are all supposed to be innocent until *proved* guilty) they are an outrage. The courage of the imprisoned innocent astounds me. When Gerard Conlon of the Guildford Four finally came out of the Old Bailey he protested his innocence, hand held high, and defied the whole system which had wasted his youth behind bars. I salute such courage.

The least that we can do is to match that courage and to keep their hope alive. The key is not turned for one reason only. The Establishment does not want to lose face. Establishments, national, political and even ecclesiastical never do. The British system of justice cannot be seen to have made a major mistake in its response to those callous murders of innocent people in the Birmingham pubs in 1974. The scapegoat principle is at work. Well, minds do change, perseverance can pay off and decency can sprout like grass through official concrete. So it was with the Guildford Four. So it must be with the Birmingham Six. The Gospels are full of hope for the hopeless. *'He has sent me to announce good news to the poor, to proclaim release for prisoners. . .'* said Christ in the Nazareth synagogue. *'He looked down from heaven to the earth that he might hear the groans of the prisoners . . .'* says Psalm 101. But miracles are not made to order. Giving hope to the hopeless depends on us.

Our views on the Irish political situation are entirely irrelevant to this issue. Nor is this a case of special pleading. By all the rules of reasonable justice these six men are not guilty. The prosecution has not proved its case and the jury made its decision on evidence now shown to be worthless. I appeal to those who have the power that I do not have, to admit that a terrible mistake was made. To admit mistakes is not to discredit the system but to make it more credible. Judges, Lawyers, Prison Officers and Chaplains – you know that these men are innocent in law and in fact. They and their families have suffered dreadfully. Please help us to get them out, free and compensated, in so far as anything can compensate for those lost years.

MARIE-THÉRÈSE KERSCHBAUMER

Gesicht

seht: brennend werden wir untergehn
brennend in der siedenden Kälte
des toten Dürreschnees

brennend das Gesicht zum Himmel
dem gnadenlosen hinabgeneigt
dem tobenden leblosen Nichts

Vision

look: burning we shall perish
burning in the seething cold
the dead snow of drought

burning our faces turned heavenward
to pitiless heaven below
the raging lifeless abyss

(Translated from the German by Maria E. Clay-Jorde.)

MARIE-THÉRÈSE KERSCHBAUMER

Excerpt from *Der Schwimmer (The Swimmer)*

which class had Messalina Barbara come to betray can anyone tell which class Messalina Barbara has come to betray now that Saint Patrick has also deserted her none has come to prop up her emaciated hands (and yet she was confident amen) in these emaciated hands the two sisters carry dangerous weapons that is why they must fast that is why they must eat that is why pea soup must be brought in for lunch for dinner and many useful tubes from boxes and cases they must not fast the shaven girls' heads fell down the girls' heads fell forward the Bengal mother was frying her child and no poet has ever reported this deed only in the emaciated heads bent forward into emaciated hands three thousand comedies arose subsidised volumes of poetry a betrayal of the authors oh there will be no pea soup for lunch there will no longer be little children and no more slates here in the north this is how it must be because this is how it has always been it is strict to be sure but just that is why Saint Patrick must burn in our entrails all for the greater glory of the queen who is dishing out soup

once upon a time said Orfeo the female captive there was an Italian count who lived in Pisa (Corriere della Domenica) he was very powerful and he was a traitor who that is powerful is not a traitor and not himself being betrayed and he was overlord of large tracts of land in the salt-marshes of Pisa he was bailiff of the king of Sardinia and of other domains and he betrayed first one side then the other and then his own grandson and the bishop pretended to side with the old man and had the grandson expelled who in vain had sought help from his grandfather therefore *Ugolino* the count returned to Pisa he wanted to be lord of Pisa and the bishop pretended to negotiate with him but at the bishop's instigation the people rebelled and threw *Ugolino* into the tower together with his sons *Gaddo* and *Uguccione* and the grandsons *Nino detto Brigata* and *Anselmuccio* from the beginning of July they were held captive and in March of the following year they were starved to death why therefore is *Ugolino* sitting down there in the ice with the traitors for you must know he is sitting in the ice and is gnawing his enemy's skull he an instrument of the law the bishop therefore the *odious meal* of him whom he betrayed you must know he is gnawing the bishop's skull because it was he who allowed him to be starved to death you see and the bishop's head does not utter a sound it is only there as a skull and as a traitor for it was the bishop who betrayed the count the traitor and when the poet walked by with his hands buried deep in his pockets and queried (queried) the count answered *I was Conte Ugolino and he is Archbishop Ruggieri* the two tenses of the verb on the temporal axis *I was he is* the transitoriness of the traitor betrayed and the eternity of the murderer who kills with a stroke of his pen

I can no longer bear listening groaned one of the sisters I can no longer bear listening how the old traitor gnaws his betrayer's skull I can no longer bear listening how successful poets are incessantly quoted that remains to be seen said the doctor and prepared the soup and prepared the feast and prepared the bomb for the sister's entrails heave ho! shouted the gaoler heave ho! shouted the queen heave ho! the home secretary you must be good and obedient and close-shaven everywhere so that you cannot hide anything Saint Patrick where is the count Saint Patrick where is the bishop Saint Patrick and the Bengal mother who fried her child on the Bengal fire Saint Patrick who is gnawing the children's betrayers that too will happen Saint Patrick I have always eaten everything one spoonful for mummy and one for daddy I had no daddy Saint Patrick it will get better my daughter and for my aunt and my uncle heave ho! and then I vomited once and had to eat my own vomit now be good and do what I say it is only your skull yes bishop we have to break your skull and this is also why you will enter the icy realm of heaven heave ho! and onwards the journey goes into the country and where are the blue eyes one of them says and gnaws with her teeth and where the green fields and swallows with her throat and where is the deep ice ask both of them doctor it was you who wrote the prescription a prescription of four words where are you from was written there when what you should have asked was where to and it wasn't meant to be Saint Patrick I do not want to gnaw the skull Saint Patrick what was your price

(Translated from the German by Maria E. Clay-Forde.)

THOMAS KINSELLA

Verse Translations

SÉATHRÚN CÉITINN (1580-c.1644)

Rugadh an Céitinneach in aice le Cathair Dhúin Iascaigh, Co. Thiobraid Árann. Chaith sé tamall ina shagart i mBordeaux, mar ar bronnadh dochtúireacht le diacht air. Ina dhiaidh sin d'fill sé ar dheisceart na hÉireann, agus chaith a dhúthracht le seanmóireacht agus le scríbhneoireacht. Is é an saothar mór staire agus seanchais aige, *Foras Feasa ar Éirinn,* an saothar próis is mó a chuaigh i bhfeidhm, b'fhéidir, ar scríbhneoirí na Gaeilge ón 17ú céad i leith.

Bíodh is nár chum sé líon mór dánta, caithfear Séathrún Céitinn a áireamh ar dhuine de na húdair mhóra is túisce a bhain leas as na meadarachtaí 'nua' aiceanta i gcuid shubstaintiúil dá shaothar fileata. Tá *Óm sceol ar ardmhagh Fáil* ar cheann de na dánta iomadúla a scríobhadh san 17ú haois ag caoineadh 'an milleadh d'imigh ar mhórshleachta na hÉireann'. Is dócha gur tar éis Teitheadh na nIarlaí (1607) a cumadh é, agus is inspéise go molann an file sa cheathrú dheireanach go mb'fhéidir gurbh fhearr uaisle uile na nÉireann a chruinniú le chéile agus iad a sheoladh an cuan amach. . .

Tá na cúig ghuta aiceanta céanna i ngach líne den dán, rud a fhágann déanamh an-ornáideach air. Mar seo atá tríd síos:

v / ó v / á v / á v / o v / í v

Eascraíonn cuid mhaith de mhaorgacht an chaointe seo ón gcodarsnacht idir rialtacht righin na meadarachta, agus éascaíocht rithimiúil na línte mar a labhraítear iad. Tá blas an Bhíobla ar an mbunsamhail a úsáideann an Céitinneach: an 'cogal' eachtrannach atá ag truailliú an tsíl dúchais.

Óm sceol ar ardmhagh Fáil

Óm sceol ar ardmhagh Fáil ní chodlaim oíche
's do bhreoigh go bráth mé dála a pobail dílis;
gé rófhada atáid 'na bhfál ré broscar bíobha,
fá dheoidh gur fhás a lán den chogal tríothu.

A Fhódla phráis, is náir nach follas díbhse
gur córa tál ar sháirshliocht mhodhail Mhíle;
deor níor fágadh i gclár do bhrollaigh mhínghil
nár dheolsad ál gach cránach coigríche.

SÉATHRÚN CÉITINN (1580-c.1644)

Céitinn, priest and scholar, was born near Cahir, Co. Tipperary. Having spent some time in Bordeaux, and taken a doctorate in Divinity, he returned to Munster where he preached with great zeal and worked at his writings, notably the highly influential history of Ireland, *Foras Feasa ar Éirinn*.

His poetical output is not large, but he in one of the first major literary figures to write a substantial part of his verse in the 'new' accentual metres. *Óm sceol ar ardmhagh Fáil* is one of a series of poems from the seventeenth century bewailing the downfall of the great families of Ireland.

The poem was probably composed after the Flight of the Earls (1607), and it is a matter of interest that Céitinn in the last verse feels it may be necessary to 'gather and winnow' all the nobles of the land, and send them into exile.

Each line of the poem conforms to a very ornate five-beat pattern of vowel sounds:

v / ó v / á v / á v / o v / í v

The majestic elegiac feeling it achieves owes a great deal to the manner in which the rigid metrical form is counterpointed by the freer rhythmic cadences of the lines as spoken. The Biblical image of the 'cockle' growing through pure Irish seed establishes the basic tone of the poem.

At the news from Fál's high Plain

At the news from Fál's high plain I cannot sleep.
I am sick till doom at the plight of its faithful folk.
Long have they stood as a hedge against hostile trash
but a lot of the cockle has grown up through them at last.

O brazen Fódla, it is shameful you do not see
it were fitter to nourish Míle's sweet high race.
Not a drop is left in the plain of your smooth bright breast
– drained dry by the litter of every alien sow.

Gach treod gan tásc tar sál dá dtogair síneadh
go hóirlios álainn ársa Chobhthaigh Chaoil chirt,
is leo gan ghráscar lámh ár ndonna-bhruíne,
's gach fód is fearr dár n-áitibh eochar-aoibhne.

Atáid foirne ag fás san gclársa Logha líofa
dár chóir bheith táir gé hard a rolla-scaoileadh;
síol Eoghain tláith 's an Tálfhuil bodhar cloíte
's na hóig ón mBántsrath scáinte i gcoigríochaibh.

Na tóisigh tháisc ón Nás gan bhogadh bhrí-nirt
i ngleo gér gháifeach ágh na lonna-bhuíne –
fá shróin an stáit ba gnáth a gcogadh i ndíormaibh;
ní dóibh ba nár ach cách gan chomhall dlí ar bith.

Dá mba beoga ardfhlaith Áine is Droma Daoile
's na leoghain láidre ón Máigh do bhronnadh maoine,
dar ndóigh níorbh áit don táinse in oscaill Bhríde
gan gheoin is gártha os ard dá dtoghaildíbirt.

Muna bhfóiridh Ceard na n-ardreann pobal chrích Chuirc
ar fhoirneart námhad ndána n-ullamh ndíoltach
ní mór nárbh fhearr gan chairde a bhfoscaindíolaim
's a seoladh slán i bhfán tar tonnaibh Chlíona.

PÁDRAIGÍN HAICÉAD (c.1600-1654)

Sagart den ord Doiminiceánach a rugadh i gceantar Chaisil ab ea Pádraigín Haicéad. Chaith sé tamall i Lobhán is é ina ógfhear; nuair a d'fhill sé ar Éirinn, chomh maith lena ghnó sagairt a dhéanamh, ghlac sé páirt i gcúrsaí polaitíochta. Bhí sé ar dhuine de na filí ba luaithe agus ab éifeachtúla a chum véarsaíocht aiceanta. Tá saothar substaintiúil filíochta againn óna lámh ach tá cuid mhaith de gafa le cúrsaí reatha a linne féin, agus rian na bolscaireachta polaitíochta air. Ní mór na dánta aige atá slán ná sásúil ar fad iontu féin; acht tá fuinneamh ollmhór intleachta le brath ar a shaothar trí chéile. Uaireanta, mar is léir ó *Do chuala inné*, bíonn a chuid véarsaí ag cur thar maoil le gangaid dá naimhde, idir naimhde eaglasta agus naimhde polaitiúla.

Any worthless crew that thought to cross the sea
to the fair, gold, age-old *lios* of Cobhthach 'the just'
– theirs without struggle of hands our mighty mansions
and the choicest swards of our lovely-bordered places.

There's a new sort growing in the plain of Lugh the lithe
who are base by right, though they flourish their 'rolls' on high
– Eoghan's seed exhausted, Tál's blood troubled and broken,
and the youth of Bántsrath scattered in foreign lands.

From the worthy chiefs of Nás not a stir of strength,
though fierce that awesome army's fire in battle
– manoeuvring often under the nose of the State.
(Not theirs the shame that the law is honoured by none.)

If that high prince lived, of Áine and Drom Daoile,
or the great gift-generous lions of the Máigh,
this horde would have no place in the bend of the Bride
– smashed, driven out, with outcry and loud wails.

If the Craftsman of Stars protect not Ireland's people
from violent vengeful enemies, bold and ready,
better gather and winnow them now without delay
and sail them out wandering safe on the waves of Cliona.

PÁDRAIGÍN HAICÉAD (c.1600-1654)

A Dominican priest from the area of Cashel, Co. Tipperary, Haicéad spent some time in Louvain before returning to Ireland to become actively involved in pastoral work and in national politics. He was one of the earliest and most accomplished of the poets to write accentual verse. A good deal of his substantial poetical *opus* is centred on topical events of his day and is inclined to be propagandist. While he has few completely satisfying poems, all his work is informed by an enormous intellectual energy and sometimes, as in *Do chuala inné,* by a great cantankerousness against his enemies, both political and clerical.

Do chuala inné

Iar gclos gur hordaíodh i gcaibidlibh na hÉireann gan bráthair do dhéanamh rainn ná amhráin.

Do chuala inné ag maothlach muinteardha
mar nuadhacht scéil ó chéile Chuinn is Chuirc
gur duairc le cléir an Ghaeilge ghrinnshlitheach,
suairceas séimh na saorfhear sinseardha.

Ní bhuaileabh féin i gcléith a gcointinne
ó chuaigh an ré 'narbh fhéidir linn friotal
gach smuaineadh d'éirgheadh d'éirim m'intinne,
uair fár bhaoghal faobhar m'intleachta;

go suaithfeadh sé gan saobhadh slimfhuinnimh
fá thuairim thaobh na gcléireach gcinsealach
nó anuas fá a mblaoscaibh maola millteacha
crua-ghlac ghéar do ghaethibh innlithe.

Fuaifidh mé mo bhéal le sring fhite
's ní luaifead réad dá bpléid bhig sprionlaithe,
ach fuagraim tréad an chaolraigh chuimsithe
's a bhfuath, a Dhé, tar éis mo mhuintire.

DÁIBHÍ Ó BRUADAIR (c.1625-1698)

Is é Dáibhí Ó Bruadair an chéad duine d'fhilí aitheantúla an 17ú céad a rinne iarracht ar dhul le filíocht mar ghairm bheatha, mar ba nós roimhe sin ag filí na scol. Rugadh é i mBarrachaibh Móra, Co. Chorcaí, ach chaith sé formhór a shaoil i Luimneach faoi scáth pátrún ar nós na nGearaltach. Timpeall na bliana 1674, tharla céim síos éigin sa saol dó agus b'éigean dó dul le sclábhaíocht feirme. Chríochnaigh sé a shaol faoi ainnise agus faoi dhólás.

File antorthúil ab ea Ó Bruadair, a raibh líofacht éachtach teanga agus cumas samhlaíochta thar an gcoitiantacht aige. Rinne sé cumasc fuinte ina chuid filíochta de sheanteanga liteartha na bhfilí agus de bheotheanga labhartha a linne féin. Tá tábhacht thar meon ag baint lena dhánta, ní hamháin mar aistí filíochta, ach mar thuairisc ar stair na hÉireann agus ar bhraithstint daoine sa dara leath den 17ú haois.

I heard from a decent man the other day
On hearing it has been ordered in the chapterhouses of Ireland that the friars make no more songs or verses.

I heard from a decent man the other day
a piece of news from the 'spouse of Conn and Corc':
that the Church condemns our Gaelic's subtle paths,
the polished pleasure of our noble fathers.

I will not spring at the flank of their argument
now that the time is past when I could utter
each thought erupting from the scope of my mind
– when the edge of my intellect was a thing to fear

showering with no loss of pliant force
into the general flank of those arrogant priests
or down on top of their bald malignant skulls
a hard sharp fistful of accomplished darts.

I will stitch my mouth up with a twisted string
and say no word about their mean complaining,
merely condemn the herd of narrow censors
and the hate they bear my people, O my God.

DÁIBHÍ Ó BRUADAIR (c.1625-1698)

Ó Bruadair is the first of the well-known seventeenth century poets to try to live completely out of verse, in the manner of the medieval professional poets. He was born in Barrymore, Co. Cork, and spent much of his adult life in Limerick, supported by patrons such as the Fitzgeralds. But by the year 1674 he appears to have been reduced to labouring in the fields. He ended his life in misery.

Ó Bruadair was a prolific poet of formidable eloquence and imaginative powers who blended the rich colloquial language of his time with the older literary diction. His poems, apart from their intrinsic poetic worth, are a valuable record of the history and sensibility of the second half of the seventeenth century.

D'aithle na bhfileadh

Do chlainn Chon Connacht Uí Dhálaigh

D'aithle na bhfileadh n-uasal,
  truaghsan timheal an tsaoghail;
clann na n-ollamh go n-eagna
  folamh gan freagra faobhair.

Truagh a leabhair ag liatha,
  tiacha nach treabhair bhaoise;
ar ceal níor chóir a bhfoilcheas,
  toircheas bhfear n-óil na gaoise.

D'aithle na bhfileadh dár ionnmhas éigse is iúl
is mairg de-chonnairc an chinneamhain d'éirigh dhúinn:
a leabhair ag titim i leimhe 's i léithe i gcúil
's ag macaibh na droinge gan siolla dá séadaibh rún.

AOGÁN Ó RATHAILLE (c.1675-1729)

Rugadh Aogán Ó Rathaille ar Screathan an Mhíl, i ndúiche sceirdiúil Shliabh Luachra, deich míle éigin lastoir de Chill Airne. Fuair sé scolaíocht mhaith ina óige, ní foláir, mar bhí eolas nár bheag aige ar Laidin, ar Bhéarla, ar stair agus ar litríocht na Gaeilge. Bhain a mhuintir, a bheag nó a mhór, leis an aicme phribhléideach: b'fhéidir gur de shliocht Mhic Aogáin a mháthair, cine ar díobh na hollúna oidhreachtúla ag an gCárthach Mór. D'fhéadfadh, go raibh an stráice talún ar Screathan an Mhíl ar cíos íseal ag muintir Rathaille ó Sir Nioclás Brún.

Tar éis bhriseadh na Bóinne (1690), toisc gur Chaitilicigh agus Seacaibítigh iad na Brúnaigh a bhí báúil leis na SeanGhaeil, coigistíodh an t-eastát ollmhór a bhí acu (c.400,000 acra) fad ba bheo Sir Nioclás. Lean de sin gur ruaigeadh an Rathailleach chomh maith as a cheantar féin; do mhair sé tamall ina dhiaidh sin faoi ainnise in aice le Tonn Tóime, Caisleán na Mainge.

Plandálaithe a tháinig go hÉirinn in aimsir Eilíse ab ea na Brúnaigh. Ghabh siad tailte na gCárthach i gCúige Mumhan de réir a chéile – ach ina dhiaidh sin sheas siad leis na Cárthaigh agus uaireanta thug siad talamh saor ó chíos dóibh. Cé go raibh Aogán Ó Rathaille mór go maith le Brúnaigh, ní raibh a chroí chomh ceangailte iontu in aon chor agus a bhí ins na Cárthaigh. Cuireann an dá dhílseacht seo – a bhí uaireanta ag teacht trasna ar a chéile – a chuid fílíochta ar tinneall. Níor réitigh sé an scéal sin ar fad dó féin go dtí deireadh a shaoil.

Ina shaothar rinne Aogán Ó Rathaille iarracht chuthaigh ar theacht

The high poets are gone

For the family of Cúchonnacht Ó Dálaigh

The high poets are gone
    and I mourn for the world's waning,
the sons of those learned masters
    emptied of sharp response.

I mourn for their fading books,
    reams of no earnest stupidity,
lost – unjustly abandoned –
    begotten by drinkers of wisdom.

After those poets, for whom art and knowledge were wealth,
    alas to have lived to see this fate befall us:
their books in corners greying into nothing
    and their sons without one syllable of their secret treasure.

AOGÁN Ó RATHAILLE (c.1675-1729)

Aogán Ó Rathaille was born in Screathan an Mhíl (Scrahanaveel), in the rugged Sliabh Luachra district some ten miles east of Killarney. He appears to have received a good formal schooling, being versed in Latin and English as well as in Irish literature and history. His parents – due perhaps to some marriage connection with the Egans, traditional *ollaves* to the McCarthymore family – seem to have been reasonably prosperous; they may have held the rentals of a large parcel of land from Sir Nicholas Browne for a modest fee.

The Brownes, of old Elizabethan planter stock, were Catholic, Jacobite and favourable to the native Irish. After the defeat of King James at the Battle of the Boyne in 1690, their vast estates (c.400,000 acres) were confiscated for the lifetime of Sir Nicholas. Ó Rathaille, in consequence, had to leave his native district. He lived for a time in poor circumstances at Tonn Tóime, at the edge of Castlemaine Harbour, some twelve miles west of Killarney.

For all his close links with the Brownes, Ó Rathaille was more emotionally involved with the McCarthys, whom the Brownes supplanted (and thereafter often supported). This twin – and sometimes contradictory – allegiance caused a tension in his poetry which he does not seem to have resolved until the end of his life.

ar thuiscint éigin ar an léirscrios a bhí déanta air féin agus ar mhuintir na tíre. An chuid is fearr den bhfilíocht sin, is filíochta mhaorga mhórthaibhseach í ina bhfuil uaigneas anama do-inste.

Tá Aogán Ó Rathaille curtha i dteannta na gCárthach i Mainistir Mhucrois, i gCill Airne.

Gile na Gile

Gile na gile do chonnarc ar slí in uaigneas,
criostal an chriostail a goirmroisc rinn-uaine,
binneas an bhinnis a friotal nár chríonghruama,
deirge is finne do fionnadh 'na gríosghruannaibh.

Caise na caise i ngach ribe dá buí-chuachaibh,
bhaineas an cruinneac den rinneac le rinnscuabadh,
iorra ba ghlaine ná gloine ar a broinn bhuachaigh,
do gineadh ar ghineamhain di-se san tír uachtraigh.

Fios fiosach dom d'inis, is ise go fíor-uaigneach,
fios filleadh don duine don ionad ba rí-dhualgas,
fios milleadh na droinge chuir eisean ar rinnruagairt,
's fios eile ná cuirfead im laoithibh le fíor-uamhan.

Leimhe na leimhe dom druidim 'na cruinntuairim,
im chime ag an gcime do snaidhmeadh go fíorchrua me;
ar ghoirm Mhic Mhuire dom fhortacht, do bhíog uaimse,
is d'imigh an bhruinneal 'na luisne go bruín Luachra.

Rithim le rith mire im rithibh go croí-luaimneach,
trí imeallaibh corraigh, trí mhongaibh, trí shlímruaitigh;
don tinne-bhrugh tigim – ní thuigim cén tslí fuaras –
go hionad na n-ionad do cumadh le draíocht dhruaga.

Brisid fá scige go scigeamhail buíon ghruagach
is foireann de bhruinnealaibh sioscaithe dlaoi-chuachach;
i ngeimhealaibh geimheal me cuirid gan puinn suaimhnis,
's mo bhruinneal ar broinnibh ag broinnire broinnstuacach.

D'iniseas di-se, san bhfriotal dob fhíor uaimse,
nár chuibhe di snaidhmeadh le slibire slímbhuartha
's an duine ba ghile ar shliocht chine Scoit trí huaire
ag feitheamh ar ise bheith aige mar chaoin-nuachar.

Ar chloistin mo ghutha di goileann go fíor-uaibhreach
is sileadh ag an bhfliche go life as a gríosghruannaibh;
cuireann liom giolla dom choimirc ón mbruín uaithi –
's í gile na gile do chonnarc ar slí in uaigneas.

His poetry, the best of which has a heroic desolation and grandeur, is in many ways a result of his effort to come to terms with the chaos in which he and his people found themselves.

Ó Rathaille is buried with the McCarthys in Muckross Abbey, Killarney.

Brightness most bright

Brightness most bright I beheld on the way, forlorn.
Crystal of crystal her eye, blue touched with green.
Sweetness most sweet her voice, not stern with age.
Colour and pallor appeared in her flushed cheeks.

Curling and curling, each strand of her yellow hair
as it took the dew from the grass in its ample sweep;
a jewel more glittering than glass on her high bosom
– created, when she was created, in a higher world.

True tidings she revealed me, most forlorn,
tidings of one returning by royal right,
tidings of the crew ruined who drove him out,
and tidings I keep from my poem for sheer fear.

Foolish past folly, I came to her very presence
bound tightly, her prisoner (she likewise a prisoner. . .)
I invoked Mary's Son for succour: she started from me
and vanished like light to the fairy dwelling of Luachair.

Heart pounding, I ran, with a frantic haste in my race,
by the margins of marshes, through swamps, over bare moors.
To a powerful palace I came, by paths most strange,
to that place of all places, erected by druid magic.

All in derision they tittered – a gang of goblins
and a bevy of slender maidens with twining tresses.
They bound me in bonds, denying the slightest comfort,
and a lumbering brute took hold of my girl by the breasts.

I said to her then, in words that were full of truth,
how improper it was to join with that drawn gaunt creature
when a man the most fine, thrice over, of Scottish blood
was waiting to take her for his tender bride.

On hearing my voice she wept in high misery
and flowing tears fell down from her flushed cheeks.
She sent me a guard to guide me out of the palace
– that brightness most bright I beheld on the way, forlorn.

An Ceangal

Mo threighid, mo thubaist, mo thurainn, mo bhrón, mo dhíth!
an soilseach muirneach miochairgheal beoltais caoin
ag adharcach foireanndubh mioscaiseach cóirneach buí,
's gan leigheas 'na goire go bhfillid na leoin tar toinn.

Tionónta dealbh ar eastát an Bhrúnaigh ab ea Aogán Ó Rathaille i ndeireadh a shaoil. Ní hamháin go raibh a shúil curtha de chabhair an Stíobhartaigh aige, ach ní raibh aon dóchas anois aige, ach oiread, go bhfóirfeadh Sir Vailintín Brún air. Déanann sé achoimre ar a mhothú i leith na mBrúnach i véarsa 5 anseo, agus ar a mhothú i leith na gCárthach i véarsa 6; agus sa véarsa deireanach, mar chríoch ar a scéal, toghann sé an tsíoraíocht a chaithamh i dteannta na gCárthach, na seanphátrúin shinseartha.

Is dóichí gur chum Aogán *Cabhair ní ghairfead* ar bhás an Chárthaigh Mhóir (c.1729) – an té deireanach arbh fhiú an teideal a thabhairt air. Bhí an file féin, dealraíonn sé, ag saothrú an bháis san am sin chomh maith.

Cabhair ní ghairfead

Cabhair ní ghairfead go gcuirthear mé i gcruinn-chomhrainn –
dar an leabhar dá ngairinn níor ghaire-de an ní dhomh-sa;
ár gcodhnach uile, glac-chumasach shíl Eoghain,
is tollta a chuisle, 'gus d'imigh a bhrí ar feochadh.

Do thonnchrith m'inchinn, d'imigh mo phríomhdhóchas,
poll im ionathar, biora nimhe trím dhrólainn,
ár bhfonn, ár bhfothain, ár monga 's ár mínchóngair
i ngeall le pinginn ag foirinn ó chrích Dhóbhair.

Do bhodhar an tSionainn, an Life, 's an Laoi cheolmhar,
abhainn an Bhiorra Dhuibh, Bruice 'gus Bríd, Bóinne,
com Loch Deirg 'na ruide 'gus Toinn Tóime
ó lom an cuireata cluiche ar an rí coróinneach.

Mo ghlam is minic, is silimse síordheora,
is trom mo thubaist 's is duine mé ar míchómhthrom,
fonn ní thigeann im ghaire 's mé ag caoi ar bhóithre
ach foghar na Muice nach gontar le saigheadóireacht.

The Knot

Pain, disaster, downfall, sorrow and loss!
Our mild, bright, delicate, loving, fresh-lipped girl
with one of that black, horned, foreign, hate-crested crew
and no remedy near till our lions come over the sea.

Ó Rathaille, an impoverished tenant of the Browne estate, despaired at the end of his life not only of Stuart intervention in Irish affairs, but also of any restoration of his own status by Sir Valentine Browne. *Cabhair ní Ghairfead* was composed during the poet's last illness, most likely on the occasion of the death of the last effective McCarthymore (c.1729). Ó Rathaille sums up his feelings for the Brownes in stanza 5 and for the McCarthys in stanza 6 and opts in the last stanza for an eternity with his family's ancestral patrons, the McCarthys.

No help I'll call

No help I'll call till I'm put in the narrow coffin.
By the Book, it would bring it no nearer if I did!
Our prime strong-handed prop, of the seed of Eoghan
– his sinews are pierced and his vigour is withered up.

Wave-shaken is my brain, my chief hope gone.
There's a hole in my gut, there are foul spikes through my bowels.
Our land, our shelter, our woods and our level ways
are pawned for a penny by a crew from the land of Dover.

The Sionainn, the Life, the musical Laoi, are muffled
and the Biorra Dubh river, the Bruice, the Bríd, the Bóinn.
Reddened are Loch Dearg's narrows and the Wave of Tóim
since the Knave has skinned the crowned King in the game.

Incessant my cry; I spill continual tears;
heavy my ruin; I am one in disarray.
No music is nigh as I wail about the roads
except for the noise of the Pig no arrows wound.

Goll na Rinne, na Cille 'gus chríche Eoghanacht,
do lom a ghoile le huireaspa ar díth córach;
an seabhac agá bhfuilid sin uile 's a gcíosóireacht,
fabhar ní thugann don duine, cé gaol dó-san.

Fán dtromlot d'imigh ar chine na rí mórga
treabhann om uiseannaibh uisce go scímghlórach;
is lonnmhar chuirid mo shrutha-sa foinseoga
san abhainn do shileas ó Thruipill go caoin-Eochaill.

Stadfadsa feasta – is gar dom éag gan mhoill
ó treascradh dragain Leamhan, Léin is Laoi;
rachad 'na bhfasc le searc na laoch don chill,
na flatha fá raibh mo shean roimh éag do Chríost.

That lord of the Rinn and Cill, and the Eoghanacht country
– want and injustice have wasted away his strength.
A hawk now holds those places, and takes their rent,
who favours none, though near to him in blood.

Our proud royal line is wrecked; on that account
the water ploughs in grief down from my temples,
sources sending their streams out angrily
to the river that flows from Truipeall to pleasant Eochaill.

I will stop now – my death is hurrying near
now the dragons of the Leamhan, Loch Léin and
the Laoi are destroyed.
In the grave with this cherished chief I'll join those kings
my people served before the death of Christ.

LOUIS LE BROCQUY

Condemned Men

As a very young man I knew the medical doctor who attended our rare executions by hanging. He had not a good word to say for them.

My own small protest, *Condemned Man,* was painted in Dublin in 1944, but it was in London many years later that the sustained effort of the Howard League for Penal Reform at long last persuaded the British people to abolish the inhuman ritual of capital punishment.

One of our arguments against such premeditated killing by the State was that error, sincere or contrived, did in fact occasionally occur and – ever dependent on human evidence – remained likely to recur. The appalling finality of such institutional error is obvious but, you may ask, who can restore a *wasted* life? Who can revive those dead years of imprisonment, of physical and mental suffering caused by the repeatedly sustained conviction of six men, each one of whom remains beyond doubt innocent of the obscene multiple murder for which he stands condemned?

'It was better that some innocent people should remain in prison than that the system of justice should be brought into disrepute.' This reported statement by Lord Denning (a comparatively enlightened Judge in the fifties) is in itself sufficient to bring the practice of British law into disrepute. Elsewhere Lord Denning continues: '. . . We shouldn't have all these campaigns to get the Birmingham Six released if they'd been hanged. They'd have been forgotten, and the whole community would be satisfied.'[1]

Will no English Zola be heeded by his countrymen when he denounces such brutal jostling of Justice and attempts to return to the Lady her fallen blindfold?

1 Interview by A. N. Wilson. *England, his England,* the Spectator, London 18 August 1990.

FRANCO LOI

În lī

În lī ch'j ghigna cume smentegâ,
un'aria ch'a passà suffia la mort,
vàrden i facc da l'aria suffegâ,
sifùlen, stan nascest dré d'una porta.
În lur che par che derma e par che spetta,
lur che par speren de mai pü svelìàss,
lur per viltâ cumpagn de la vendetta,
gent sensa faccia, morta sensa nass.

There They Are

There they are, grimacing as if forgotten,
like air that in passing breathes death;
watching the features of the air choke,
they whistle – hiding behind a door.
There they are, who seem to sleep and seem to wait,
who seem to hope never again to wake,
whose mean minds make them friends to vengeance,
featureless people, dead though never born.

(Translated from Milanese via Italian by Pearse Hutchinson.)

ANNE MADDEN LE BROCQUY

Antigone

A fusion of inner and outer worlds, the figure of Antigone burying Polynices appears in my painting inspired by a Greek pietà of the 5th century BC. Perhaps she is a metaphor for the creative process. She gathers the fragmented body to make it whole, to bury and thus ensure its rebirth. As Nietzsche said, 'There is no burial without resurrection.' In the back of my mind lurks Antigone's relationship with Power and Death. Totalitarian power claims rights over the body, alive or dead. She stood against the repressive edicts of Creon and the City, against old men who send youth to be slaughtered. She takes the unjust practice of the law into her own hands and consequently is walled up alive. Antigone stands as a figure of human justice outside the law of her time.

HUGH MAXTON

Bukharin's Fox

I

At Leningrad terminal
the undercarriage clattered
on the tarmac like the huge
claws of an arctic eagle
a metre short of its prey.

A fox turned blandly to go.
The birch that shadow themselves
with bruised growth stood open
on the edge of the airport –
the emigrés, the accused.

Can the Truth cease to be true?
Better – how long does it take
for demon or beast to die
reaching his old, iced-up haunts?
And Nature, does it close ranks

when the word barely goes out
annulling the enterprise?
Dialectic and divorce,
he had known each to be shrewd
visiting Madame Stalin.

II

Pavlov called again, amazed
at my commissar's grasp of
biology. His lectures
were based on research commenced
when I was just eleven.

Osip's brother has been lifted.
Poet and wife have me plagued.
He thinks Gorky's not gifted,
has slapped Tolstoy in the bake.
Brother, I pray, save thyself.

Remember, Koba, the arm-
wrestling, the falls and throws
when we were young and comrades?
I won by means of my height.
Shortly, I am in the throes.

Your wife? Put this posthumous
note in the drawer with Lenin's
crisp rebuke of your pawing
his missus. I suppose mine
can with-stand another death.

III

A wisp of smoke rose from the box
hiding the same hands. The court
took note of the confessions,
and Rosengolts breaking down
into daft unfinished song.

On the day no documents
existed. The accused were
the competent witnesses.
By the year's end, a poet
who mocked the gunman's stubby

fingers died naturally.
How the truth rang hollowly,
how the prisoner returned
each question as its answer,
how the song swallowed itself

as a beast enters its lair.
Beast and truth, nature and lair,
one slips into the other.
Vomit and motiv – please
choose, quickly enter your pleas.

IV

In the Taynitsky Gardens
after he ceased to exist
the grass annually hardens
and forgives like the tourists
with their guilt-ridden questions.

Memoirs of Koba's daughter
speak of the gods and the good
as if the one might pardon
the other party without
snorts of demonic laughter.

The guides so-call Government
Hotel where some two per cent
of the nomenklatura
survived intact the era
with only a loss of face.

Gold leaf, red square, black market.
The dealers have adjusted
to the rues of history
and its leavings, to point out
the detachment of soldiers.

V

Three times the beast to its lair,
I returned to my office.
Three times my gun in my mouth,
Lenin turned to his statue.
The engines race to reverse.

He loved a crippled hawk caged,
Adders sunned themselves in jars,
frogs, hedgehogs, and Pavlov's dogs.
Spring, and summer, then the fall.
Nature has its own career.

For the best part of six months
I, Anna Larina, stood
in iced-water, warming it
with piss and menstrual blood.
Then released into the camps

for another eighteen years.
Meanwhile the fox hid and sought
in the Taynitsky Gardens
throughout the long war with naught
but monuments for comfort.

NELL McCAFFERTY

A Visit to Edinburgh

From 1970, the year I entered journalism in Ireland, until 1989, I travelled happily and often to Britain, as a holiday visitor or on foot of invitations to give lectures there. I was usually invited to speak on feminism or the politics of Northern Ireland where I was born and reared. Despite all that Britain had done to the North, I retain an affection and respect for that country's broad tradition and achievements. Unlike most Irish people, I grew up steeped in British education and history in my home-town of Derry. Much of that heritage was, and is, fine.

Travel to that island, since 1989, is no longer a carefree experience. In that year I went over on a publicity tour for the British edition of a book, written by me, which was originally published in Ireland. *Peggy Deery* is the true story of how a Derry woman and her family have coped with the war which has been going on in the North since 1969. I had a copy of the book in my luggage as I flew from Dublin to Edinburgh airport.

Plain-clothes Scottish police officers scrutinised the queue of Irish people waiting to go through customs. I was one of a few individuals selected to explain the nature of our visit there. Given the collective ordinariness of our appearance, I think the selection was random. I explained that I was going to give a lecture. The officers wanted to know where, to whom, and on what topic. Stranger as I was to that city, I had to fish in my handbag for the letter of invitation, which gave such details as the venue, the list of speakers, and the names of the organizing group. The group was called 'Troops Out'. It is a legitimate organization, sponsored by many members of the British Parliament. Upon hearing the details, the two officers requested me to step into a nearby room. It was more of a broom-closet than a room, to judge by the mop and pail in the corner. The officers, saying not another word, opened an inner door and went into a room where I glimpsed a computer and people in police uniform. Shortly afterwards, a policewoman came into my closet and sat with me at a table. I introduced myself to her by name, extended my arm for the customary handshake, and was left talking to thin air. She would not tell me her name or take my civil hand. I thought that was rather rude. So far, none of these people had acted like your local friendly British bobby, yet for all they knew I could have been a distant relation of the Queen. One of her nieces, for example, Marina, the daughter of Princess Alexandra, has just married the son of a Derrywoman,

Catherine Hegarty, who lives near my Derry home. The Queen and I are practically neighbours. One of the two men came into the closet and asked me to describe my luggage. They were going to search it, they said. This worried me just a little bit. If they were upset at the 'Troops Out' letter, how would they feel when they saw the Virago cover of my book? The British edition shows a photograph of Peggy Deery and two of her sons. The sub-title, 'A Derry family at War', is prominently lettered. The photo, the title, and the sub-title are imposed on a background wall-mural of masked IRA men firing rifles.

I calmed myself by repeating firmly, like a mantra, the names of the British MPs which were in the letter of invitation. Clare Short and Maria Fyffe, of Labour, are women to be reckoned with, and fine company to be in at any meeting. I began to feel just grand. I had committed no crime. I did feel like a little bit of a quisling when I also mentally reassured myself that I wasn't a member of any political party, and certainly not a member of Sinn Féin. The Prevention of Terrorism Act – for under such I was being detained – has that effect upon a person. You begin to abandon every principle you've known. Who, me? A terrorist? What do you take me for, a member of Sinn Féin? . . .

The effect is insidious. You know, or at least you believe, that you're not going to be detained, for long, or charged, or framed. The Birmingham Six affair was an aberration; well, at least they lived in Birmingham, unlike me who didn't live anywhere over there. Giuseppe Conlon was the father of Gerry Conlon, and Gerry had been implicated in someone's confession . . . that is the kind of stuff you tell yourself, though actually you only tell yourself that long after the event, when you rationalize backwards.

At the time, in the broom closet in Edinburgh, what frightened me, and also saddened me, was that the police might decide, arbitrarily, to put an exclusion order upon me – that is to say, issue an edict that I might never again set foot in Britain. That is done often enough to people who are not sympathetic to the British Army's conduct in, or British government policy on, Northern Ireland. I could certainly be described as lacking such sympathy. *Peggy Deery* makes that clear.

Fear of exclusion from Britain under the PTA is based on several factors. I have many relatives in Britain. If the police viewed me unfavourably, might they not adopt a similar attitude to them? At the very least, pay them a visit, and undermine their otherwise certain sense of security and contentment there? I earn a portion of my living in Britain. Impoverishment for the sake of the Irish cause does not attract me. A black mark on my character, stamped there by Britain, might be noted by America, where I also earn an income from writing.

Not to mention that the implications of an exclusion order, under the PTA, would be noted by certain elements in the North.

The sadness was rooted in the thought of never seeing Britain again. My parents reared me on stories of the great hunger march from Jarrow, of the benefits of the British Welfare State which gave us health and education, of the struggles of the miners. Some of the happiest days of my life have been spent in London, where I was first introduced to the glamorous concept of freedom – freedom from parental supervision, uncensored freedom to read and speak as I wished, freedom to stay up all night in a city which was always wide-awake, freedom to visit all those concerts and night-clubs and theatres and sad cafes. 'If you're tired of London you're tired of life,' Samuel Johnson rightly said. Britain? I could write a hymn of love to Britain.

I love Ireland even more, but imagine being trapped here, on an offshore island of Europe for the rest of your life, unless you're got sufficient wealth to fly direct from Dublin to foreign places. Imagine not being able to avail of the cheap bucket-shop tours from London. Imagine being locked up with SPUC and their moral paratroops for evermore.

Ah, no, I thought that day in Edinburgh.

Half an hour after being detained I was set free and on my way into Edinburgh. I was elated. Two days later, on my way home, the same police officers made a point of speaking to me as I checked in for my flight to Dublin. Nothing heavy, nothing threatening; they even smiled at me. They smiled as they let me know that they were keeping an eye on me; that they had not forgotten me; that I was on their list now.

I've been frequently in Britain since. I worry every time I arrive in a British airport. If I'm randomly selected from the queue, and they check my name on the computer, and the number of confirmations mount up, well – I'd be suspicious of me, too.

Under the PTA, these people have ways of making you squeak. You do get worried. You begin to wish you were just going there on holiday. You begin to have qualms about invitations to speak on the North. You begin to silence yourself and then you recover courage, and then you become resigned. The exclusion will come some day. Won't it? Will it? It certainly could, for no reason at all. None at all. It has already happened to many others, and there is no appeal against it. You begin to behave oddly – you memorise the names of the organizers, the address of the meeting place, and you clear out your handbag and luggage of letters and books – your own books, written by yourself. You censor yourself, doing their work for them. And you insist that the organizers put you up in a hotel, not in one of their homes, so that if you're asked where you're going, you avoid drawing unwelcome attention to them, and you at least sound like you're going on a holiday. That might allay suspicion; forestall any more questions; relieve you of the temptation to lie, because once you tell a lie, you're really inviting trouble. The police would be quite justified in suspecting liars. So you demand hotel expenses, and the organizers can't afford them, and so the invitations to speak become fewer and fewer.

The ramifications and effects of the Prevention of Terrorism Act are huge. All they need to do is detain you for a lousy ten minutes. You remember it, ponder upon it, and fear it for the rest of your life.

ENDA O'BRIEN

Excerpt from *On the Bone*

When dogs bark
I think of you
And dogs bark
The world over
Even in ochre-veined Mexico
Where the women scrape the cacti
And offer them
Like Manna
With heads bowed.
On those nights of the vehement dogs
I think of you –
Oh Mother
Is there still such a long way
To go
Even though the end has been?
Ours was a lonely wine
A lonely trail,
Without dalliance
Without men-folk.
I travelled far
Changed my name,
Anything to forget you.
Rooms. Bed-sitting rooms.
A hovel in MacDoughall
Where we built castles
From a pauper's pipe
Our brains amok
In the violet air.
Then that island
Where they ate orchids
And cooked a sheep on the
Muslin sea-shore.
Now and then
A five-star hotel
With a message on a salver
'Come to lunch
Or
Come to tea
There will be James and Jonathan

And you and me,
We are all getting old, you know,
Darling'.
Duologues and Dialogues
Much the same,
Climbing the next bit of missing stairs,
Coming on you unawares
Like a gate hasp
Or a paw.
Oh Mother without mercy,
I am back now
I am here to stay.
Ours was a lonely wine
A lonely trail
I would make it again
For the sake of the song
For the sake of the rose.
Let us fold it together
Petal upon petal
Glorious
Ancestral
Menstrual
Rose
Made red
From
The pool
Of our
Being.

JULIA O'FAOLAIN

Mad Marga

'Lady to see you. A Miss . . .' The porter fumbled the name: 'Babyblacker? Something like that. She's at the gate lodge. They rang through.'

'Now?' queried James. It was ten p.m.

'She rang,' the porter said vaguely, 'last night, was it? I told her you'd be working late this evening. I meant to mention her to you, but it slipped my mind.'

'What does she want?'

The man shrugged or maybe suffered a tremor. He had some sort of palsy. 'She's American,' he offered.

It was the policy of the Blumfontein Art Institute to give low-level jobs to men who might have had trouble getting them anywhere else. James, the director, had no say in the matter.

'It's a condition of Mr. Blumfontein's will,' the chief trustee had told him. 'Philanthropy. Shouldn't affect your end of things since it only applies to unskilled personnel.'

'What if one of your charity cases goes berserk and attacks the paintings?' James had asked.

The trustee had a smile for this. 'We're businessmen, James. You may rely on us to protect the Institute's property.' He had gone on to explain about burglar alarms.

James felt put in his place and that probably his place, in the mind of the chief trustee, would not be far from that of the disabled porter. The trustee had been an associate of the Institute's founder – a tough, not to say brutal, South African who had made his money in unsavoury ways. When the Institute first opened, there had been some picketing and articles in the radical press. James, who had accepted the directorship about then, was not, he told friends, condoning Blumfontein's crimes, just glad that good should come of them. Anyway, wasn't there a nice symmetry to this buccaneer's leaving loot for fifteenth-century Italian art, just as fifteenth-century usurers used to leave theirs to the church?

'Am I to send her away, then?' The porter spoke like a man used to being in the wrong. 'She said she was a friend of yours.'

'What was the name again?'

'Foreign name. Bavylacca?' The man's arms opened as though to embrace a box.

Suddenly James knew who it was. 'A stout lady?'

'That's right.'

Marga Bevilacqua! James hadn't seen her for – oh, a dozen years. How like her not to write and turn up at such an hour. No nous, no grace: the old Marga. At the same time, a warm feeling bubbled up in him.

The porter's gesture reminded him of his own first impression of her: girth. She was calling herself Peg then, and the name went badly with her Italian surname. 'A square peg,' had been James's thought, 'jiggling round a hole!' The erotic implication was too cruel for laughter, and because he couldn't dispose of her that way he'd given her a second glance. What he saw was a plain, passionate girl who had begun to fear that she was unfitted for the only destiny she could imagine for herself – matrimony. Poor Square Peg! He had advised her to call herself Marga.

'All right,' he told the porter. 'Phone through that they can let her come.'

James had rescued her – this became a shared joke – from the bullying KKK dream of Küche, Kinder, Kirche: a good act, since she could never have achieved it. Maybe things would have been different if she had married at eighteen? By the time he met her she had become a yearner with an appetite so keen that its scope was metaphysical. James was fascinated and eager to steer this force into appropriate channels. To be fair to himself, his main motive had been kindness. But in a way he couldn't put his finger on, he had, for a time, become dependent on Marga. Odd. James laughed at the oddness of it.

Marga would be on her way up the long avenue. Should he have sent a car? Surely she would have one? He had no idea what she did for a living. When they'd met she'd been a typist and he an art historian employed by an American foundation. Their salaries were princely by London standards, and hers went almost entirely on her back. She spent nothing on food, eating perhaps one yogurt for lunch in the subsidized canteen. She was involved in an all out struggle with her recalcitrant flesh.

'Like an old-time saint,' James had teased. His field was the quattrocento, and extremes of asceticism and carnality excited him. Both met in Marga, whose preoccupation with her anatomy was stern. Once or twice she came to work unmade-up, and he remembered marvelling how, as the day wore on, her wistful travesty of a *Vogue*-ish ideal was assembled step by step. Identities fractured before his eyes: the one she wanted, the one doing the wanting, and – touching as a child's drawing – the bright, crude mask with which she ended up. By noon, with her eyelashes on, she was starting to remind him of a cow called Maybelle who had promoted processed cheese in the ads of his boyhood. These had appeared in American magazines which reached England at a time when the things they promoted were unavailable, making post-war schoolboys like James salivate over such pictured marvels as pineapple, Hershey bars, and something golden, phallic, and unknown called corn on the cob. When an American soldier gave James an actual Hershey bar, the discovery that it was less good than ordinary English chocolate shattered a sustaining faith.

Peg subscribed to the very magazines which had dazzled him. He saw them furled in the bucket bags she slung about her. These made her look even more like Maybelle and Gladys. There had been a whole family of those cows, he remembered now, all chewing cheese, a sort of auto-destructive cycle – surely eating the product of your udder was next thing to eating yourself? Peg's udders jutted like dispensing-machine spouts. She came from a place in Iowa called Council Bluffs and would never have left it if her fluent Italian, learned from immigrant parents, had not got her a job in this Renaissance institute where she served sulkily, like a slave ravished on the eve of her nuptials and sold into bondage. Longing for domesticity, she had no career ambitions at all. She never looked at the paintings or bothered to attend lectures on art. Yet to James she seemed an embodiment of the artistic impulse: working against the grain of her nature, striving, pursuing a dream. When she told him she only stayed here because she had got used to the money, he could not believe this, and when one of the other American employees told him she thought Peg an ordinary small-town girl, he was astonished.

'Surely not?'

'I promise you,' said the girl. 'Peg's maybe not too pretty, but she wants what girls from those places want: a man, a house, babies.' The girl laughed to deprecate disloyalty and distinguish herself from Peg, who was only a typist – whereas she, the speaker, having a glorious degree from Vassar College, wore flat shoes, no lipstick, and didn't have to try. The implication was that she could get these same goodies with one hand tied behind her.

'Oh,' said James. 'It's like dreaming about unobtainable Hershey bars.' He saw that this girl, whose mind had been alerted to Freudian symbols at Vassar, supposed he was being smutty. Like Peg, she was programmed, but as her programme was working for her she was unlikely to see its limitations.

Peg was acutely aware of hers. She sloshed paint across her face in a superstitious rather than a hopeful spirit. Her hair had recently been dyed pink and her clothes bought rather as fetishistic symbols than with an eye to suitability. Distrust in her system was blatant. 'All things betray thee, who betrayest Me,' quoted James in his own mind, and was reminded of paintings of the young Saint Francis throwing off the raiment of his wastrel days. Peg's passion must be working towards its peak and turning-point. He felt an urge to hasten it along and asked whether she had ever considered cutting her hair short. Something severe.

'It would suit you. Play up the strength of your face.'

Attention thrilled her – she got so little. Yet – he saw doubt move across her face – might his be the wrong sort? She knew James had taste. Everyone said so. They also said that he had special preferences, and mightn't the ones undermine the other? Was he trying to make her mannish? Well, thought James, we'll just have to get past that one, won't we?

It must have been about then that he introduced her to the boy he was living with. Gio, an apprentice waiter in a Soho restaurant, looked anything but mannish. He had long Bernini curls. They suited *him*; a Bernini boy all over. Beautiful and self-regarding, he might have been made of bronze or, no – some more ductile, re-usable material like wax. This was unkind. Gio was sharp, in a ferret-like way, but dealt fairly with James. It was just that he lacked a dimension: sensibility? soul? Some northern requirement. The lack left gaps in James's emotional life and James used Marga's friendship to fill them in.

That autumn, on a trip to Florence – it was a treat for Gio, whose family lived there – James lay on the rim of a Giambologna fountain staring up Neptune's thigh at soul-made-stone: tensile and denying its own essence, tremulous with the life it didn't have. Soul, he decided, was dissatisfaction. It was revolt against the imperfections which hem us in and figure death. Gio, it was clear, didn't have it. Peg did. Frustration had bred it in her. She knew that longing which, missing its object, was apt, in earlier ages, to leap up and fasten on God. On what should it fasten on now?

Across from James, on the stage set of the Loggia dei Lanzi, a bronze Judith held up Holofernes' dripping, severed head. Sabine women in greyed marble were ravished as Peg surely dreamed of being ravished: held aloft in palpitating curves of passive grace. Hold *her* that way and she'd look like a removalman's burden: an upside-down armchair or a toppled Pegasus. Oh dear, another Peg joke.

Yet back in London she became his private Pegasus, lifting him up, providing respites from the quarrelsome carnality of his life with Gio. Unable to free himself from his lower nature, he launched a campaign against hers.

'You've got to be freed from thinginess, Marga,' he instructed.

Her room, which she now let him visit, proved to be a temple to the flesh, a prop-shop filled with gadgets for curling, massaging, slimming, opening pores, humidifying, and procuring a winter tan. He recognized these as the instrument of despair, something like the emblems displayed in the portraits of the saints and martyrs of his period. She was irredeemably ugly. But what did that matter, he thought. If only she could see that it didn't matter at all.

Came the spring of 1968, and anti-consumerism was in full spate on the walls of Paris where James, back from another trip to Florence, stopped off with Gio. He noted a number of slogans which Peg/Marga ought, he told her, to take to heart. She should, he exhorted, live up to the battling abbess's face, which was hers now that she had shed her frizz of hair. He lent her books, extolled collective over individual passion, and took her to demos in Trafalgar Square. Demands for gay, minority, and women's rights were riding a tide of festive energy and goodwill.

Society, James wrote on Marga's bathroom mirror, *is a carnivorous flower.*

Shriek, he advised. *Yell.*

Advertising has you in thrall.

Some of the Paris slogans didn't translate well. *Man screws objects,* he tried, then *Objects screw men.*

French was a better language for this sort of thing, he assured her. Italian too. Maybe she should spend her summer vacation in her parents' old country instead of visiting them in Council Bluffs? Things were brewing in Italy, he told her. Energy was like ozone in its air. Last month in Florence, coming from a church full of Masaccio frescoes, he had stepped into a crowd of demonstrators. In the stony light, their faces resembled the ones he had just been admiring: dour, shrewd Tuscan faces, one or two with jaws like hers. A man had called James *compagno.*

'If you get politicized,' he told her, 'you'll never be alone.'

'Right now, you're stuck,' he accused her, 'stuck in consumerism like a fly in jam.' Flipping derisively through one of her glossy magazines, he mocked its advice on how to hook your man, how to become Mrs. X or Mrs. Y. 'You,' instructed James, 'should have the nerve to just be you.' He was gratified by the way she blossomed under his attention.

He must have seen her on less emphatic occasions. He forgot. Shortly after that conversation, he left his job, having been appointed to look after the art collection of a small New England college. When he returned to England, Marga had left it. Perhaps they had crossed in mid-Atlantic, square-dancing between continents? He heard that she had tried life in Council Bluffs for a while, hoping perhaps to settle with some ageing boy-next-door? Then he ran into the Vassar girl at a party and heard some garbled gossip.

'Did you hear that Peg joined the Weathermen, or was it the PLO?' The girl, now a woman, had changed identities in that effortless way some Americans could. Painted and maternity gowned, she alighted beside him between the coffee and liqueurs. '*You've* got a lot to answer for,' she chid him brightly. Peg, it seemed, had been involved in some scandal – a kidnapping or perhaps only a sit-in. Anyway, her name had got into the papers: Marga Bevilacqua. 'That was your idea, wasn't it? Such an operatic name!' reproached the ex-Vassarite. 'It seems to have gone to her head. What did a girl like that have to be dissatisfied about? She had a good job. Her father was only a truck driver, you know. And where did all that protest get anyone in the end?' She'd heard rumours that Peg had had to go underground, but maybe they weren't true? She hoped not. In America, she told James, change and social mobility came to those who waited. No need for impatience. An Englishman mightn't be aware of that. 'Of course Peg,' she added absolvingly, 'was never well balanced.'

'Miss Bevilacqua,' announced the porter with practised accuracy. Marga must have won his heart.

'Marga!'

'Jim!'

They kissed, then held each other at arm's length.

'You've changed,' she yelped.

'For the worse?' James was vain. Then he realized that she had deflected his scrutiny of her. Clever old Marga! '*You've* regressed,' he noted with surprise. Her head was once more aureoled with yellow frizz.

'A wig!' She pulled it off. 'I'm in my bourgeois gear. Your porter wouldn't have let in a weirdo, would he? By the way, I've got a friend downstairs.'

'The porter shouldn't have let him in,' James remarked. 'Shall we have him brought up?'

'Her. Later, perhaps, I have a way with porters. Fortunately. Getting in here was like crashing a party in the Kremlin.'

'Well, you could have written. What are you doing in these parts?'

'What are *you*?' Firm scrutiny. She began to circulate around James's study, staring at walls and furniture. Dumpy as ever, she was tied like a flour sack into an old camel coat. Her bourgeois gear? The hair she had uncovered was tufty, grey and short. She had a large shoulder bag, and her legs were thrust into stumpy brogues.

'I heard you became a revolutionary,' he said, uncertain whether to tease.

'Your lot don't think much of us here,' he observed to her back. She was examining the place like a surveyor. 'We were picketed,' he admitted, wanting Marga to agree that he'd been right to take this job and hadn't succumbed to what they used to call the three middles: middle age, middle class, and middle of the road. He couldn't put his case though, until she turned around. You had to see a person's expression, try to make them smile.

'Is that a cupboard?' She tapped a door with her knuckles. 'Or does it lead somewhere?'

'It's a false door,' he told her. 'It goes with the panelling. Bog oak and holly. We had it brought from a house in Buckinghamshire. Marga, darling, you're making me babble! I wish you'd sit down. Anyone would think you were casing the joint for a burglary.'

She sat. 'You're not far out.'

'Were you really an activist?' he asked. 'That female – the one with buck teeth who shared an office with you – told me you were. She couldn't remember any details.'

Marga shrugged.

How old she's got, he thought. She was leaning back, eyes closed the way you saw overworked people do on late-night buses. Hadn't the porter said something about her working late? At what? She didn't look like a secretary. She looked like an Oxfam lady who wore the best of the charity clothes herself.

She probably needed the catnap she was taking, yet James couldn't resist trying to rouse her. Like a child throwing a nut at a somnolent zoo animal, he asked whether he had been responsible for politicizing her.

She answered without opening her eyes, 'Oh you needn't bear that guilt. If it hadn't been your advice I took, it might have been my horoscope's. No' – James had made hurt sounds – 'I'm not forgetting your kindness.' She opened her eyes and he remembered that they were her one good feature. Deep blue and large, they looked as though they belonged to someone else. 'You gave me the first push,' she told him. 'You felt I wasn't fit for ordinary living, so I'd better be extraordinary. You thought I *could* be. You were wrong, but that's another matter.'

Again her lids drooped, shutting in that bright, vivacious blue. James, filtering jocularity into his tone, said he'd heard rumours about her having been involved in some violence. The remark about his thinking her unfit for ordinary living embarrassed him. Yet he'd been fond of her. He still felt a connection with her, as though she had been his child or mother or some aspect of himself which had fallen on the thorns of life while he, home and dry, had been able to go on enjoying his profession. She looked derelict, sitting in that Gothic chair.

'*We* never chose violence,' she said firmly. What did she mean by 'we'? Who were 'we'?

'You mean,' he remembered the current rhetoric, 'that it was part of the system?'

'What was?'

'Violence.'

She gave a half-snore. Was she going to fall asleep?

Talk! he wanted to shout. You came here to make contact, I presume? Ask me about Gio. No don't. Gio was now the father of four and the sweaty part-owner of a restaurant in Bagno a Ripoli. How much of whose money went into all that chrome and neon, James had wondered, foolishly visiting the place last summer.

'You respond to institutionalized violence,' he reminded her, 'with revolutionary violence. Isn't that the argument?' Words rolled off his tongue. Irony seemed to coat them. 'You choose the lesser evil in an attempt to eliminate the greater one.' It sounded like a send-up. It was his fluency. His accent perhaps? That sort of speech had to be made as if you were dragging thought from some painful depth of your soul. A third-world person could deliver it best, or dotty old Marga, but the poor cow seemed to be asleep. Frightening to remember that she was younger than he. Two years younger. God!

'James!' She had roused herself and was leaning forward. 'Is there a back way out of this room?'

'No. Why do you ask?' He waited, then launched his joke: 'You're not on the run, I hope?'

'Listen.' She had lowered her voice. 'I'm sorry to spring this on you, but I couldn't have written or anything because you might have told the police.'

Oh God! Trouble. What kind? The grey-faced woman, Marga, was sweating that peculiar smelly sweat which meant fear. James had encountered it in Italy. Once he had agreed to be the outside examiner in an exam for tourist guides and been confronted with what the comfortable jokingly call 'the great unwashed'. Peasant boys from farms, girls with only this single hope of getting out of husbandless small towns had competed for a very few places and sweated sour terror across the examiner's table at James. It had befuddled him then. It was doing so now.

'Marga, you know I'll . . . are you really in trouble?'

She had opened her handbag and was taking out a gun. It was a nasty-looking thing with a snout. James knew from cinema experience that the snout was a silencer.

She laid it on his desk. 'Take it. The woman downstairs is armed too: Annie. They don't trust me. We were sent to destroy your Pieros. They picked me because they know I used to know you. I couldn't say "no".'

The four pictures by Piero della Francesca were the collection's pride and its core. James felt seized by a curious rigidity. His brain had not adjusted to the situation.

'Hear me out,' said Marga, and added that she had never for one moment intended going through with the plan. 'It's the kind of dumb gesture *they* go in for. They – the people who set this up – claim to be anti-materialistic, but you become the thing you fight: object-obsessed . . .' James's brain seemed to divide. Half of it monitored her babble about the people who had her in their control. The other part of his brain was passive, overrun by emotion. 'I'm wanted in Italy,' he heard Marga say. 'If they denounce me, or if the cops here get me, I could be extradited.'

'What room is this woman in?' asked James's alert self. 'How many of you are there?' The Pieros, he was thinking – oh God, the Pieros. Their luminosity became fractured inside his head. The two sides of his mind clashed like cymbals.

'There's a car outside the gate, but there are only us in the house. Annie has a machine gun in her briefcase. It doesn't take her thirty seconds to assemble it. She's in the hall where the fountain is. These people think they're God . . .'

She went on speaking, saying other things, telling who the groups were. There were several groups, he gathered. They lent each other people. She had been lent. International co-operation within the framework of . . . Meanwhile he was seeing the woman down in the hall, waiting. Would she get impatient? There were two fourteenth-century *predelle* right there for her to destroy. His heart raced. The precarious quality of beauty had always pained him, and here was brutal justification for his fear. Rubbish. No. She'd come for the Pieros. She'd have more patience, more control than he. How long *had* Marga been here? The keys to the Piero room were in his pocket. The women must have known that. Damage to the *predelle* – anonymous, much less newsworthy – would be a waste of their expedition. She won't do it. James. Keep *calm*.

'You knew I had the keys?' But he'd guessed the answer before she told him: the porter. His foot edged toward the burglar alarm button in the floor. No. *Wait*. He was sweating now. Marga had begun pulling on her doll-like wig. He let her talk. Coldly he waited for useful facts, his foot poised near the alarm button.

She was afraid of extradition, she said, pulling wisps of frizz over the hairline. If the Italians got her they'd lock her up and throw away the key. She'd been framed by her fellow militants. 'That's policy. You get someone implicated in a crime, then they can't get away from you.' Fiddling with the bangs of her Mrs. Middle-America wig, Marga claimed that she only wanted to be ordinary, but now they wouldn't let her. She had been with a feminist group who had shot a gynaecologist in the legs. 'It was in Rome. Maybe you heard of the case? He used to charge extortionate fees to perform abortions on poor women, so it was decided that he should be made to see what it was like to be imprisoned in your body. They crippled him,' said Marga, but said that she had not known of the plan in advance. 'If I had, I might have gone along with it anyway. I don't know. It was like a punishment out of Dante. You remember *la legge del contrapasso*: you are punished even as you sinned?' James winced. Was he to be punished in the pictures, then? Marga had been press-ganged into joining further expeditions. In short, she had a record.

What about the woman downstairs, James asked. Wouldn't she be getting impatient?

'No,' said Marga. 'She'll give me time to chat with you. Then I'm to ask you if you'll show us both the Piero room. I'm to say she's an art student. If you refuse, I'm to bring you down at gunpoint with the keys.' However, she had a counterplan: James must agree to show the pictures. Annie would then be off-guard and, on the way to the Piero room, Marga and he would disarm her. Explaining her change of heart, Marga talked obsessively about herself. 'I,' she said, 'I.' Had she always been so self-centred, he wondered impatiently. Had *he* done this to her? Made a Frankenstein of her? He picked up the gun. She seemed not to notice. Had she invented the whole thing? Did the woman, Annie, exist? 'You're my link with the old life,' she was saying. '. . . A new start,' he heard, 'if you'll help me, James . . . help me to get away from them is all I ask.'

All, he thought, *all*? She must be insane. Maybe she always had been? If she was his creation, his Miss Frankenstein, then he had nothing to be proud of. Banalities poured from her. She unreeled the ragged frieze of her life while the four paintings dazzled his inner eye and he held her gun on his lap, trained on her but concealed by the desk. Why shouldn't she go to gaol, he thought. He had not the slightest pity for her.

'Things,' she said, 'Pictures are only things.'

He was aghast.

'*You* taught me,' she repeated, 'not to be fetishistic about material things. You said . . .' Laboriously she reported what she thought he had said. Had he? It sounded distorted in her mouth. 'But to destroy material things gives them importance,' she argued triumphantly, refuting her new mentors' arguments with what she took to be his. 'A form of idolatry,' she concluded. Christ, thought James, *Jesus Christ!* Art was like Christ's face glowing on Veronica's towel: the soul's graphic mark, the imprint of its passion, worth more than the botched lives of endless women like this.

Her face was rosy now, almost beautiful as she planned her treachery towards her confederate. James was to keep the gun in his pocket. 'She'll think it's your keys, see. I'll be behind and she'll think I've got you covered. Then you wave her ahead towards the Piero room. She'll expect you to do that for a lady. Then you stick the gun in her back.' Annie would then be handed over to the police while Marga herself was to be let quietly go. She'd be free of the law and of her terrorist companions. 'I'll just disappear,' she said, sounding for all the world like a woman in a soap opera of the sort she should have been watching at home in Iowa if she'd never left it. Then she was talking *about* Iowa, and how she would go back there where she had no record and used a different name.

It struck him that of course she had planned this – maybe even offered herself as go-between. She must have put the paintings at risk deliberately, in the hope that he would help her get away from her companion. How *could* the terrorists have known she knew James unless she had told them so herself? He had tried to groom her, to take away her ordinariness, and now he owed it to her to restore her to her habitat. She was actually saying something like this.

'No, but they used to call me your fag hag. Don't look hurt. Well, you wouldn't have wanted them thinking we were having an affair, right? You were so admired, and who was I in that outfit? Miss Nobody from the bottom of the barrel. I guess it amused you to pick me out to have lunches with: the prince and the goose girl. It amused you to surprise people. No, don't be offended, James. I was, I am grateful to you. Only, you see, I *am* a sort of goose girl. I really am. I want to go home to my own place.'

'Isn't that just fantasy? I thought you had tried living back in Council Bluffs?'

'It was too soon. Now I could. I was too radicalized then, and dressing the way you'd taught me, and I kept arguing with straight people. Now I'd love it. I just want to be where I know people, know the way they are, you know, and the rhymes the kids are skipping rope to, and where the teenagers go for their coke or dope or whatever. Feeling my way into them. Knowing their features from their parents.' She spoke rapidly, lyrically. Energy flowed back into her. She laughed. 'I could be the lady bank clerk in one of those dinky one-storey banks, or the saleslady at the health-food store looking out the window at green lawns and the white frame church. "Miss Bevilacqua?" people would say. "Sure, she's from here. Knew her dad. She went to Europe for a bit but she's home now . . ."'

James's foot pressed the button on the floor. He'd been meaning to do it, but when he did he surprised himself the way you can when you find you've turned off a radio programme without thinking: something cheap and invasive, maybe an ad or a tear-jerker that gets to you on levels of yourself which you don't like to acknowledge. Good, he thought, feeling back in control. The police station was less than a mile away. They'd be en route in no time, dousing their blue light on the last stretch and approaching the house with maximum discretion. The trustee had explained the drill. The woman, Annie, would not suspect a car or two coming quietly up the drive. Even if she did, she'd be disarmed before she knew it and Marga would, of course, have to be taken into custody. No deals. How could there be? Anyway, he doubted if she was quite sane. Years had passed since he'd known her. She'd probably taken drugs of various sorts, shot her brain to bits.

'Why don't you put on a light?'

'What?'

'It's dim here.' She indicated his green reading light, the discreet lamps. 'Or shall we go down now?'

'No, no,' he had to say. Then, 'Tell me more about Council Bluffs.'

She laughed, amused, unsuspecting. What a hopeless revolutionary she must have been. A hopeless human being. But were revolutionaries not mostly that? The rank and file of them anyway, the wretched background figures?

'Tell me,' he said, an image of the travelling police cars in his mind's eye. They'd be at the crossroads any minute. He must hold her here until they had dealt with the woman, Annie, and if there was no such person then no harm was done. He would have done the prudent thing. 'Is there a river there?' he asked.

'River?'

His mind swam. Why had he asked that? 'In your hometown?' Was he thinking of some song?

But it seemed that there was one, the Missouri River. There were oaks and sumac bushes, and above all the lawns – she returned to these – were unfenced. James strained his ear for the sounds of a car. How would he know it was the right one? Better wait here until that door behind her opened and the police walked in. He tried to think of the pictures she had come to destroy, but instead of their familiar pallor something neon bright and soda-pop vivid spun into his vision: lime-juice-green lawns and crème-de-menthe foliage, Marga's dream. Nostalgic, lost – canvases by Hopper, Wyeth, Norman Rockwell filled the frame of his mind's eye. American Gothic: an old couple rocking on a gingerbread porch, her parents waiting for her, who would not be back. Was that the car? No . . . Magazine art, *New Yorker* covers, pictures for people who didn't understand art but liked what they liked danced fervently as she talked. Mad Marga, he thought. She did have fervour, only lacked direction, and whose fault was that? Lonely – it had been her loneliness he had loved, he remembered now – why shouldn't she want to go home as Gio had? Fat Gio, proud of his restaurant and calling James *il mio dottore*. James was Marga's *dottore* too, and derelict in his duties.

'Come and visit me there,' she was saying, 'why don't you?' – while the purr of the police car on the drive made James adjust his grip on the gun, which was pointed at her in case there should be a moment's confusion when the cops slipped in the door.

'I will,' he promised before his divided mind could send the signal to the rest of him that the place where he would have a chance to visit her would not be Council Bluffs.

NUALA O'FAOLAIN

Can the Judges Understand them?

Snow on the ground, on this last day, and bright Christmas decorations in the windows around the Old Bailey. In the lifeless world of the courtroom the appeal ends, as evenly and undramatically as everything has been for weeks and weeks. There is no climax. It just stops, with a few words from Lord Lane.

No one expected anything other than a reserved judgment, except the families. They couldn't help believing that if a retrial was being even contemplated, the men would have been let out now, today.

Three of the wives sat together in the cafeteria afterwards trying to get the courage to go out and face the cameras. Their raincoats are too thin for this icy weather. They were bowed, sagging. In an hour or so they will be nobodies again.

It has been an arid experience to attend the hearing. It did not, as the Kerry Babies Tribunal did, when it sat in Tralee, or as the original trial in Lancaster seems to have done, create its own world and its own camaraderie. This was just one, tiny, event in the huge life of London. By five minutes after the end of each day, everyone had dispersed, back to their larger lives. The pubs are still closed at 4.30.

It has not had the human and sociological interest that many court proceedings have. We haven't heard and have barely seen, the men whose liberty is at stake here. There was very little witnesses evidence, and most of that was on the forensic side. Of the forensic witnesses, only Dr. Skuse was other than colourless.

There are differences in style between the judges and between counsel.But they are all lawyers: they all share the same language, and no-one matters to them except each other. The law has, over its long evolution, become a form of commentary on real life, a commentary purged of passion and accident and prejudice. What matters is the perfection of the commentary in itself. By definition, this repels lay observers, whose sense of life is based on experience or on art.

A vast amount of labour underpinned the appeal.

In and around the courtroom there are all or part of the following: 10 volumes of trial depositions, 19 volumes of trial transcript and the approximately 300 statements collected into three volumes by the Owen Inquiry. There are 21 volumes from the prison officers' trial, one volume from the civil action, and approximately 25 volumes of the 1,000 statements taken during the Devon and Cornwall inquiry into police conduct. This is to leave aside the various law-books which have figured so largely in arguments about precedent.

The procedure by which the bench constantly writes down what counsel have just read, from what they wrote down, and the huge pile of paper that surrounds the principals, harks back to the world of parchment and quill, and seem all the more odd when journalists leave the court to use cellphones, and lap-top keyboard terminals, and Fax machines.

The judges take all these words away now, and continue their work. For everyone else it is on to the next job. This is particularly true of the broadcasters: their miles of film and video now become archive. The press is more open to returning to the subject, as the *Guardian* did in the seventies.

Our own two reporters, Carol Coulter and John Armstrong, have filled just under 60 shorthand notebooks. They've spent about 125 hours dictating copy over the telephone to Angela Doyle in the newsroom in Dublin. Further countless hours have been spent on sub-editing and lay-out.

For what? Why? Why are we all so involved? These are not six Nelson Mandelas in the dock: these men were never valued by anyone except their families and friends. They were – it varies from man to man – sympathisers with the IRA. They are British citizens, duly convicted by a jury of their peers. The appeal just concluded was argued by counsel, on both sides, of the highest calibre, and before a bench remarkable for its alertness. Justice has been seen to be done.

But what if the men are not guilty? What if they did nothing? If they were terrorised by the police, if confessions were cynically planted on them, if they have spent all these years deprived of any life worth living, and with the terrible burden of coming to terms with their powerlessness in the face of injustice? What if these six men are innocent?

These are not the first men to have been dragged from their private lives to face an incomprehensible public punishment. Nor is what is alleged to have been done to them specific to one country.

Human rights cases rise above the local and the temporary. The argument that this appeal is an important episode in Anglo-Irish relations, because of the present debate about extradition, is not logically sustainable, though this case does, of course, issue from the unhappy history of these islands, and it is always coloured by historical suspicions. But it is much more sound to base one's view of this case within the context of human rights in general.

The Birmingham Six and their families have been fortunate in attracting sustained and intelligent support from people whose only interest in them is from the point of view of basic human rights. On Fridays, the Campaign Committee discreetly gave envelopes to the families, who could not otherwise afford the fares and the time off work that visiting the court for every day of six weeks involves. This money, meagre though it is, has been collected publicly and honourably by the hard work of the committee. They ask for nothing in return.

On another level, but more importantly in the public world, the Hierarchy has been a weighty presence in the courtroom itself. One takes their commitment as a guarantee that moral issues, and not mere cultural or procedural ones, have been relevant to the proceedings just ended.

Cultural understanding is, nevertheless, the issue here. The further fate of the men is in the hands of three judges who would have to make great imaginative leaps to be able to conceive of an innocent interpretation of the sequence of events so ably put to them by Mr. Igor Judge for the Crown. It will be hard to wait for the judgment.

No matter what happens, the appeal has reaffirmed two of the great positive values in ordinary human life. One is, as touched upon above, the disinterested goodness of outsiders who work for strangers in the name of justice. The other is the amazing strength and beauty of family ties. Not many people are called upon in the way the wives and children of these men have been called upon, to live out their vows. Such love and loyalty is, one hopes, its own reward.

That this appeal ever happened at all is important. But in itself it hardly addressed the central issue, the core of the case, as it is perceived in both Britain and Ireland. The core is the confessions. It is noticeable that when observers here argue for the men's total or partial guilt, and no matter what point they start from, they come within a minute or two to a reliance on the truth of the confessions. If the confessions are true, then it doesn't matter about Dr. Skuse or anything else. If the confessions are not true, then there is little or nothing to prove the guilt of the men.

And if the confessions are not true, then not one or two or five, but tens of police officers are thoroughly corrupt, and habitually corrupt, since their absolute silence on this matter has lasted for thirteen years.

This is the Dreyfus factor, and the real, if unspoken reason, for British media interest in this case. It is extremely unlikely, but it is just possible, that these six men will be instruments of sensational revelation about the British police. If it were to become publicly known that the police are not just as unworthy, but as incompetent as this case might show them to be, then British society would be shaken as no IRA bomb could ever shake it.

Counsel for the men in this appeal have asked for a retrial. If it is granted, the men may well be reconvicted. If it is not granted, this is the end of the line. No other proceedings are in hand or contemplated.

There are four grandfathers in the dock already. Soon they will all be grandfathers. It is possible that while they live out their captivity, the Birmingham bombers are free, and that as it happens, the IRA found perfect partners in the Birmingham police in pulling this off. The casualty list from those IRA bombs must read, no matter what happens now – 21 dead, 162 wounded, and these six walking dead.

LIAM Ó MUIRTHILE

'Upon the Mercy of Government'

Bhí sé phribhléid agam a bheith i láthair im cháilíocht mar fhinné, thar ceann an phobail in Éirinn, sa Chúirt Achomhairc san Old Bailey i Londain seachtain is an lá inniu.

Bhíos tar éis Baile Átha Cliath a fhágaint an mhaidin sin ag a cheathrú i ndiaidh a seacht ar eitilt go Luton agus thuigeas ionam féin ag a deich a chlog go mba gheall le míorúilt é a bheith suite anois mar a rabhas: díreach taobh amuigh den dronuilleog de ghloine philéardhíonach ag ceann an staighre a lig ceathrar Ghuildford aníos as an duibheagán leathuair a chloig ina dhiaidh sin chun aghaidh a thabhairt ar an dTiarna Príomh-Ghiúistís Lane agus a bheirt chomhghleacaí.

De réir gach córas loighce dar ceapadh riamh, níor chóir go mbeinn i ngaireacht glaoch teileafóin láimhe don gCúirt. Amuigh sa tsráid bhí na barracáidí curtha in airde ag na póilíní agus orduithe crua tugtha fanacht taobh istigh díobh: cró na gceamaraí teilifíse agus nuachtán cúpla céad slat suas ó phríomhdhoras an Old Bailey; cró an phobail caoga slat ar aghaidh an phríomhdhorais amach; agus scuaine iriseoirí ag síneadh síos céad slat ar feadh an chasáin ag feitheamh le súil go gcuirfidís cos thar tairseach isteach san Old Bailey féin, gan trácht ar dhul isteach sa Chúirt Achomhairc. Ina lár seo go léir bhí scafall in aghaidh foirgnimh trasna ón Old Bailey, agus ardaitheoir ag imeacht suas síos lena thaobh lán d'oibrithe tógála Éireannacha féna hataí crua ag filleadh ó bhriseadh tae na maidne.

Dá gcuimhneoinn i gceart ar an radharc ní thabharfainn fé in ao'chor. Ach múineann an tsráid instinn duit agus táim buíoch anois don dtógaint sráide a mhúin scileanna áirithe iontrála dhom i sorcais nuair nach raibh an praghas iomlán agam; i bpáirceanna imeartha nuair a déarfadh fear an gheata liom greadadh isteach as a radharc, agus in ócáidí foirmeálta nó ceiliúrtha nuair ba chóra gur cic sa tóin amach an doras cúil a gheobhainn in áit a bheith ag teacht i dtír mar chách ar bhia nó ar dheoch in aisce. Instinn ghlan a thug ormsa an t-éasc a aimsiú sa chóras agus sleamhnú ón gcúl fé láimh shínte an chonstábla a bhí ag scaoileadh cúigear sa turas isteach i *carousel* an Old Bailey.

B'éigean dom mo dhintiúirí a bheith agam ar ndóigh. Litir ó m'fhostóir; mo chárta tuairisceora; pas taistil. Ní raibh agam go fóill. Isteach liom ina dhiaidh sin i gcapsúl séalaithe i gcomhair cá bhfios cén x-ghathú crómasónach. Amach liom chun ligean dóibh x-ghathú a dhéanamh ar mo bhagáiste. Suas in airde staighre go dtí scuaine eile agus striopáil leictreonach ar gach luid éadaigh agus gach fearas dá raibh ar iompar agam. Peann agus leabhar nótaí ar nós an daichead tuairisceoir eile a bhí fágtha agam nuair a shuíos sa chúirt tar éis na striopála leictreonaí.

Is deacair liom fós cur síos ar na tonnta éagsúla mothúchán, maidhmeanna a scuab tríom le linn na héisteachta. Bíonn tú ró-ghnóthach ag iarraidh coimeád suas leis an bhfianaise agus á breacadh síos – ag déanamh nótaí fírinneacha comhuaineacha – chun aon cheann a thógaint de. Ach ó am go chéile b'éigean dom stopadh de bheith ag scríobh – mar nárbh fhiú bheith ag glacadh nótaí ar aon nós d'fhírící áirithe a bhí ar eolas againn cheana féin – chun nach mbrúchtfadh an fhearg tríom aníos ina racht.

Le croitheadh móiréiseach a chinn b'iúd é an Tiarna Príomh-Ghiúistís Lane ag slogadh mar fhírinne, fianaise a raibh diúltaithe aige féin di mar dheargéitheach roimhe sin. B'iúd é maorlathas dlíthiúil ceannais ar taispeáint, á chréachtadh go smúsach ní de bharr sceimhlitheoireachta ach de thoradh coiriúlacht thiarnúil aicmí den mhaorlathas féin. Óm thaobhsa de, is í an mhórcheist atá anois le freagairt ná cen fhaid a shíneann géag lofa na coiriúlachta san? Ach ní móide go nochtfaidh na téarmaí atá tugtha don mBinse Fiosraithe Oifigiúil an cheist sin go brách, mar chun í a fhreagairt chaithfí an bhunchloch a bhaint as struchtúr an mhaorlathais cheannais féin.

Ní lú ná san na ceisteanna breise is gá a chur i dtaobh aon tsocruithe eiseachadtha idir Baile Átha Cliath agus Londain; ní lú ná san na ceisteanna is gá a chur i dtaobh gnéithe fianaise d'ár gcóras dlíthiúil féin, go háirithe nuair a ghlactar le focal neamhdhearbhtha Cheannfort sa Gharda Síochána chun duine a chiontú i gcásanna ar leith. Ina theannta san ní foláir aird níos mó ná riamh a dhíriú ar an Acht um Sceimhlitheoireacht a Chosc sa Bhreatain, mar gurb iad na daoine is leochaillí agus is imeallaí – cuid de na daoine sin a dhíbrímid féin amach as an dtír againne ar imirce – is mó atá i mbaol de réir feidhmiúlacht an Achta san. Ná ní dhearmadfadsa ach go háirithe, radharc den Aire Dlí is Cirt againn féin ag réabadh isteach in óstán i bPort Laoise i naoi déag seachtó ceathair – nuair a gabhadh ceathrar Ghuildford mar a tharlaíonn – agus drom armtha le Uzis á ghardáil faid a bhí sé ag ól cupa tae: bhí faoistiní á mbatráil as príosúnaigh an uair sin leis fé mar a bheadh Dia á rá leo.

Ach gan trácht in ao'chor ar ghaolta na bpríosúnach fadfhulaingeach, tá creidiúint nach beag ag dul d'abhcóidí áirithe Sasanacha i ngeall ar a misneach agus cás cheathrar Ghuildford a throid nuair ab ionann drannadh leo, i súile a gcomhghleacaithe, agus lobhair a láimhseáil. Tá creidiúint leis ag dul do pholaiteoirí áirithe thall, agus do Tom McGurk agus iriseoirí FIRST TUESDAY a dhein na cláracha faisnéise ar Ghuildford. Sheasaimh scáthghrúpaí den Eaglais Chaitliceach go diongbháilte leo. Bhí cúis acu. B'fhéidir gur scaipeadh téacs óráid Naomh Oilibhéar Pluincéad ag Tyburn sular díothaíodh é, orthu. Bhí chúig seachtaine faighte ag an bPluincéadach ó Thiarna Príomh-Ghiúistís an ama – 1681 – chun a chás a ullmhú. Theip air. Loirg sé a thuilleadh spáis: 'Ansan d'athchainíos go truamhéileach dhá lá déag eile do thabhairt dom do chum mo thriala; gidh eadh, do dhiúltaigh an Tiarna Príomh-Ghiúistís mé agus leis sin do tugadh chun mo thriala mé agus do tugadh suas mé (ionann agus dá mbeadh mo lámha ceangailte) fé chumhachta meirdreach na mbréag do thug leabhar éithigh do chum an anama do bhuain asam . . .'

Ceathrar Ghuildford

'. . . do tugadh suas mé fé chomhachta meirdreach na mbréag do thug na leabhair éithigh do chum an anama do bhuain asam. . .'

Oilibhéar Pluincéad, Tyburn, 1681

Coinnítear iad ar bís i mbéal an duibheagáin
aisteoirí ar na cliatháin, cipíní briste na héagóra;
Tá greim fáiscthe acu ar mhugaí gorma plaisteacha,
fé shrathair ag ordú grod ó pheiriúic an achomhairc.
Aimsímid súile a chéile ag léimnigh ag stánadh
trín bpána piléardhíonaithe ar líonrith an phóna;
Táim gafa go brách ag aonfhéachaint thruamhéileach amháin –
níl aon phúicín fós acu do fhuinneog súl chéasadh anama.
Nuair a tugtar iad ar aghaidh Abadón ar an mbinse
is trína súile siúd óna gcúl a chímse os mo chomhair é;
Tá ciníocha iomlána daortha ag éitheach a dhlínse,
tíoránacht an treascróra fé chlóca ceannais na córa.
Sa chúirt chliniciúil tá géaga morgtha ag úscadh,
le hordóg neamhchiontach feasa d'fhéadfaí iad a theascadh.

SEÁN Ó TUAMA

Christy Ring

Do thriail sé an ní dodhéanta
formhór gach Domhnach ar an bpáirc,
is uaireanta rith leis.

Ar leathghlúin dó
teanntaithe i gcúinne
nuair las a shúil –
réamhchríostaí, leictreonach –
's gur dhiúraic an liathróid uaidh
thar trasnán,
chrith an t-aer le hiontas.

Nuair thug gan coinne
aon ráig ghlan fiain
trí bhulc na bhfear
's gur phléasc an sliotar
faoi smidiríní solais
sa líontán
do liúigh an laoch
san uile dhuine.

Aon neomat buile amháin
in earr a ré
is é Cúchulainn
bhí 'na ionad
ar an bpáirc –:
d'at a chabhail
i radharc na sluaite,
do bholgaigh súil
's do rinc ar mire,
bhí cnagadh is cleatar,
liútar-éatar,
fir á dtreascairt,
fuil ag sileadh –
's nuair rop trí cúil isteach
bhí seandéithe Éireann uile
ag stiúrú a chamáin.

Dúirt bean os cionn a choirp
tráth a bháis anabaidh:
'ba mhór an peaca é
an fear san a adhlacadh'.

Christy Ring

He aimed at the impossible
each Sunday on the pitch;
sometimes he suceeded.

Down on one knee,
trapped in a corner of the field,
when his prechristian electronic eye
lit up in combat,
and the ball, a missile,
sped from him straight above the bar,
the air shook in awe.

When a driving lunge
brought him clear beyond
the ruck of men,
and the ball, propelled,
self-destructed in the net
to smithereens of light,
our cheering became a battle cry.

In one moment of raw frenzy
as his playing days ran out,
he summoned Cú Chulainn
to aid him on the pitch:
his trunk swelled up
in sight of thousands,
one eye bulged
and danced, demented,
through clash and crash
hue and cry
men were toppled
hot blood spurted
and as he rammed in
three lethal goals
all the gods of ancient Ireland
lent his hurley a guiding hand.

Looking at his corpse laid out,
the day of his untimely death,
a woman said:
'It would be a sin to bury such a man.'

Ní féidir liomsa fós
Christy Ring a adhlacadh. . .
Samhlaím é uaireanta
is é ar buanchoimeád,
sínte ar leac na honóra
i mBrú na Bóinne
is Aonghas Mac an Daghda á choimhdeacht
go dtí an leath-uair bheag gach Geimhreadh
go soilsíonn ga gréine go hómósach
ar a chúntanós.

Ach ní fhéadfadh aoinne againne
a mhair faoi bhriocht ag Christy Ring
é leagadh uainn go buan faoi ghlas
i measc míorúiltí na seanmhiotas –
mar, ó na míorúiltí
chonaiceamar dáiríre
is a chúntanós faoi loinnir
formhór gach Domhnach
Geimhreadh is Samhradh
ar an bpáirc.

I have not managed yet to bury Christy Ring
Sometimes I imagine him
being venerated
in the care of the great god, Aengus,
on a slab at Newgrange
and at each winter solstice
for just one half an hour
a ray of sunshine
lighting up his countenance.

But no friend of his could think
of laying Christy Ring eternally to rest
locked in with ancient miracles –
for oh the miracles of the living flesh
we saw when his countenance lit up
Winter days and Summer days,
Sundays in and Sundays out,
on the playing pitch.

BERT PAPENFUSS-GOREK

revolver

von innen betrachtet
die hand ein handschuh
schwarzglänzend über mir
der schädeldecke firmament

der rippen kathedrale
überspannt serpentinen
des gedärms in wallung
jeder furz höhlt mich aus

dem herzen dargebracht
menschenopfer zu beklagen
zerrkrampft ein praller ball
vollgesogen der sonne schwamm

am litoral gespannt
fährst du immer wieder
als gae bolga in mich &
errichtest deine stacheln

ich bin ein revolver
& gehör in jedes bett
schwaden schwarzen blutes
stocken über den eingeweiden

revolver

described from within
  the hand a glove
    black glittering above me
      the skull's firmament

the rib's cathedral
  overstretched serpentine
    of guts tied in knots
      every fart hollows me out

offered up to the heart
  human sacrifices to lament
    crumples up a blazing ball
      the solar plexus soaked

arched at the lido
  you drive again & again
    as gae bolga into myself &
      raise your hackles

I am a revolver
  & belong in every bed
    swathes of black blood
      stick over the innards

(Translated from the German by Karen Margolis.)

TOM PAULIN

Excerpt from *The Break on Ulster*, a stage-play in progress

(The play is set during the negotiations which led to the signing of the Anglo-Irish Treaty in December 1921. This scene comes near the end of the negotiations.)

(*Lights come up on delegates sitting round the table – flamboyant aggression from Churchill and Lloyd George, steely confidence on Irish side like a football team working together after a sticky first half.*)

Churchill: Look at the tribunals the Russian government has devised!

Collins: Right comrade!

Churchill: Give the judges universal scope –

Collins: And if you can't get judges?

Churchill: Generals – we'll put the entire island under martial law!

Collins: Then you'll need what? – quarter of a million men.

(*Lloyd George, sensing danger, looks for an opening.*)

Churchill (turning to the map of the world): Look at our Empire! We can put a soldier in Ireland for every man woman and child.

Childers: But you'd have to keep them there –

Collins: For ever and ever.

Lloyd George: Gentlemen, let us not debate mere hypotheses – I put it to you that you must concede to the Crown the harbours and foreshores of Ireland –

Collins: You'll be wanting our foreskins next.

Griffith: You persist in treating us as if we were a new nation –

Churchill: And are you not?

Griffith: We most emphatically are not. If we were a new nation – if we were settlers far from the centre of power – then, yes, we might accept Dominion Status – we could wait then – what? – five, six, seven generations – wait for power to devolve back to us. But we are not (*taps table*) a new nation – we are an ancient and spirited nation – a nation whose soul and being has lived underground, has become invisible – gone out on the roads or into exile – for so many, many generations –

Collins: Correct.

Childers: Absolutely true.

Griffith: – and it is for this reason that we cannot accept – we can *not* accept a limited, a curtailed, freedom upon a merely verbal promise of a less limited, a less constrained, freedom in the future – it is for this reason that the concept of External Association – Association *with* mark you – not *without* the British Commonwealth – is a fixed mark we cannot depart from –

Lloyd George: You will swear an oath of allegiance?

Collins (banging the table): Oath of Allegiance be damned! You're offering us something shapeless – it's neither fish nor flesh!

Churchill: The Crown, gentlemen, the Crown – the Crown is the symbol of everything that keeps the nations of the Empire together – it is the keystone of the arch in sentiment –

Griffith: We are prepared to recognize the Crown as head of the . . . the *Association* of the two states.

Churchill (shaking his head): The Crown is the symbol of common citizenship –

Lloyd George: No one can be a subject of two states.

Collins: No way we'll recognize the Crown as head of our state.

Lloyd George: Oh but you must.

Collins: Never.

Childers: Never.

Griffith: Never.

(*Lloyd George signals to Stevenson. She brings him a document*)

Lloyd George: Let me read you the proposed Oath of Allegiance – (*reading*) 'I – dot dot – do solemnly swear true faith and allegiance to the Constitution of the Irish Free State and to recognize the King of Great Britain as Head of State' – well?

Childers: Utterly impossible.

Griffith: Don't you see – we Irish cannot swear direct allegiance to your King –

Churchill (*getting up abruptly*): It's the King or nothing!

Collins (to Lloyd George, slowly getting up): It's war is it?

Lloyd George (thrown off guard): No . . . it can't be war.

(*Everyone stands up, except Stevenson*)

Collins: What d'you mean it can't be war?

Churchill (*intervening*): You didn't hear what the prime minister said.

Collins: For sure I did – he said 'it can't be war'.

Lloyd George: As a matter of **public** record I said we can't comtemplate war. (*gesturing*) Pray be seated gentlemen. I fear we've all been a trifle hasty.

Collins (*exchanging exasperated look with Griffith and Childers and sitting down*): Contemplate my asshole!

Griffith (*soothing*): In that case, prime minister, perhaps we could return to the vexed question of the oath – I propose we substitute 'to the Treaty of Association' after 'Free State' and replace 'the State' with 'the Association'.

Lloyd George: I don't follow your drift.

Childers: Perhaps you could write it down?

(*Lloyd George is momentarily lost. Stevenson brings him a document*)

Lloyd George (*writing*): Could you repeat the words, Mr. Griffith?

Griffith: 'I – dot dot – do solemnly swear true faith and allegiance to the Constitution of the Irish Free State, to the Treaty of Association, and to recognize the King of Great Britain as Head of the Association'.

Collins: We can go no further.

Lloyd George (*passing document to Churchill*): Winston?

Churchill (*reading*): It . . . it might be feasible.

Lloyd George: Two crowns, two parliaments.

Collins: So? A parliament in Dublin – and in London.

Lloyd George: No.

Collins: I don't understand.

Lloyd George (*coldly laying out his proposal*): As from the day we sign a treaty of peace between the two islands there shall be established a parliament in Dublin *and* a parliament in Belfast.

Childers (*standing up*): Never, never, never!

Collins (*gathering his papers and standing up*): All this way – for this! What a fool's errand!

Lloyd George: You don't accept my proposal?

Griffith: We do not accept your proposal.

Lloyd George: Yet you have given me your personal pledge.

Griffith: You tricked me.

Lloyd George: The cry of the Irish down the centuries! (*exasperated*) Listen to me now – each one of you must make up your own mind – and make it up tonight (*suddenly he produces two letters and holds them up, one in each hand*) – I have to communicate with Sir James Craig tonight – here are the letters I have prepared – one enclosing the Articles of Agreement – the Treaty we have hammered out here in this room – (*gestures with letter*) – the other stating that the representatives of Sinn Fein refuse to come within the Empire. I will send one (*shakes second letter*) or other (*holds it still*). If I send this (*second letter*) it is war – and war within three days – which – which letter am I to send? Whichever letter you choose goes by special train to Holyhead and by destroyer to Belfast . . (*menacing*) the train is waiting – waiting with steam up – at Euston. If this (*gesture*) or this (*gesture*) is to reach Sir James Craig in time I must know your answer by 10 tonight. I tell you it is no longer possible to sit hovering on the fence – tell me – and tell me now – is it peace or war?

Griffith: We won't be browbeaten.

Lloyd George: I am giving you an ultimatum.

Griffith: We will discuss your ultimatum.

Lloyd George: Very well, Mr. Churchill and I will withdraw again – you have half an hour.

(*Exit Lloyd George and Churchill*)

Collins: Worse and worse! (*paces the room*)

Childers: We're in their house!

Collins: Impaled on their terms.

Griffith: They're the best terms we'll get.

Collins: Are they fuck. They're useless.

Childers: They have us in a trap – all we can do now is fight – with guns, not words.

Collins: It'll be a relief after this nightmare.

Griffith: You think so? you think so?

Collins: I know so.

Griffith (*walking the room thoughtfully*): Last March – only what? – only eight months back I was locked in Kilmainham – (*he sits down with a slow, exhausted thoughtfulness*) – the 12th of March – we all remember that day . . . poor Paddy Moran – (*gets up, goes to empty chair by table, leans on the table*) – him and five other brave fearless lads – oh those poor boys! (*shudders*) – we called it the Hang House. D Wing, the Hang House – there were so many that went to their deaths there . . . stinking kip it was . . . Paddy Moran was first (*walks*), then Jim Bradley (*walks*), then Tomás MacKenna (*walks*) . . . Charlie Cassidy (*walks and stops*), Inan McHugh (*walks and stops*). Last of all – last of all was Ned Coughlan – remember Ned Mick – on the hour and the half-hour they dropped them. Oh God! One by one they dropped them through the trap. And you call **this** a trap! (*reminiscing*) You know, early on – just after dawn – I looked through the spyhole – coffins – one after the other – empty coffins – they were bringing them up from the workshops . . . new they were, cheap and plain – rope-handles nailed on the sides . . . and those poor lads still living – still on God's earth! But you know? (*he looks at them*) – you know worse – what was worse than that? was I saw the hangman in a grey overall – walking with a screw beside him – and the screw carrying this long canvas bag – they walked so slowly – and the hangman wearing these wash-leather gloves – they walked so slowly – slowly but firmly – and I was sick, sick beyond anything – I was so sick I couldn't for a moment give the signal . . . but I did and we beat the walls, we beat the pipes and the bars . . . we wrecked our cells – all that long terrible morning we chanted – chanted and sang as they took those six lads out one by one and dropped them. O God spare us, spare us, spare us . . . (*he breaks down*)

Collins (after a pause): Jesus God what can we do?

Childers: I tell you we must not sign.

Collins: Ned Coughlan, he was my dearest friend – I can't bear to send more men to their deaths.

Childers: They are prepared to die. We must fight.

(*Griffith sighs*)

Collins: If we start fighting tomorrow the Brits will walk all over us. We're too weak to fight them a second time. You know that.

Childers: If we concede the principle of partition then Ireland will forever be divided.

Collins: Principle! You're forever harping on principles when it's the lads on the ground that count! (*gets up*) You're like a field under water – dead, barren!

Griffith: We have to sign.

Childers: You said you would sign – neither of us did.

Collins: Don't sound so smug! Isn't it obvious? Arthur said he'd sign – we all have to sign. The damage is done now. We'd look ridiculous.

Childers: I'm not signing.

Collins: Well I'm for signing.

Griffith: Erskine– I'm pleading with you . . .

(*Blackout*)

GABRIEL ROSENSTOCK

Leanbh Gréine

Thángthas air i gcró na gcearc
áit ar choinnigh sí é. Ní raibh
ar a chumas faic a rá.

Nuair a lonraigh an laindéar,
Buíocán solais
Ina gcúlfhuinneog,
Chuir an páiste sa chró
Súil le scoilt –

A gharsúinín na gcearc,
Aghaidh bhiorach ort mar úrghealaí
Sa chuimhne, do ghrianghraf fós
Mar a bheadh spléachadh ar chreimire
Ar urlár m'aigne.

A Dhomhnaillín na gealaí
I ngeimhle agus dílis
Ag bun an chlóis,
Do chruth faon, solasmhar,
Gan mheáchan, ag corraí an dusta,

Líonta an damháin alla, seanchacanna
Faoi bhun na bhfaraí
Agus bolaithe tíortha ón bhfuílleach
A chuireadh sí tríd an gcomhla chugat
Maidin is tráthnóna.

D'éis na gcoiscéimeanna úd, tost;
An fuireach, an t-aonarachas, an troscadh,
Deora neamhbhaiste,
Dáimh mhearbhlach le solas.
Ach labhraíonn tú anois sa deireadh,
Aithris aduain

Ar ní éigin is mó ná foighne,
Cruthúnas béalscaoilte gan bhriathra uait
Ar achair ghealaí
A taistealaíodh thar gean amach.

Pionós

Tig liom tarraingt
an tsealáin ar bhaic a muiníl
a bhrath, an ghaoth
ar a brollach nochta.

Séideann sí a siní
ina coirníní ómra,
Croitheann seoltrioc briosc
na n-easnacha.

Tig liom a corp báite
a fheiceáil sa phortach,
meáchan na cloiche,
slat is craobh ar snámh.

Faoin uile ar dtús
ba bhuinneán feannta í
a baineadh
ina dairchnámh, feircíninchinn:

a cloigeann bearrtha
mar choinleach dubh arbhair,
bindealán salaithe a púicín,
fáinne an sealán

a thaiscfeadh
cuimhní seirce.
A adhaltraín,
sular chéasadar tú

Bhí d'fholt ar dhath an lín,
bhís gannchothaithe, is b'álainn
d'aghaidh ar dhath an tarra.
Is a sceilpín gabhair,

is láidir nach bhfuil mé i ngrá leat
ach dhéanfainn féin, is eol dom,
clocha an tosta a theilgean.
Is mé voyeur na gcleas

ag faire cíora nochta
dorcha d'inchinne,
rabhaisc na matán
is an uile chnámh áirithe:

mise a sheas im bhalbhán
is na siúracha leat san fheall
faoina gcaipíní tarra,
ag gol cois ráillí,

a chúlcheadódh
le halltacht shibhialta
ach fós a thuigfeadh díoltas
cruinn dlúth na treibhe.

(Dánta le Seamus Heaney aistrithe ón mBéarla ag Gabriel Rosenstock)

GERTRUDE DEGENHARDT

JÜRGEN SCHNEIDER

Federico

Immer noch trinken die des Goldes
Silberwhisky neben den Vulkanen,
Ihre Städte aus Draht und Tod
Ihr Leben ein langer Sonntag.
Immer noch mordet Hautptmann Nestares, Schädel aus Blei
Sein Name austauschbar Seelen aus Lack,
Gräber im Sand und Wiesen aus altem Blut,
Viznar überall.

Tränen, wenn wir allein sind,
Offene Augen und bittere Wunde,
Die entzündet.
Kein Vergessen gibts.
Unter den Hyazinthen und Binsen,
Du, Bruder aller,
Dein morgen, morgen, morgen
Feuer aus deinen Händen
Verkündend die Auferstehung
Der sezierten Schmetterlinge.

Federico

Those men of gold still drink
Silver-whisky next to the volcanos,
Their cities of wire and death
Their life a life-long Sunday.
Captain Nestares murdering still, Lead-head
His name exchangeable Souls made of gloss,
Graves in the sand and meadows of old blood,
Viznar everywhere.

Tears when we are alone,
Open eyes and a bitter wound,
Inflamed, inflaming.
There is no forgetting.
Under hyazinths and reeds,
You, brother of all,
Your tomorrow, tomorrow, tomorrow
Fire from your hands
Proclaiming the resurrection
Of the dissected butterflies.

(Translated by the author.)

RALF SOTSCHECK

Letter to the Lord Chief Justice

Dear Lord Chief Justice Lane,

wait a minute
i'd better leave out 'lord chief justice'
start again

Dear Lane

come to that
i'll leave out the 'dear' too
try again

Lane,

I am quite aware
of the situation in Britain
all the crime
is a crime is a crime
and the pressure
on the police
and on judges
to obtain confessions
and convictions
however
does this really justify to
MANIPULATE
INTIMIDATE
INTERROGATE
INCRIMINATE
VIOLATE
FLAGELLATE
INCARCERATE
innocent people?

I am quite aware
of the situation in Britain
the inflation and unemployment
that if you lose your job
you won't get another
therefore I fully understand
how anxious you must be
to hang on to yours
but for a man of your education
there must be openings

you could even go on the dole
temporarily
although I realise
you could not maintain yourself
at the level to which you are accustomed
nevertheless
many of us fare worse
in Gartree, Long Larton, Full Sutton

a judge is a busy man
he probably won't have time to read all this
i'd better start again

Lane,
you creep

(Adaptation of a poem by Nigel Gray.)

FRANCIS STUART

The prisoner

Tears cannot recall thee, nor sweat,
The holes in thy hands ran slime
As they held me, the walls were wet
With the ooze of ages, and thine
Were we, Lord and Ghost,
Companion of the lost,
Where there is silence and the brine
Of silence turned to a cry
That is neither 'sweet Christ' nor 'alas',
Neither 'my love' nor 'why?'
But a choking on time
That does not pass.

A. J. P. TAYLOR

Excerpt from *How Wars End**

The Conference of Potsdam in July 1945 was the last of the great gatherings, though not great in terms of number of assembly. Potsdam was simply the last meeting of the so-called great powers: the United States, Soviet Russia, Great Britain. Later, though some of their representatives met again, the heads of state never met in grandeur as they had done in Teheran, in Yalta and in Potsdam. And the Potsdam Conference, far from leading to any conclusion, led to estrangement. One very significant thing was that when President Truman went to Potsdam it was the first time he had ever been out of the United States. This in itself marked a very great change. One distinguishing feature of President Roosevelt was that he, in his skilful way, had wanted to be on good terms with Russia and had managed to be at the Teheran conference and at the Yalta conference. Indeed, one could go further and say that Yalta was the only meeting of the three great powers and therefore the only meeting of the great world powers in history which was a success, where all three wanted to work together and reach agreements.

Already at Potsdam Russia and the United States wanted to encourage conflict and to win against each other. There has never been, from that day to this, a really satisfactory meeting of the great powers; of their more modest representatives perhaps, but never of the great rulers again. When Truman came to Potsdam, he had with him a piece of secret knowledge. He believed that the first nuclear weapon would be used in the course of the summer, but until it was used he could not be sure it would succeed. It had never been tried out. When Truman was on the way back to America, he got the news on board ship that the nuclear bomb had been dropped over Hiroshima and he exclaimed, 'This is a great day in the history of the world!' He had no idea how great it was going to be and what troubles it was going to cause.

Why was the nuclear weapon used over Japan? Japan was seeking to make peace. She had sent her messages through Russia, which the Russian government had not passed on because they did not want to – they wanted to get their blow of war in. The American army and the American navy both offered eventual solutions, but there was something more than this. The scientists and technical advisers who had developed the nuclear bomb insisted that if it were to be tried, it must be tried on a real target, so that Congress should be satisfied with all the money that it had paid. Therefore the first bomb was dropped on Hiroshima not to lead to the collapse of Japan, or even to lead to peace offers from Japan, because Japan was only too eager now to make peace offers. It was dropped as a demonstration to the American Congress.

Nobody knew what it was going to be like. Nobody had conceived the terrible devastation that was caused. What is more, the Japanese did not immediately respond by unconditional surrender. Indeed they tended to take the view, 'Well that's a bomb. We've lost 50,000 people and more killed at Hiroshima, but now the situation is as before.' The Americans had two bombs: one they could use at Hiroshima, and had done; the second, they said they must use, otherwise the Japanese would think that the Hiroshima bomb was the only one, whereas if they used two the Japanese would be overwhelmed. Even though the Japanese might have said after the dropping of the bomb on Nagasaki, 'All right, that's it. We'll stand these two catastrophes and continue with the war.' As it was – this is a very dramatic episode in history – the Japanese government ministers were fully clear that there must be unconditional surrender. None of them dared do it because they said, 'If any of us takes the lead and offers unconditional surrender to the Americans, we shall be massacred by nationalistic Japanese fanatics.' The Emperor who had never given a lead in policy in his life, or one might say also in history – the Emperor was a figurehead – asserted himself for the first and last time. In the late days of August 1945 he went on the air and announced unconditional surrender. But, as I said earlier, it was not until 1951 that the peace treaty with Japan was signed, simply because the Russians put forward terms to which the allies would not agree and eventually Japan had to make a separate treaty with Russia.

Meanwhile, the other treaties went forward, and there are great curiosities there. Italy had been, for something like three years, an enemy. One Italian government, though not a government which exercised authority over all Italy, not at any rate until the last days in 1945, had come over and was accepted somewhat grudgingly as an ally, or at any rate as a co-operator with the allied forces. The other one technically remained an enemy although it did not do anything as an enemy. When, in 1947, a peace conference was held in Paris, Italy was the first country that the allies dealt with. There were two territorial topics which concerned the allies. One was whether any of South Tyrol should be restored to Austria, bearing in mind that it was inhabited by Germans or German-speaking people. It was easy enough for the allies to decide this, since they could say, 'No, Italy should have it, because she's been an ally for a short time and the Austrians were never allies.' Much trickier was the fact that the Yugoslavs, who had been our allies throughout the war, were laying claim to Trieste. But now the Yugoslavs were taking a Commmunist line of their own, and as Communists they could not be given Trieste; it had to go to the former enemy, Italy, and that was the arrangement of the treaty which was finally made in 1947. There remained plenty of other treaties to make. Romania and Bulgaria made peace fairly quickly and there was nothing much one could dispute, except Transylvania. Hungary was accepted.

Austria was a difficult case. It was like Germany, or rather it had been part of greater Germany but had managed to jump aside in time, and before the end of the war it had again become independent under Chancellor Renner (who had also made Austria an independent republic at the end of the First War in 1918). Austria was now a small independent republic. Who should garrison it? The four powers agreed that it should pass under their combined authority. Each had a zone of occupation, all four of them occupied Vienna. It was the only place where full allied co-operation continued for ten years after the war. To have a picture of Vienna under allied occupation, remember the Orson Welles film *The Third Man*. The other remarkable thing about Austria is that the allies actually agreed in the end that she should be a neutral state. She was not allowed to join any of the alliances; she could have her own army and so on, but she was to remain totally independent of the coalitions. She was not an associate of the British and Americans, she was not an associate of the French, she was not an associate of the Russians. She was a guaranteed neutral independent state, which you might think set an example to a number of the other small independent states. It certainly worked in the case of Austria.

But the biggest problem, one which almost goes on to the present day – something of it is certainly still with us – was Germany. It was not for some years that the American Congress resolved that a state of war with Germany had ceased to exist. It was not until 1955 that the Americans actually recognized that Federal Germany should have its own independence. Eastern Germany was under Russian occupation and has remained to this day a separate state, completely under Russian control and accepting Russian direction more than the independent Communist states such as Czechoslovakia and Hungary and Romania do. These were not the only problems that came up. In the centre of the two conflicting states there was Berlin, which was divided into four, three of them belonging to the three parts of Germany belonging to the western powers, one part under Russian control. And Berlin has become not gradually more united but more divided. Berlin was divided in 1960 at the great wall which still exists there. There was an alarm in 1948 when the Russians stopped land transport, road transport and rail transport, from western Germany into Berlin, to which the allies replied, to everyone's astonishment, successfully with an air lift, which went on for something like a year. The American and British air forces carried everything into western Berlin. Western Germany maintained its independence or separation from Russian control and has retained it.

However, Europe still bears the scars of the Second World War and now seems as if it is resigned to them. There are still millions of Germans who complain at being evacuated from their home all those, nearly 40 years ago. There are hundreds of thousands of Hungarians who grieve at being expelled from their homes in Czechoslovakia. One could go on reciting the various things that have happened. But the greatest legacy we have had from World War Two is without doubt the development of nuclear fission, and the transformation of this into nuclear weapons. This has now become the most terrifying, the greatest and most threatening danger that hangs over civilisation.

However, do not worry. The Third World War will be the last.

* This article is from *How Wars End* published in 1985 long before the major political events in Europe in 1989. – Editor's note.

GERTRUDE DEGENHARDT

GERTRUDE DEGENHARDT

WILLIAM TREVOR

A Bit of Business

On a warm Saturday morning the city was deserted. Its suburbs dozed, its streets had acquired a tranquillity that did not belong to the hour. Shops and cafés were unexpectedly closed. Where there were people, they sat in front of television sets, or listened to transistors.

In Westmoreland Street two youths hurried, their progress marked by a business-like air. They did not speak, until they reached Stephen's Green. 'No. On ahead,' one said when his companion paused. 'Off to the left in Harcourt Street.' His companion did not argue.

They had been friends since childhood; and today, their purpose being what it was, they knew better than to argue. Argument wasted time, and would distract them. The one who'd given the instruction, the older and taller of the two, was Mangan. The other was a pock-marked sallow youth known as Lout Gallagher, the soubriquet an expression of scorn on the part of a Christian Brother ten or so years ago. Mangan had gelled short hair, nondescript as to colour, and small eyes that squinted slightly, and a flat, broad nose. 'Here,' he commanded towards the end of Harcourt Street, and the two veered off in the direction he indicated.

A marmalade cat sauntered across the street they were in now; no one was about. 'The blue Ford,' Mangan said. Gallagher, within seconds, forced open the driver's door. As swiftly, the bonnet of the car was raised. Work was done with wire; the engine started easily.

In the suburb of Rathgar, in Cavendish Road, Mr. Livingston watched the red helicopter touch down behind the vesting tent in Phoenix Park. Earlier, at the airport, the Pope's right hand had been raised in blessing, lowered, and then raised again and again, a benign smile accompanying each gesture. In Phoenix Park the crowds knelt in their corrals, and sang 'Holy God, We Praise Thy Name'. Now and again the cameras caught the black dress of clergymen and nuns, but for the most part the crowds were composed of the kind of people Mr. Livingston met every day on the streets or noticed going to Mass on a Sunday. The crowds were orderly, awed by the occasion. The yellow and white papal flags fluttered everywhere; occasionally a degree of shoving developed in an effort to gain a better view. Four times already the cameras had shown women fainting – from marvelling, so Mr. Livengston was given to understand, rather than heat or congestion. Somewhere in Phoenix Park were the Herlihys, but so far Mr. Livingston had failed to identify them. 'I'll wave,' the Herlihy twins had promised, speaking in unison as they always did. Mr. Livingston knew they'd forget; in all the excitement they wouldn't even know that a camera had skimmed over them. It was Herlihy himself who would be noticeable, being so big and his red hair easy to pick out. Monica, of course, you could miss.

Mr. Livingston, attired now in a dark-blue suit, was a thin, grey-haired man in his sixties, only just beginning to go grey. His lean features, handsome in youth, were affected by wrinkles now, his cheeks a little flushed. He had been a widower for a year.

Preceded by Cardinal Ó Fiaich and Archbishop Ryan, the Pope emerged from the papal vesting chamber under the podium. Cheering began in the corrals. Twice the Pope stopped and extended his arms. There was cheering then such as Mr. Livingston had never in his life heard before. The Pope approached the altar.

Mangan and Gallagher worked quickly, though with no great skill. They pulled open drawers and scattered their contents. They rooted among clothes, and wrenched at the locks of cupboards. Jewellery was not examined since its worth could not even roughly have been estimated. All they found they pocketed, with loose change and notes. A transistor radio was secreted beneath Gallagher's jacket.

'Nothing else,' Mangan said. 'Useless damn place.'

They left the house that they had entered, through a kitchen window. They strolled towards the parked blue Ford, Mangan shaking his head as though, having arrived at the house on legitimate business, they disappointedly failed to find anyone at home. Gallagher drove, slowly in the road where the house was, and then more rapidly. 'Off to the left,' Mangan said, and when the opportunity came Gallagher did as he was bidden. The car drew up again; the two remained seated, both their glances fixed on the driving mirror, 'O.K.,' Mangan said.

Mr. Livingston heard a noise and paid it no attention. Although his presence in the Herlihy's house was, officially, to keep an eye on it, he believed that the Herlihys had invited him because he had no television himself. It was their way to invent a reason; their way to want to thank him whenever it was possible for all the baby-sitting he did – not that there wasn't full and adequate payment at the time, the 'going rate' as Monica called it. Earlier that morning, as he'd risen and dressed himself, it had not occurred to him that Herlihy might have been serious when he said that it was nice to have someone about the place on a day like this when the Guards were all out at Phoenix Park. The sound of the television, Herlihy suggested, was as good as a dog.

'A new kind of confrontation,' stated the Pope, 'with values and trends which, up to now, have been unknown and alien to Irish society.'

Mr. Livingston nodded in agreement. It would have been nice for Rosie, he thought; she'd have appreciated all this, the way she'd appreciated the royal weddings. When his wife was alive Mr. Livingston had hired a television set like everyone else, but later he's ceased to do so because he found he never watched it on his own. It made him miss her more, sitting there with the same programmes coming out, her voice not commenting any more. They would certainly have watched the whole of the ceremony today, but naturally they wouldn't have attended it in person, being Protestants.

'The sacredness of life,' urged the Pope, 'the indissolubility of marriage, the true sense of human sexuality, the right attitude towards the material goods that progress has to offer.' He advocated the Sacraments, especially the Sacrament of Penance.

Applause broke out, and again Mr. Livingston nodded his agreement.

Gallagher had wanted to stop, but Mangan said one more house. So they went for the one at the end of the avenue, having noticed that no dog was kept. 'They've left that on,' Mangan whispered in the kitchen when they heard the sound of the television. 'Check it, though, while I'm up there.'

In the Herlihy's main bedroom he slipped the drawers out softly, and eased open anything that was locked. They'd been right to come. This place was the best yet.

Suddenly the sound of the television was louder, and Mangan knew that Gallagher had opened the door of the room it came from. He glanced towards the window in case he should have to hurry away, but no sound of protest came from downstairs. They'd drive the car to Milltown and get on to the first bus going out of the city. Later on they'd pick up a bus to Bray. It was always worth making the journey to Bray because Cohen gave you better prices.

'Hey,' Gallagher called, not loudly, not panicking in any way whatsoever. At once Mangan knew there was a bit of trouble. He knew, by the sound of the television, that the door Gallagher had opened hadn't been closed again. Once, in a house at night, a young girl had walked across a landing with nothing on her except a sanitary thing. He and Gallagher had been in the shadows, alerted by the flush of a lavatory. She hadn't seen them.

He stuffed a couple of ties into his pockets and closed the bedroom door behind him. On the way downstairs he heard Gallagher's voice before he saw him.

'There's an old fellow here,' Gallagher said, making no effort to speak privately. 'Watching His Holiness.'

Gallagher was as cool as a cucumber. You had to admire that in him. The time Mangan had gone with Ossie Power it had been nerves that landed them in it. You couldn't do a job with shaking hands, he'd told

Power before they began, but it hadn't been any use. He should have known of course.

'He's staying quiet,' Gallagher said in a low voice. 'Like I told him, he's keeping his trap tight.'

The youth in the doorway was wearing a crushed imitation suede jacket and dark trousers. His white t-shirt was dirty; his chin and cheeks were pitted with the remains of acne. For an instant Mr. Livingston received an impression of a second face: a flat, wide nose between two bead-like eyes. Then both intruders stepped back into the hall. Whispering took place but Mr. Livingston couldn't hear what was said. On the screen the Popemobile moved slowly through the crowd. Hands reached out to touch it.

'Keep your eyes on your man,' a voice commanded, and Mr. Livingston knew it belonged to the one he had seen less of because it was gruffer than the other voice. 'Keep company with His Holiness.'

Mr. Livingston did not attempt to disobey. Something was placed over his eyes and knotted at the back of his head. The material was rough, like tweed. With something similar his wrists were tied in his lap. Each ankle was tied to a leg of the chair he occupied. His wallet was slipped out of the inside pocket of his jacket.

He had failed the Herlihys; even though it was a pretence, he had agreed to perform a small and simple task; the family would return to disappointment. Mr. Livingston had been angry as soon as he realised what was happening, as soon as the first youth appeared. He'd wanted to get up, to look around for something to use as a weapon, but only just in time he'd realised it would be foolish to do that. Helpless in his chair, he felt ashamed.

On the television the cheering continued, and voices described what was happening. 'Ave! Ave!' people sang.

'Pull up.' Mangan said in the car. 'Go down that road and pull up at the bottom.'

Lout Gallagher did so, halting the car at the opening to a half-built estate. They had driven further than they'd intended, anxious to move swiftly from the neighbourhood of their morning's work. 'If there's ever a squawk out of you,' Mangan had threatened before they parted from Mr. Livingston, 'you'll rue the bloody day, mister.' Taking the third of the ties he'd picked up in the bedroon, he placed it round the old man's neck. He crossed the two ends and pulled them tight, watching while Mr. Livingston's face and neck became suffused. He released them in good time in case anything went wrong.

'You never know with a geezer like that,' he said now. He turned his head and glanced out of the back window of the car. They were both still edgy. It was the worst thing that could happen, being seen.

'Wouldn't we dump the wagon?' Gallagher said.

'Drive it in on the site.'

They left the car behind the back wall of one of the new houses and since the place was secluded they counted the money they'd trawled. 'Forty-two pound fifty-four,' Mangan said. As well, there were various pieces of jewellery and the transistor radio. 'You could be caught with that,' Mangan advised, and the transistor was thrown into a cement mixer.

'He'll issue descriptions,' Mangan said before they turned away from the car. 'He'll squawk his bloody guts out.'

They both knew that. In spite of the ugliness Mangan had injected into his voice, in spite of the old man's face going purple, he would recall the details of the occasion. In the glimpse Mangan had caught of him there was anger in his eyes and his forehead was puckered in a frown.

'I'm going back there,' Mangan said.

'The car's hot.'

Mangan didn't answer, but swore instead, repeatedly and furiously; then they lit cigarettes and both felt calmer. Then Mangan led the way from the car, through the half-built site and out on to a lane. Within five minutes they reached a main road and came eventually to a public house. High up on the wall above the bar a large television set continued to record the Pope's presence in Ireland. No one took any notice of the two youths who ordered glasses of Smithwick's and crisps.

The people who had been robbed returned to their houses and counted the cost of the Pope's personal blessing. The Herlihys returned and found Mr. Livingston tied up with neck-ties, and the television still on. A doctor was summoned, though against Mr. Livingston's wishes. The police came later.

That afternoon in Bray, after they'd been to see Cohen, Mangan and Gallagher picked up two girls. 'Jaysus, I could do with a mott,' Lout Gallagher had said the night before, which was how the whole thing began, Mangan realising, he could do with one too. 'Thirty,' Cohen had offered that afternoon, and they pushed him up to thirty-five. They felt better after the few drinks. Today of all days a bit of fecking wouldn't interest the police, with the headaches they'd have when the crowds headed back to the city. 'Why'd they be bothered with an old geezer like that?' Mangan said, and they felt better still.

In the Esplanade Ice-Cream parlour the girls requested a Peach Melba and a Sundae. One was called Carmel, the other Marie. They said they were nurses, but in fact they worked in a paper mill.

'Bray's quiet,' Mangan said.

The girls agreed it was. They'd been intending to go to see the Pope themselves, but they'd slept it out. A quarter past twelve it was before

Carmel opened her eyes, and Marie was even worse. She wouldn't like to tell you, she said.

'We seen it on the television,' Mangan said. 'Your man's in great form.'

'What line are you in?' Carmel asked.

'Gangsters,' said Mangan, and everyone laughed.

Gallagher wagged his head in admiration. Mangan always gave the same response when asked that question by girls. You might have thought he'd restrain himself today, but that was Mangan all over. Gallagher lit a cigarette, thinking he should have hit the old fellow before he had a chance to turn round. He should have rushed into the room and struck him a blow on the back of the skull, with whatever there was to hand, hell take the consequences.

'What's it mean, gangsters?' Marie asked, still giggling, glancing at Carmel and giggling even more.

'Banks,' Mangan said, 'is our business.'

The girls thought of Butch Cassidy and the Sundance Kid and Bonnie and Clyde, and laughed again. They knew that if they pressed their question it wouldn't be any good. They knew it was a kind of flirtation, their asking and Mangan teasing with his replies. Mangan was a wag. Both girls were drawn to him.

'Are the ices to your ladyships' satisfaction?' he enquired, causing a further outbreak of giggling.

Gallagher had ordered a banana split. Years ago he used to think that if you filled a room with banana splits he could eat them all. He'd been about five then. He used to think the same thing about fruit cake.

'Are the flicks on today?' Mangan asked, and the girls said on account of the Pope they mightn't be. It might be like Christmas Day, they didn't know.

'We seen what's showing in Bray,' Marie said, 'In any case.'

'We'll go dancing later on,' Mangan promised. He winked at Gallagher, and Gallagher thought the day they made a killing you wouldn't see him for dust. The Mail boat and Spain, posh Cockney girls who call you Mr. Big. Never lift a finger again.

'Will we sport ourselves on the prom?' Mangan suggested, and the girls laughed again. They said they didn't mind. Each wanted to be Mangan's. He sensed it, so he walked between them on the promenade, linking their arms. Gallager walked on the outside, linking Carmel.

'Spot of ozone,' Mangan said. He pressed his forearm against Marie's breast. She was the one, he thought.

'D'you like the nursing?' Gallagher asked, and Carmel said it was all right. A sharp breeze was darting in from the sea, stinging their faces, blowing the girl's hair about. Gallagher saw himself stretched out by a blue swimming-pool, smoking and sipping at a drink. There was a cherry in the drink, and a little stick with an umbrella on the end of it. A girl with one whole side of her bikini open was sharing it with him.

'Bray's as great place,' Mangan said.

'The pits,' Carmel corrected.

You could always tell by the feel of a girl on your arm, Mangan said to himself. Full of sauce the fat one was, no more a nurse then he was. Gallagher wondered if they had a flat, if there'd be anywhere to go when the moment came.

'We could go into the bar of the hotel,' the other one was saying, the way girls did when they wanted to extract their due.

'What hotel's this?' he asked.

'The International.'

'Oh, listen to Miss Ritzy!'

They turned and walked back along the promenade, guided by the girls to the bar in question. Gin and tonic the girls had. Gallagher and Mangan had Smithwick's.

'We could go into town later,' Carmel casually suggested. 'There'll be celebrations on.'

'We'll give the matter thought,' Mangan said.

Another couple of pulls of the tie, Mangan said to himself, and who'd have been the wiser? You get to that age, you'd had your life anyway. As it was, the old geezer had probably conked it on his own, tied up like that. Most likely he was stiffening already.

'Isn't there a disco on in Bray?' he suggested. 'What's wrong with a slap-up meal and then the light fantastic?'

The girls were again amused at his way of putting it. Gallagher was glad to hear the proposal that they should stay where they were. If they went into town the whole opportunity could fall asunder. If you didn't end up near a mott's accommodation you were back where you started.

'You'd die of the pace of it in Bray,' Marie said, and Mangan thought: a couple more gins and a dolop of barley wine with their grill and chips. He edged his knee against Marie's. She didn't take hers away.

'Have you a flat or rooms or something?' Gallagher asked, and the girls said they didn't. They lived at home, they said. They'd give anything for a flat.

A few minutes later, engaged at the urinals in the lavatory the two youths discussed the implications of that. Mangan had stood up immediately on hearing the news. He'd given a jerk of his head when the girls weren't looking.

'No bloody go.' Gallagher said.

'The fat one's on for it.'

'Where though, man?'

Mangan reminded his companion of other occasions, in car parks and derelict buildings, of the time they propped up the bar of the emergency exit of the Adelphi cinema and went back in, of the time in the garden shed in Drumcondra.

Gallagher laughed, feeling more optimistic when he remembered all that. He winked to himself, the way he did when he was beginning to feel drunk. He spat into the urinal, another habit at this particular juncture. The seashore was the place; he'd forgotten about the seashore.

'Game ball,' Mangan said.

The memory of the day that had passed seemed rosy now – the empty streets they had hurried through, the quiet houses where their business had been, the red blotchiness in the old man's face and neck, the processions on the television screen. Get a couple more gins into them, Mangan thought again, and then the barley wine. Stretch the fat one out on the soft bloody sand.

'Oh, lovely,' the fat one said when more drinks were offered.

Gallagher imagined the wife of a businessman pleading down a telephone, reporting that her captors intended to slice off the tips of her little fingers unless the money was forthcoming. The money was a package in a telephone booth, stashed under the seat. The picture of Spain began again.

'Hi,' Carmel said.

She'd been to put her lipstick on, but she didn't look any different

'What d'you do really?' she asked on the promenade.

'Unemployed.'

'You're loaded for an unemployed.' Her tone was suspicious. He watched her trying to focus her eyes. Vaguely, he wondered if she liked him.

'A man's car needed an overhaul,' he said.

Ahead of them, Mangan and Marie were laughing, the sound drifting lightly back above the swish of the sea.

'He's great sport, isn't he?' Carmel said.

'Oh, great all right.'

Mangan turned round before they went down the steps to the shingle. Gallagher imagined his fancy talk and the fat one giggling at it. He wished he was good at talk like that.

'We had plans made to go into town,' Carmel said, 'There'll be great gas tonight.'

When they began to cross the shingle she said it hurt her feet, so Gallagher led her back to the concrete wall of the promenade and they sat down with their backs to it. It wasn't quite dark. Cigarette packets and chocolate wrappings were scattered on the sand and pebbles. Gallagher put his arm round Carmel's shoulders. She let him kiss her. She didn't mind when he twisted her sideways so that she no longer had her back to the wall. She felt limp in his arms, and for a moment Gallagher thought she'd passed out, but then she kissed him back. She murmurmed something and her arms pulled him down on top of her. He realised it didn't matter about the fancy talk.

'When then?' Marie whispered, pulling down her clothes. Five minutes ago he'd promised they would meet again; he'd sworn there was nothing he wanted more; the sooner the better, he'd said.

'Monday night,' he added now. 'Outside the railway station. Six.'

It was where they had picked the two girls up. Mangan could think of nowhere else and it didn't matter anyway since he had no intention of being anywhere near Bray on Monday night.

'Geez, you're great,' Marie said.

On the bus to Dublin they did not say much. Carmel had spewed up a couple of mouthfuls, and in Gallagher's nostrils the sour odour persisted. Marie in the end had been a nag, going on about Monday evening, making sure Mangan wouldn't forget. What both of them were thinking was that Cohen, as usual, had done best out of the bit of business there'd been.

Then the lean features of Mr. Livingston were recalled by Mangan, the angry eyes, the frown. They'd made a mess of it, letting him see them, they'd bollocksed the whole thing. That moment in the doorway when the old man's glance had lighted on his face he had hardly been able to control his bowels. 'I'm going back there,' his own voice echoed from a later moment, but he'd known, even as he spoke, that if he returned he would do no more than he had done already.

Beside him, on the inside seat, Gallagher experienced similar recollections. He stared out into the summery night, thinking that if he'd hit the old man on the back of the skull he could have finished him. The thought of that had pleased him when they were with the girls. It made him shiver now.

'God, she was great,' Mangan said, dragging out of himself a single snigger.

His bravado obscured a longing to be still ordering the girls gins at the bar, and talking fancy. He would have paid what remained in his pocket still to taste her lipstick on the seashore, or to hear her gasp as he touched her for the first time.

Gallagher tried for his dream of Mr. Big but it would not come to him. 'Yeah,' he said, replying to his friend's observations.

The day was over; there was nowhere left to hide from the error that had been made. As they had at the time, they sensed the old man's shame and the hurt to his pride, as animals sense fear or resolution.

Privately, each calculated how long it would be before the danger they'd left behind in the house caught up with them.

They stepped off the bus on the quays. The crowds that had celebrated in the city during their absence had dwindled, but people who were on the streets spoke with a continuing excitement about the Pope's presence in Ireland and the great Mass there had been in the sunshine. The two youths walked the way they'd come that morning, both of them wondering if the nerve to kill was something you acquired.

KATHARINA WILCZEK

Wie kann man es wagen
auf würdige Weise
in einer Werkstatt der Folter
die schwarzblauen Früchte
die Herbstes zu preisen!

How
in a workshop of torture
could one dare to praise
the blackish-blue fruits
of autumn with dignity!

(Translated from the German by Jürgen Schneider.)

Warum bin ich gekommen
was will ich – was ich weiss?

Das Aufhören von Taubsein
der Weg durch die auseinander –
gebogenen Zweige der Gartenhecke
das Alter unter dem Zug im Gesicht
geraten die Menschen in Bewegung
unter den Farben des Bildes
hören sie scharf den Beweis.

Why have I come
What do I want – what I know?
The ceasing of being deaf

The way through the multi-
bent sprigs of the garden hedge
the age under the tension in the face
people get moving
under the picture's colours
they sharply hear the evidence.

(Translated from the German by Jürgen Schneider.)

VOLKER WILCZEK

Volker Wilczek

VOLKER WILCZEK

Volker Wilczek

BOB WOFFINDEN

The Birmingham Six

There is, on the one hand the group of imprisoned men now known to millions as the Birmingham Six; and there is, on the other, the legal system which established exacting standards for the administration of justice, which has been renowned and even revered for its unimpeachable principles, and which became the model for criminal justice law in jurisdictions the world over. The two have now stood in opposition for over fifteen years. From this epic confrontation, the judicial system has emerged battered and bloodied, its historic reputation in shreds; it is the men who have come through it all unbowed, with honour intact.

The Birmingham Six are all clearly innocent: why were they even arrested?

All miscarriages of justice arise from police misapprehensions, misconceptions, mistakes or misconduct. Ironically – in view of all that was to follow – the initial misapprehensions of the police in this case were explicable, however inexcusable. The five Belfast-bound men who arrived at Heysham late in the evening of 21 November 1974 *could* have been making a swift escape from Birmingham after planting the two bombs that had exploded in the city centre soon after 8.00 p.m., killing 21 people. When they were detained, they naturally withheld the information that the purpose of their visit to Belfast was to attend the funeral of an IRA activist, James McDade; when police discovered the Mass Cards in John Walker's baggage then, equally naturally, they thought they were on to something. When Frank Skuse announced that his scientific tests proved that Paddy Hill and Billy Power, two of the detained men, had recently been handling explosives, flickering suspicions were immediately fired into raging certainty. From that moment, the police treated the five men – together with a sixth, Hugh Callaghan, who had seen the others off on the train – as callous murderers; and responded to what they understood to be their wanton brutality with some wanton brutality of their own.

The Birmingham Six are all clearly innocent: why were they ever convicted?

There never was any doubt that they would be convicted. The British judicial system is best perceived as a central myth supported by a number of ancillary myths. One of these is that a trial can take place uninfluenced by outside factors. In this case, admittedly, it was accepted that, with local feeling running so high, the trial could not be held in Birmingham. However, this problem could be no more than marginally ameliorated by holding it anywhere other than Birmingham. The bombings had obviously attracted national attention and, indeed, national outrage.

The trial was moved to Lancaster, and held there in the 900-year-old castle. It was common knowledge that an important reason for the choice of Lancaster was that the castle housed a prison, and thus the men could be held there in secure conditions. For the duration of the trial, parking was prohibited within a quarter-mile radius of Lancaster castle, and all the other now-familiar elaborate security precautions were put into operation. All this is bound to make at least a subconscious impression on the local community, and hence on its members who are serving as the jury: why, they will be bound to ask themselves, is such absolute security necessary, if not because the men in the dock are genuinely guilty?

No one would deny that security measures have to be implemented. They could, however, be discreet. For high-profile cases of particular sensitivity, they are deliberately ostentatious. The panoply of security thus becomes another of the administrative pressures to which a jury is subject, and a most effective means of pre-empting its deliberations. It is merely stating the obvious to say that it vitiates the principle of the presumption of innocence.

That whole notion, in any case, was another of those supposed sturdy tenets of British justice which crumbled on close examination. More often than not, there was a presumption of guilt. The more dignified, the more laborious the court procedure, the more difficult it was to believe that it was all being undertaken in error; and English court procedure was very dignified, and very laborious.

This observation is less pertinent today, in 1990, after a decade of public disquiet engendered by a succession of fiercely-disputed convictions – those of the Birmingham Six not least among them – and rapidly declining confidence in the competence and trustworthiness both of the police and the judicial processes. In 1975, when the six Birmingham men stood trial, few juries came equipped with a decent scepticism.

The court proceedings in Lancaster must have been a formality (albeit an exceptionally protracted one; the trial lasted from 9 June to 15 August). Oblique confirmation of this was provided when, on 2 August, the *Daily Mirror* splashed photographs of the six men across its front page. The trial was then still in progress, and the *Mirror* was the country's biggest-selling daily newspaper. A more flagrant contempt of court is hard to imagine; yet no one bothered to do anything about it. No need on this occasion to be fastidious about the rights of defendants; after all, these men were just Irish bombers.

The Birmingham Six are all clearly innocent: why did their appeal fail?

As a rule, appeals always do fail. Originally, the English judiciary only accepted the concept of an appeal court with considerable reluctance. Now that it has been in existence for most of this century, there still seems to be some misunderstanding concerning its precise functions. Parliament and the public would like to believe that it is there to remedy miscarriages of justice. On the whole, it isn't; and even if it is, it doesn't. (The appropriate piece of legislation here is the 1968 Criminal Appeal Act, which has been conspicuously ineffective. It is a moot point whether this is because the act was too loosely framed to start off with, or because appellate judges very quickly emasculated it.)

The judiciary considers that it is no part of its remit to contradict jury decisions. Whether in principle (constitutionally, the jury is the tribunal which must determine guilt or innocence) or in practice (the jury has actually heard all the evidence and seen all the witnesses), the position is clear-cut. There can be no realistic possibility of organizing matters differently. Even leaving aside the principle, it would in practice be unrealistic to expect the appeal court to re-try cases, hearing the evidence and seeing the witnesses all over again.

That line of argument is the nearest thing to an honourable reason which appeal court judges can provide for their consistent failure to remedy miscarriages of justice. They do not, of course, admit to the plethora of dishonourable reasons. Foremost among these is the consideration that the overturning of a conviction necessarily reflects discredit on aspects of the legal machinery; something, somewhere, obviously went very wrong. As a whole, the legal profession seems to resent criticism as profoundly as it abhors change; certainly, it invites neither.

Judicial attitudes have merely been more entrenched in the consideration of Irish cases, which combine the random slaughter characteristic of all terrorism with acute political sensitivities, in particular the overwhelming need of the English state to maintain its credibility in regard to the conflict in Northern Ireland.

In 1976, applications for leave to appeal in the Birmingham pub-bombing case were brusquely dismissed. In retrospect, it can be seen that the judgment of Lord Widgery, then the Lord Chief Justice, gave abundant indication of the lack of care, the lack of either legal or intellectual rigour with which the Court approached cases that it was more than usually predisposed to reject. The men had been convicted largely on confession and forensic science evidence. The latter must have been especially compelling, after Frank Skuse had said on oath that he was '99 per cent certain' that Hill and Power had been handling explosives. Yet the evidence was virtually set aside at this first appeal. 'This is not a point, as we see it, of great importance in the case,' said Widgery.

He was, of course, correct to dismiss this evidence (albeit for reasons he could hardly have suspected). The case was left resting on almost the sole foundation of the confessions. Hence, the alleged ill-treatment of the men in police custody acquired an enhanced significance. Yet something which could have had a direct bearing on this – John Walker's black eye – was dealt with dismissively by Widgery: 'the origin of [the eye injury] I have forgotten, but I do not think it matters very much anyway.' Whether in terms of judicial logic, or intellectual rigour, or mere common sense, the judgement in this appeal was utterly inadequate. Sometimes the Court of Appeal does manage to put up a credible façade of administering justice; on this occasion, it didn't even manage that.

The Birmingham Six are all clearly innocent: why did it take so long to stimulate public concern?

Looking back, this question is one of the hardest of all for a British journalist to answer. Why did it take so long? All of us in the media must bear a heavy responsibility. Certainly, one important factor was the loss of the investigative zeal of the *Sunday Times*, after its purchase by Rupert Murdoch in 1981. Under the editorship of Harold Evans, the *Sunday Times* had been the acknowledged leader in the field of campaigning journalism, and it proved, in the short term, irreplaceable. This was, perhaps, merely one of the more obvious symptoms of the shifting political sands, and the chillier climate which confronted journalists.

There was also a feeling of powerlessness. To give just one example, Tom Sargent, the *eminence grise* of British justice campaigns until his death in 1988, once wrote that he thought the political sensitivities in the Irish cases (Birmingham, Guildford and the Maguires) were so overwhelming that they would never be rectified. (Sadly, it must be pointed out that, in respect of Birmingham, and also the Maguires, he has yet to be proved wrong.)

This is not to suggest that he underestimated their gravity; on the contrary, he once described them to me as the most serious miscarriages of all. He considered, however, that in his position as secretary of the Justice Organization he could more usefully devote his last years to cases which stood a better chance of being resolved.

Overall, perhaps, the simple reason for the long delay in bringing the case to public scrutiny was that, faced with the enormity of the injustice, journalists were just as incredulous as everyone else.

Finally, Granada Television's World in Action did put together a major re-examination of the case, which was transmitted on 28 October 1985. Public attention was further alerted with the publication the following summer of Chris Mullin's book, *Error of Judgement.* Mullin had taken the idea to Granada in the first place, and then researched the case together with Charles Tremayne.

Granada, having set the ball rolling, reinforced their exemplary work with a second World in Action on 1 December 1986, which presented the fresh evidence of Tom Clarke, the former policeman who had observed some maltreatment of the six men in police custody.

Television programmes are transmitted one day, and gone the next. They can be truly effective as campaigning journalism only in conjunction with newspaper reports. Television provides the impact and the mass audience; newspapers give the story a longer life and also tend to carry weight with those in positions of authority, very few of whom ever admit to watching television, let alone being influenced by it.

In this respect, the media landscape changed significantly in the latter part of 1986 with the launch of the *Independent,* which quickly assumed the position formerly cocupied by the *Times*, as the country's most widely-respected serious newspaper. Almost from the outset, the *Independent* provided continuing coverage of these stories of injustice and helped to give them a public prominence which was soon reflected throughout almost the entire media. Until then the *Guardian* had been a solitary voice. The particular importance of the arrival of the *Independent* was that it resisted political pigeon-holing. It reported keenly on Birmingham and other cases not because it had any political axe to grind; but because it understood, and was not afraid to discharge, the quintessential functions of a newspaper.

With the book, TV programmes and press interest, the case became increasingly prominent throughout the latter part of 1986. Chris Mullin had been active in Ireland in explaining the situation, and he and other campaigners thus ensured that the case became a *cause célèbre* not just within the United Kingdom, but also beyond it. Douglas Hurd, then the Home Secretary, agreed to examine the case closely; and on 20 January 1987 he exercised his right to send a case giving rise to serious doubts back to the Court of Appeal.

The Birmingham Six are all clearly innocent: why was this second appeal, conducted against a background of national and international concern, not successful?

At the time I wrote that this 1987/8 appeal represented the greatest challenge that the judicial system had ever faced. Not surprisingly – given the disheartening precedents – it was a challenge that British justice failed.

The hearing got underway on 2 November 1987 in a packed Old Bailey. It was the focus of considerable attention for five weeks, at the end of which judgment was reserved.

By the time of this appeal, the scientific evidence was in a state of disarray. On the one hand, it was resurrected, as it were, because all the lawyers agreed that Lord Widgery's ruling in regard to it had been, simply, wrong; on the other, the tests themselves by then seemed wholly unreliable, their credibility further undermined by the fact that Dr Skuse had in the meantime had to take compulsory early retirement, on the grounds of 'limited efficiency'.

Moreover, the confession evidence had from the outset been intrinsically flawed. Now there were a few cracks – few enough, admittedly – in the hitherto monolithic police account of the circumstances in which those supposed confessions were obtained.

In this context, the most important development was the discovery of the Reade schedule. When referring the case to appeal, the Home Secretary had asked an outside police force, Devon & Cornwall, to conduct a thorough re-examination of the evidence. It was in the course of this reinvestigation that the document dubbed the Reade Schedule came to light.

To anyone prepared to look at the case with an open mind, this provided the clinching proof that police testimony relating to the interrogations of the six men in Birmingham could not be believed. The Schedule was several pages long. When invited by Devon & Cornwall officers to say exactly what it was, former Superintendent George Reade admitted that it was in his handwriting, but fumbled around for an explanation of the circumstances in which he had drawn it up.

It did appear to be a record of interviews of the six men over that weekend, but tell-tale signs throughout suggested that it was not an actual, contemporary record, but one put together afterwards with the aim of ensuring that all the police testimony tallied. Obviously, with police supposedly recording all their actions in their notebooks, there could have been no orthodox reason for the drawing-up of this document. At the original trial, the judge made it plain that 'they (the police) must have spent many hours trying to ensure that their various lies would accord with each other' if the accusations of police aggression were to be believed. In 1975 this had seemed an impossible scenario; by 1987 there was a widespread view that a police conspiracy had taken place, and that the Reade Schedule provided the ultimate proof of this.

The widespread view was not, however, shared by the three appeal court judges – Lord Lane, the Lord Chief Justice, Lord Justice O'Connor and Lord Justice Stephen Brown. They seemed incredulous that counsel for the men should be inferring that the Reade Schedule was 'a master perjury plan'.

On 28 January 1988, the three judges took it in turns to read out the exceptionally lengthy 169-page judgment. The appeal was turned down. This came as little surprise bearing in mind the impatience they had shown during the hearing both with the appellants' counsel and with witnesses appearing on their behalf. In contrast, those witnesses supporting the Crown, epecially the beleaguered pair at the heart of the case – George Reade and Frank Skuse – had been heard with the utmost courtesy and tolerance. But if it was little surprise, it was no less a shattering blow.

Seven fresh witnesses had independently given evidence which pointed to the conclusion that the men had been maltreated in police custody. Chief among these were Tom Clarke and Joyce Lynas. It had already been anticipated that the evidence of Clarke, the star witness of the second World in Action, would be regarded with disfavour by the appeal court. He had left the police force in disgrace after being convicted of stealing from a prisoner (an offence of which he had always asserted his innocence). Prior to going public with his story, he had tried to sell it for financial gain, which also had the effect of contaminating the evidence.

Joyce Lynas gave unremarkable testimony at the appeal, but had later returned to the witness-box to give precise evidence of police brutality. She explained that she had originally withheld the more important parts of her testimony because she had received telephone calls threatening her children.

The rejection of this particular part of the appellants' case was especially disheartening, because by their actions Tom Clarke and Joyce Lynas had displayed exceptional moral courage – Clarke in being the very first of the policemen present during the interrogations of the Six to come forward; and Lynas for admitting that she had been frightened into giving incomplete evidence.

Nevertheless it was not surprising that their evidence was dismissed. Testimony that appears to be tainted or has been subject to some modification or amendment is almost bound to be dismissed. The appeal court can really only deal with fresh evidence if it is straightforward and advanced by particularly impressive witnesses. Such is the burden of overturning a case at appeal.

However, the testimony of Clarke and Lynas ought to have been considered not just individually, but also in the context of the evidence offered about police misconduct. As a critical analysis by Amnesty International subsequently pointed out, the judges made no attempt to examine the collective force of this material. In conjunction with the Reade Schedule, it should have made a telling impact.

It is at this point that the judgment ceases to be an honourable rejection of the appellants' arguments, and becomes a crude and dishonourable one. The various parts of the case against the men had collapsed; if these convictions weren't unsafe and unsatisfactory (to use the terminology of the appeal court), then none ever would be. But the ramifications of admitting error in this case were by now mountainous. If this, the most serious murder investigation in British criminal history, had gone wrong, not just at one stage, but at every stage, then what did that imply about the justice system as a whole? This consideration would have been only fortified by the fact that the case had been heard at different times by virtually a full complement of senior judicial authorities – Lord Bridge (the judge), by then a senior Law Lord; the Lord Chief Justice in 1976; the Master of the Rolls in 1980; the House of Lords in 1981, *et cetera, et cetera*. Was it now to be admitted by other eminent judges, by colleagues, that all these esteemed figures had been oblivious of the true nature of this case and had helped to perpetuate such an unprecedented injustice? And, beyond that, what about the implications for the British establishment if error on such a grand scale was to be confessed?

The judicial hierarchy is one area of British society which is self-evidently leak-proof. No confidences are shared with the press or otherwise imparted to the public. We can only make an intelligent guess at what happened; and the intelligent guess must be that, faced with such a battery of utterly uncomfortable repercussions, the judges determined that the appeal would have to be turned down. The liberty of six innocent men had to be measured against the requirements of the authorities; and, in this particular arena, it was an unequal struggle.

Even so, there was some discomfort for the judges in actually having to present a public case for keeping these men in prison. There was no serious possibility of their being able to present rational and well-founded arguments for upholding the convictions. All they could say in respect of the Reade Schedule, for instance, was that Reade 'did not seek to deceive the Court'. As an assessment of a central piece of evidence, it was blithely inadequate, as they themselves must have realized.

The judgment concluded with a parting shot to the Home Secretary: 'as has happened before in references by the Home Secretary to this Court, the longer the hearing has gone on, the more convinced this Court has become that the verdict of the jury was correct'. Clearly, the judges did not want other cases of high political and judicial sensitivity referred to appeal.

The Birmingham Six are all clearly innocent: why do they remain in prison still?

The most encouraging aspect of the judgment was that hardly anyone believed a word of it. The more unsavoury elements of the British press made token attempts to re-criminalize the Six. The Murdoch-owned *Sunday Times* published a front-page headline story, 'New Clues Confirm Guilt of Pub-Bombers' (31 January 1988). This appeared only in the first editions, and was almost straightaway dropped from the paper. Even a crusading right-wing newspaper could come up with no grounds on which the convictions could be justified. The judgment hadn't rebuilt the case against the Six; it had merely piled further disrepute on an already discredited judicial system. In doing so, of course, it became an extra contour in the 'appalling vista' identified by Lord Denning; every time an opportunity to do something about this case was spurned, it provided an additional reason to do nothing about it the next time round. The injustice was reinforced at each stage of the process.

After the case was refused consideration at the House of Lords, solicitors for the men, having exhausted all legal remedy nationally, were able to send the case for consideration by European judicial authorities. Although European courts have tended to dispense a more rigorous standard of justice than British ones, they have traditionally been unwilling to interfere with criminal cases when a country appears to have carried out all its own procedures properly. Moreover, the European route is a lengthy one. How many more years of imprisonment were these men expected to endure?

The case became a focus of increasing concern, with campaign groups springing up throughout Britain. In 1989 two developments re-focused attention on it: the disbandment in August of the West Midlands Serious Crimes Squad (some of the officers implicated in misconduct such as extracting false confessions had worked on the pub-bombings investigation); and the quashing of the convictions of the Guildford Four in October. Both seemed to have a direct bearing on the situation of the Birmingham Six, although the authorities publicly maintained that this was not so. In fact, the West Yorkshire police inquiry into the activities of the Serious Crimes Squad specifically precluded cases prior to 1986.

The cabinet reshuffle which followed the Lawson resignation also seemed discouraging, because the new Home Secretary, David Waddington, appeared a less sympathetic and imaginative man than his predecessor, Douglas Hurd. Nonetheless, such was the continuing pressure of public opinion, he did take some – albeit limited – sympathetic and imaginative action, in authorising a change in the prison status of the men, taking them off the high-risk category 'A' register.

In December 1989 solicitors for the men submitted to the Home Office a dossier of fresh evidence. Once this became publicly known, in January 1990, Waddington said straightaway that the material was being closely examined. In March he announced another inquiry into the case, again by Devon & Cornwall police, although this was to be restricted to an examination of the fresh evidence.

By this stage, the case was unique. It was some considerable time since any independent observer had stated in public that the men were actually guilty. No one any longer believed that. If pressed on the matter, spokesmen for the legal establishment would equivocate, and perhaps restrict their remarks to comments along the lines of 'well the jury found them guilty . . .'

Government in Britain often seems to be conducted on the principle of short-term embarrassment limitation. This explains why the authorities tend to be so intractable. Usually, it is safer to do nothing. Accordingly, campaigners need to ensure that it becomes more embarrassing for those in authority to continue to do nothing than to do something. In the Birmingham case, this point seems to have been reached. The powers-that-be probably recognize this, but their actions are inhibited by two considerations. First of all, they remain preoccupied with trying to minimise the embarrassment of releasing the men; and, secondly, they also have the practical difficulty of working out how they can release the men without straining to breaking point the constitutional understandings that underpin the British state. Who is responsible, in the last analysis, for rectifying miscarriages of justice? The judiciary, or the executive? No one seems to know. Undoubtedly, what the authorities need is either a fall guy – very unlikely, in these particular circumstances – or a magic formula of words which somehow absolves everyone of blame. There is also scant prospect of this.

So, a case which began as the most serious murder investigation in British history continues, becoming almost as longstanding a sore on the national fabric as inflation or balance of payments problems.

The saga will serve as a permanent reminder not of the crime, or the criminals (some of whom have never been caught), but of the wretched hypocrisy on which the British judicial system is founded. The case has exposed its *raison d'être* to be not justice, but expediency; and every day that the men remain in prison, its reputation is tarnished a little more. The men will be set free one day soon; for the proud traditions of British justice, there is no escape.

The Birmingham Six are all clearly innocent.

DONALD WOODS

The Birmingham Six

Having lived in Britain for twelve years in exile from South Africa, I considered that in terms of tolerance, humour and political maturity the British are among the most civilized people in the world. They have, however, one major flow – an apparent inability to come to terms with the question of Ireland and the Irish.

Let any element of the Irish equation enter national debate, and this otherwise kindly old country bares its mediaeval teeth and reverts to the darkest ages of its past, its national elders and officials striking attitudes more appropriate to Cromwellian times than to the eve of the 21st century.

They reflect a national neurosis on the subject, one based on an unwillingness to confront the present in terms of the past, and it has astonished me as a foreigner travelling the length and breadth of Britain to discover the depths of ignorance of Irish history or Irish aspirations.

It is less an aversion than a total lack of interest, an unwillingness to seek out or understand. It is a kind of subconscious disengagement – an avoidance of thinking the thing out – which may conceivably stem from feelings of guilt over their treatment of these troublesome cousins. Not one person in ten in Britain knows the details of the 1921 boundary dispute over north-eastern Ulster, though the consequences of it have cost the British taxpayer billions, and not one in ten knows, or cares, about details of the preceding centuries of British-Irish contention.

From time to time there is outrage over a bombing or some other act ot terrorism, and at such times there is an overwhelming tendency to lump together the issue of Irish reunification with the methods of the terrorists. This reaction also serves to keep British attitudes to the overall Irish question at the most superficial level. Then the issue fades away until the next outrage, mass interest in it sustained only occasionally by the funeral of yet another victim from one or the other side.

It is a formula for perpetually unresolved deadlock and, sadly, the obduracy of the British establishment is matched by the obduracy of some of the extremists among the Irish, whose failure to understand what makes the British tick is matched only by the failure of their counterparts to understand what makes the Irish tick. For example, anyone who knows the British well could have told the IRA that the most counterproductive action imaginable would be to injure a horse called Sefton.

But while I cannot imagine any national group in the world less susceptible to morale-damage by bombing or horse-injury than the British, so, too, can I not imagine any logical reason why the British should persist in their national imperviousness to Irish sensitivities.

Do the British hate the Irish? Not at all, in my view. On the contrary, I think it is the very propinquity of the two countries, and the congruity of their national interests, that complicates the problem. The British perceive the Irish at different levels on different occasions. I have watched British rugby and soccer crowds warmly, one could say affectionately, applauding Irish deeds, and their boxing fans will back an Irishman against anyone not British; British television is studded with popular Irish stars, and the chauvinism of British reporting in any kind of international contest from athletics to Eurovision songs extends to and embraces the Republic of Ireland.

In many conversations with people in all parts of Britain I have detected no broad national hatred of the Irish down the years. Nor do I believe that the presence of British troops in Ireland represents any conscious wish to impose the British will there, nor anything else beyond a misplaced sense of duty and an ill-founded sense of responsibility. Certainly the overwhelming majority of the British people don't seem to want their soldiers to be there, for a variety of reasons, and appear to tolerate the policy only through an inertial acceptance of what they dimly regard as their duty to the people of Northern Ireland to 'keep the peace'.

Whatever the reason for this national neurosis, it is what causes the kind of injustices meted out to the Guildford Four and the Birmingham Six, leading to aberrational notions of judicial equity such as have been expressed from time to time by the likes of Lord Denning.

Juridically speaking, the core of the case of the Birmingham Six is the issue of assault. It is an axiom in law, or should be, that civilized justice cannot be done on the basis of beating up an accused. The over-riding principle of civilized law in all cases where crime is alleged is that the person in the dock should not be incriminated through the medium of violent coercion. That, surely, is what the rule of law is all about – that no citizen should be punished illegally by the state.

Once let go that precious principle and the cure for crime becomes worse than the disease.

When the state accuses someone of a crime the fairness of the accusation process can only be preserved if the appropriate officials of the state marshall their evidence legally and do not themselves resort to crime.

Confessions resulting from assault or torture belong to Stalinist show-trials or Nazi tribunals, not to the ways of the country that has given the world so much that is best in judicial and parliamentary tradition.

It is because I believe in the ultimate fairness of British justice when the full light of information is turned upon it that I believe justice will ultimately be done to the Birmingham Six, provided the rest of us work hard enough to bring to the attention of the British public a clear knowledge of the injustices that have disfigured this tragic case from the beginning.

Through the media, through the written and spoken word, let it be established finally that justice administerd through illegality and violence is no justice at all, and that people not found guilty through right and proper legal process must be presumed innocent and allowed to go free.

MACDARA WOODS

Man on the Doorstep

He knocks on my door at night
the howling storm made visible
raves at me like conscience
come out he says come out
come out and see the holes in the road
the holes in the road in the rain
it is all falling down around us
holes full of water for children to fall in
and he is right –
five minutes is all it would take
take five to walk to the bottom of the hill
to see these children's graves in the rain

But I can't go out
bacause I am minding a real live child
I am father to a child
who eats and sleeps and goes to school
flies kites and brings me paintings
and keeps his margins to the edge of the page
or as near as he can at five and a half
who is not for the moment homeless
and depends on me to keep the night outside

Tá Bran ar scoil
Tá Micí ag gáire Tá Lúlú ag gol

No you can't come out says the man
but you can go to bloody Umbria –
and what are you going to do about this
Fascist descent into Anarchism?
What are the artists of Ireland doing?

Safeguard your reputation

I was here this morning in this very place
in this very place today – and
he digs his heel into the crumbling pavement –
and I said to an Indian doctor
an Indian doctor from the College of Surgeons
how can people live in this
in this city falling apart

seeing this same shit day after day and every day
head shaking like John O Gaunt
this same shit and nothing else
enough said said the doctor –

Do you realize
that in the European parliament
the whole of Europe is laughing at us?
The Germans are laughing at us
the Italians the French
the Greeks and Spaniards are laughing
laughing into their translation machines
laughing like drains
like the rain falling on Dublin they laugh
and the British shoot us

He moves away into the night –
Safeguard your reputation with Cess-Clean
says the advertisement on national radio

APPENDIX I

Lord Gifford QC

Excerpts from *Lord Gifford's opening speech at the Appeal Hearing* November 2, 1987. Selected by Carol Coulter who reported on it for *The Irish Times*. The introductory notes to each excerpt were also written by Carol Coulter.

The Appeal opened at the Old Bailey on Monday, November 2, 1987 and continued for almost six weeks. Lord Gifford, who appeared for Richard McIlkenny and Gerry Hunter, outlined the basis of the men's appeal.

From "Pillars of prosecution case 'cracked and flawed'"*The Irish Times November 3, 1987.*

Lord Gifford said that on August 15, 1975, the six appellants had been convicted by a jury at Lancaster Crown Court on 21 counts of murder. The trial had lasted 45 days. The crimes of which they were convicted concerned the placing of high-explosive bombs on November 21, 1974, in one of the greatest crimes of recent times. As well as the 21 people who died, 161 were injured. The first bomb had exploded at 8.17p.m. at the Mulberry Bush public house in the Rotunda in Birmingham and two minutes later the second bomb had exploded in the Tavern in the Town in New Street, Birmingham. At 8.11p.m. a warning had been phoned but this had been too late and too vague to be of any use in preventing loss of life.

The whole country had been affected by the horror of the bombs. Within days the Prevention of Terrorism Act had been passed through parliament in 17 hours. The shock and anger felt by people was greatest in the Birmingham area. There had been attacks on Irish homes and Irish public-houses. It was the news that there had been early arrests that enabled the anger to focus on these six men.

On November 25 that anger had boiled over. The six men had been subjected to sustained assaults by prison officers and prisoners alike. The question to be answered was whether the process of law itself had been free from the wave of emotion or whether in the circumstances of the time police officers, expert witnesses, and distinguished judges, had given of their best.

Lord Gifford said the appeal came before the court by reference from the Home Secretary under Section 17 of the 1968 Criminal Law Appeal Act. The appeal would deal with fresh evidence not available at the original trial, the scientific evidence offered against three of the men and the treatment that the men received while in police custody. In addition, there was further important material which had come to light.

The fresh evidence, at the very least, threw substantial doubt on the prosecutions presented to the jury. That prosecution had twin pillars, the first that two or three of the appellants had recently been in contact with explosives and, secondly, their confessions. Both of these pillars were cracked and flawed and could not sustain the burden of these convictions, which were unsafe and unsatisfactory.

The question would be posed whether among the victims of the Birmingham bombs might be counted these six men who had spent 13 years behind bars. If this was so, the miscarriage of justice was one of the greatest in recent times.

It was essential that there should be effective procedures for remedying miscarriages of justice. There was a need for a readiness to face up to the fact that this case might have perpetrated a terrible error.

Lord Gifford then outlined the arrest of the men, their questioning and eventual confessions, the contradictory nature of those confessions and the doubts now cast on the forensic evidence of Dr. Frank Skuse. He went on to describe new evidence on the conduct of the interviews, described as the 'Reade Schedule'. This has acquired new significance in the light of the reasons given by the Home Secretary for the referral of the case to the Court of Appeal again, the fact that an analysis of the notes of Richard McIlkenny's interviews revealed that they were not contemporaneous.

From 'Dishonest police document condemned' The Irish Times November 4, 1987.

The court was told by Lord Gifford of fresh evidence on the interviews said to have taken place. Far from having been methodically recorded, they were in fact fabricated after the event. There are conflicts of evidence on whether the interviews had taken place at the times alleged by the officers at all.

For example, Mr Hill said he was interviewed the morning, afternoon and evening of the 23rd. The prosecution alleged he was interviewed from 11.15 to 1.10 in the morning.

Mr Hunter said he was questioned for 12 hours without a break. The prosecution said he was interviewed from 10.15a.m.to 7p.m. with no different interviewers and substantial breaks. The appellants' case was that the scenario as well as a number of facts were false.

'It is in that light we are looking at a document that came to light during the Devon and Cornwall investigations which I shall call the Reade Schedule,' Lord Gifford said.

Detective-Superintendent Reade had conducted the interviews of Hunter, Walker and McIlkenny. And Hunter and McIlkenny said he was among the most violent of the interviewers.

There were two items in Reade's handwriting. One was a time schedule which was in the form of a photocopy of a photocopy which was discovered by the Devon and Cornwall police investigators and the document was in the hands of the court. There was a schedule in several columns with headings for time, names, officers, prisoners, place, code letter and one entitled 'knowledge of.'

The Lord Chief Justice asked what was the status of the document. Lord Gifford replied that the prosecution had a statement from Mr Reade saying the document was in his handwriting.

Mr Igor Judge, QC for the Crown, said there would be a statement as to where this statement came from.

Lord Gifford gave details of the entries under the different headings which related to times of interviews, places where the interviews took place, names of interviewers and times of confessions, which would be the subject of direct evidence later.

He said that one entry relating to an interview with Hill had been scrubbed out with a number of lines through it and the word 'out' underlined three times written on it. Some of the details of that entry, like the showing to Hill of McIlkenny's statement, were inserted into an earlier interview, into an entry on a preceding page, and that was how it came out in the evidence. A reference to showing Hill Callaghan's statement was inserted in a later box on the next page.

'There is no honest explanation for the writing out of a supposed interview which was never given in evidence and was never shown to exist,' Lord Gifford said, 'and the officer said in the trial he did not see Hill again.'

Lord Justice Brown asked what was counsel saying this meant.

Lord Gifford replied that the appellants' case was saying that this document was prepared as a blueprint of a scheme of interviews, a false scheme of interviews that other officers were to adhere to in preparing a concocted chronology of interviews prepared at some stage.

Lord Justice O'Connor said: 'It doesn't make sense at all, does it? The document looks as if it was prepared and later amended. We have no idea when. It might have been when putting the evidence together.'

Lord Gifford said: 'We do not say it was prepared then. We say there is no honest explanation of the insertion of the interview with Hill which was later expunged and the details we inserted into other parts of the chronology.'

The Lord Chief Justice said: 'You are saying that it is Reade's chronology which is false.'

Lord Justice O'Connor asked: 'Was it prepared before anyone was questioned at all?'

Lord Gifford replied: 'Before any notebooks were written up. At an early point, before the defendants were charged. A script had to be prepared for the trial.'

The Lord Chief Justice said: 'Let's leave it like that, we'll see how things go.'

Lord Justice Brown asked had the document any official status. He said there was no suggestion it was an official record.

Lord Gifford replied that it was his suggestion that it was an unofficial record made for a dishonest purpose. For some reason, perhaps because there was not enough time to get Callaghan's confession across to Queen's Road, it was necessary to change details, so this account was scrubbed out.

The Lord Chief Justice asked did Callaghan dispute that he made a statement, voluntary or involuntary, at about those times at Sutton Coldfield. He said it seemed there was a factual basis for the penultimate entry on that page.

Lord Gifford said there was a dispute about the time of Hunter's interview.

He referred to the record of the interviews between Superintendent Reade and officers from the Devon and Cornwall police which ranged over many topics. In relation to the Reade schedule, they had asked him to confirm that it was his. He had replied that it was a schedule he tried to keep as things happened. The officers had asked him if this was contemporaneously or later. Superintendent Reade said it was compiled as they went along, it was not bang up to date.

The officers had pointed out it was marked as a mastercopy which meant that there must have been others. Superintendent Reade had replied that there might have been individual interviews. He had continued that he did not know why he had done it, it could have been as an aid or a check. 'I see I've got one marked out, I don't know why,' Lord Gifford read from the interview record.

Lord Gifford said the superintendent had confirmed all the writing was his and had then continued: 'On reflection, I think I made this out when going through the evidence. I don't know why that is marked out, probably because I had wrong information in front of me and corrected it.'

Lord Gifford told the court: 'We maintain this is a thoroughly dishonest document, evidence of a thoroughly dishonest plan.'

Lord Gifford outlined at length the contradictions between the different confessions made by the men, and between the accounts of the interviews given by the men and those given by the police.

He pointed out that the confessions were riddled with contradictions with each other and with independent evidence.

From 'Court told of flaws in confession evidence' The Irish Times November 3, 1987:

Lord Gifford then read extracts from the written confessions of Power, McIlkenny, Walker and Callaghan. It was not clear from them how many devices there were. Power had spoken of seven plastic bags, Callaghan of six plastic bags, Walker of three parcels and McIlkenny of four plastic bags.

It was not clear who had brought the bombs to New Street. Power said Walker brought two, Hunter three, McIlkenny one and Callaghan one. Callaghan said Walker and Hunter had white plastic bags in the station bar which he hadn't seen before, though he was at the station before Walker. Walker said he, Hunter and Hill had one bomb each. McIlkenny said Walker, Hunter, Hill and himself had one bomb each.

There was a conflict in relation to the distribution of the bombs. Power had said Walker gave him one. McIlkenny gave him one and Callaghan gave Walker one. Callaghan said Hunter gave one bomb to each of them. Both Walker and McIlkenny said there had been no distribution of the bombs. McIlkenny said further that Hill had taken his bomb from his case when the others had gone.

There was also a conflict in relation to who gave the orders and who planted the devices in which places. Power said he alone placed two devices in the Mulberry Bush. Callaghan said he did it with Hunter. McIlkenny said he placed bombs in the Tavern in the Town with Hill, while Walker said he did it with Hunter. From the statements Hunter was involved with different public houses.

There was also a conflict between the statements and independent evidence. According to independent evidence referred to in the trial transcript, some sort of suitcase, briefcase or hold-all had been used to carry the devices.

He said this meant we had a remarkable feature that in the case the statements referred to plastic bags, never any other type of container to hold the bombs.

'We would submit that the assumption that plastic bags were used was made by the police for two reasons,' he said. The first of these was because the Hagley Road devices had been in two white plastic bags and the detective sergeant who questioned Power would have received that information. Secondly, the evidence of the forensic scientist, Mr Lidstone, was that before November 23 these devices were frequently in plastic bags. So these supposedly frank confessions on the vital matter of the container failed to mention what the scientific evidence actually showed.

APPENDIX II

International Association of Democratic Lawyers Submission to the United Nations Commission on Human Rights.

The submission is made in relation to six Irishmen who have been in prison in England for 15 years. They were convicted in 1975 of having murdered 21 people by causing explosions and it was said by the prosecution that they did so as part of a bombing campaign by the Irish Republican Army.

1. These six men have never been members of the IRA, nor did they ever commit the crimes with which they were charged. Powerful evidence has become available since their trial to show that they were innocent. They are all still however, in prison, in part because the English judicial system has no proper procedure for undoing injustice, but more importantly, the reasons for which they came to be arrested in the first place, the reasons for their having been convicted and for having remained in prison, together with the way in which they have been treated in prison, are only part of a pattern of unfair and discriminatory treatment in relation to Irish suspects.

2. There is a long history, well documented, of prejudice within Britain against the Irish. There has been a significant identifiable pattern over the past twenty years of discrimination in relation to Irish suspects where what is under investigation concerns the activities of or suspected connections with, Irish republican organisations. This pattern goes far beyond legitimate investigation and inquiry and amounts to persecution and deliberate manipulation of the criminal justice system by all representatives of the state involved. As a consequence, not just the six Birmingham defendants, but a significant number of others, have wrongly spent many years in prison convicted of crimes they did not commit and moreover when in prison, have suffered conditions that apply to no other prisoners.

3. Recently three other Irish men (and one English woman) convicted of identical crimes in virtually identical circumstances in 1974 have been released after documentary proof emerged that the police evidence that convicted them was deliberately fabricated. This is known as the Guildford Pub Bombing case.

4. Procedures in the British criminal justice system fall short of internationally required standards.

5. England has an adversarial system of criminal trial in which juries, 12 men and women selected at random from the population, adjudicate upon factual issues. These are people invited to use their individual common sense and instincts in weighing up the evidence presented to them. Judges exist in theory to ensure fair play and deal with questions of law. The suspect in theory has the right not to assist his adversary, (i.e. the state) in obtaining evidence from his own mouth to use against him. Because of the respective imbalance of the power of the state as against the individual, it is imperative that if a suspect chooses to say anything while in custody or at any subsequent trial, what he says has not been forced from him by any form of pressure. It is equally important that juries are free from prejudicial contamination, and that judges do not intervene in the process of factual decision-making unfairly.

6. In relation to the Irish suspect, however, special considerations have nevertheless applied and still apply today. The six Birmingham defendants were stopped and questioned initially solely because they were Irish. This does not present, under English law, a reasonable basis for suspicion. Had they been English, they would never have been detained in the first place.

7. Special considerations have applied to all Irish political suspects since 1974 which have effectively abolished the right to silence which is available to all the rest of the population. The period permissible for interrogation was extended in 1974 for Irish suspects alone by the Prevention of Terrorism Act, to up to seven days. During those seven days, until recently, access to legal advice was systematically barred. Numerous cases record instances of detainees suffering serious psychological damage as a result of such detention. The European Court of Human Rights has held the workings of the Prevention of Terrorism Act enabling this period of detention to be in breach of the European Convention on Human Rights. Following that decision there has not only been no attempt to remedy British practice, but in fact the United Kingdom government has recently lodged a notice of derogation from the Convention thus flouting the judgment. Lawyers have frequently observed detainees suffering forms of mental illness following detention including the case of one man who committed suicide as a direct result.

8. In the case of the six Birmingham suspects, they were deliberately deprived of sleep and food. They were not only questioned continuously by police for 72 hours without any lawyer present, but were threatened, terrorised and beaten by the police until they signed confessions. To date, three police officers, one doctor, two lawyers, and two prison officers have all described having seen the beatings or

the effects of beatings on the six men; the courts have discounted the whole of that evidence.

9. Periods of detention of Irish suspects are invariably used by police press departments to produce maximum prejudicial publicity until the moment that they have committed themselves either to charging or release. That publicity has one effect; to prejudice the outcome of the eventual trial by prejudicing the minds of the pool of potential jurors.

In the Birmingham case, police announced immediately that they had caught the men responsible for the bombings.

10. Appearances in court act as an extension of the prejudicial melodrama affecting the outcome of the case, taking over from the moment at which the case ostensibly becomes *sub judice*: helicopters fly overhead, sirens herald court appearances and all potential jurors receiving these subliminal messages think of the suspects as 'terrorists'. In one recent case a special plane flew continuously above the court throughout the proceedings.

11. Wholly unprecedented conditions of detention have been applied to Irish prisoners both prior to trial and subsequently. In the case of Irish women defendants, they have been held in complete isolation and under conditions of sensory deprivation apart from other prisoners. Both men and women suffer continuous intimate body searches and clear evidence exists of psychological and mental damage as a result affecting the capacity of those detainees to do justice to themselves at any eventual trial. In relation to male suspects not only have long periods of solitary confinement been applied, but it is clear that the prison system has been unable to guarantee the physical and mental safety of Irish prisoners. In the Birmingham case immediately upon entry into prison, the six men were savagely beaten in circumstances where it was fortunate that they even survived until trial. The prosecution then relied upon those injuries to suggest that the men showed no pre-existing trace of injury from their beatings at the hands of the police *before* being admitted to prison in the previous seventy-two hours and thus sought to prove that the confessions obtained as a result of police beatings, had been made voluntarily.

12. Injury and abuse to Irish prisoners (including the Birmingham and Guildford defendants) both within police stations and within prisons is extensively documented. Others have been held in extended, almost limitless, conditions of sensory deprivation: solitary confinement causing mental and physical damage.

13. Almost all cases involving Irish citizens charged with terrorist offences make use of the 'conspiracy charge' (often known as

the most useful weapon in the prosecutor's arsenal). Conspiracy charges depend upon suspicion alone without substantive evidence and allow for evidence being introduced against the defendant which is otherwise inadmissible. The atmosphere of the trial appears to be dominateed by the concern of judges to ensure that the defendants are convicted. Rulings are almost without exception made in favour of the prosecution and against the defence. Evidence is not excluded where it is improperly obtained by the police and the extensive authority of Judges to sum up their opinions as to the facts undoubtedly determines the outcome of trials. In the Birmingham case the Judge told the jury clearly that he did not believe the defendants. Prejudice often comes through. The Judge in one case frequently referred to the defendant's Irish accent as a disability and said that he had 'only himself to blame' if the jury did not understand him.

14. In Irish cases the prosecution regularly 'vets' the jury i.e. screens jurors for their political opinions, a facility not permitted to the defence whose right to challenge jurors was recently abolished. In this way direct political intrusion into the thoughts and minds of the jurors is effectively permitted. It can, however, go further; in one recent case the alleged victim of a conspiracy to murder, a Government Minister, himself gave press conferences during the trial where the defendants had chosen to exercise their right to silence announcing that the Government had taken an executive decision to abolish the right to silence because terrorists frequently relied upon it to escape the consequences of their actions.

15. The right to a fair trial is further undermined by the Court of Appeal in England, originally established to undo miscarriages of justice. When convincing new evidence is produced, as happened in the Birmingham Appeal two years ago (and as had happened in the Guildford Appeal 12 years before) the Court of Appeal consistently substitutes itself for a jury in assessing that evidence and will never order a re-trial before a jury. It also consistently expresses its disbelief in that evidence. In 1987 the Court of Appeal in the Birmingham case rejected the evidence of four police officers present at the time of the interrogation who had seen injury to the defendants. It also rejected a document written by the officer in charge of the case which had no explanation other than it was a blueprint for other officers to perjure their evidence relating to interrogation. (It was similar documentary evidence that came to light in the Guildford case that finally forced the acknowledgment that they had always been innocent and had spent 15 years wrongly in prison).

16. After conviction systematic discriminatory treatment is inflicted upon Irish prisoners perceived as being Republican. These are the *only*

prisoners who are refused consideration of serving their sentences near to their families. The Government refuses to transfer all such prisoners, as it does all others, near to their families. One of the six Birmingham defendants has barely seen his wife and children (who live in Derry in Northern Ireland) for 15 years because of the expense and difficulties of travel to prisons remote from urban areas where he has been placed.

17. It is even now impossible for Irish defendants to raise freely the fact of their wrongful convictions as other prisoners might do. A recent Government directive to the broadcasting authorities banning an elected party in Northern Ireland from access to radio and television, has even led to the banning of a song devoted to the wrongful convictions of the Birmingham and Guildford defendants. It was said by the broadcasting authority that because these people were convicted terrorists, and because the song purported to criticise British justice, it could not be broadcast.

18. We wish to raise before the Commission incontrovertible evidence to show patterns of discrimination in relation to Irish suspects violating articles of both the Universal Declaration of Human Rights and the International Covenant on Civil and Political Rights.

19. We complain that the six Birmingham defendants have no effective remedy nationally to rights guaranteed to them by international law; that they have never enjoyed a fair and public hearing by an independent and impartial tribunal; they have never been presumed innocent until proven guilty and they have never had the guarantees necessary for their defence; they have not had witnesses against them examined under the same conditions as witnesses on their behalf; they have not been treated with humanity and with respect for the inherent dignity of the human person and they have not been equal before the courts as prisoners who are not Irish.

20. We ask, therefore, that the Commission on Human Rights be seized of the issue of such cases in Britain which show a pattern of violation of internationally accepted norms of human rights. Only the focus of the international machinery of human rights can provide justice for those innocently imprisoned in Britain for what they are and not for what they have done.

Submitted on behalf of the International Association of Democratic Lawyers, 263 Avenue Albert, Brussels 1180, by Kader Asmal, The Law School, Trinity College, Dublin 2.

February 1990.

APPENDIX III

The European Parliament Resolution on the Birmingham Six

Joint resolution replacing Docs. B3-525, 526, 531, 536, 574 and 588/89

RESOLUTION
ON THE BIRMINGHAM SIX

The European Parliament,

A. having regard to the expressions by the European Parliament in previous resolutions of grave concern that a miscarriage of justice took place in the cases of the Birmingham Six and the Guildford Four,

B. noting the numerous calls for the release of the Birmingham Six,

C. noting that in a parallel case involving the conviction of four Irish and British citizens for bombings in Guildford, the authorities recently withdrew the charges on which the accused had been convicted.

D. noting that the convictions of the Birmingham Six were based in part on confessions which the accused later withdrew as having been made under pressure of brutal and inhumane treatment by the police and in part on forensic evidence since shown to be unreliable,

- that the accused have constantly affirmed their innocence,
- that other persons have since given independent investigators convincing evidence that they, and not the six who were condemned, were responsible for the Birmingham bombings,
- That when, in January 1988, the Court of Appeal dismissed the appeals of the accused, national and international observers pointed out that it had failed to take into account new evidence that had been adduced.

E. having regard to the concern expressed by Amnesty International that the most grave doubt remains regarding official denials that these prisoners had been ill-treated while in police custody and therefore about the safety of convictions based on confessions.

F. noting that the Serious Crimes Squad of the West Midlands police force, which investigated the Birmingham bombings for which the six were jailed, has been disbanded and an inquiry commenced into serious allegations surrounding its work but deploring the fact that the inquiry into the suspected misconduct of detectives in the West Midlands force has not been allowed to include the period when the Birmingham Six were arrested and convicted.

G. having regard to the grave concern in Britain expressed by numerous church leaders, internationally renowned representatives of the legal profession and the judiciary and senior politicians of all political persuasions that proper justice has not been applied in the case of the Birmingham Six.

H. supporting the call from 130 Members of the United Kingdom Parliament from all parties for a new legal mechanism to deal with all possible past or future miscarriages of justice.

I. recalling the series of European Parliament resolutions condemning the use of criminal violence in the European Community by terrorist organizations,

1. Urgently calls for a thorough review of the case of the Birmingham Six;
2. Calls for a fully independent investigation of the activities of the West Midlands Serious Crimes Squad which, in the interest of justice, must be extended to include, as a priority, the conduct of all officers who interviewed the Birmingham Six during their investigation;
3. Instructs its Committee on Legal Affairs to draw up a report on the case of the Birmingham Six;
4. Instructs its President to forward this resolution to the Commission, the Council and the British and Irish Governments.

Parliament adopted the resolution by RCV (RB):

Members voting:	114
For:	81
Against:	24
Abstentions:	9

APPENDIX IV

An Excerpt from Amnesty International United Kingdom Paper of August 1988 on the Appeal Hearing of Six Men convicted of Bombings in Birmingham.

On 30 March 1976 the men applied for leave to appeal against their convictions. The grounds were as follows:

1. That the judge displayed excessive hostility to the case of the six men and gave a clear indication of his view of the facts and the witnesses as to deprive the jury of the chance to form an independent opinion.

2. That he 'overstepped the bounds of his judicial function' in his criticism of certain defence witnesses.

3. That he failed to sum up the six men's cases adequately on the scientific evidence and also on the evidence from a doctor about injuries which he said he had found on the men.

4. That he wrongly allowed certain witnesses to be called by the prosecution in rebuttal.

The application for leave to appeal against the conviction was rejected by the Court of Appeal. As regards the allegations of beatings in police custody the Lord Chief Justice said that when the defendants had made their first appearance in court their faces seemed undamaged and that there was no evidence to suggest that they had at this stage experienced damage or knocking about 'beyond the ordinary'. The appeal court also dismissed the other grounds of appeal.

On 30 December 1975, 14 prison officers were charged with assaulting the six men during their detention in Winson Green Prison. The trial of the prison officers opened at Birmingham Crown Court on 10 June 1976. The six men testified, *inter alia,* that they had been repeatedly assaulted in the prison yard by police officers and in the reception area by prison officers and by a prisoner. All the prison officers were acquitted.

In November 1977 the six men commenced a civil action against the Home Office and the West Midlands Police for the injuries they claimed to have received while in custody. The Home Office admitted that the men were assaulted whilst in prison. The police applied for the action to be struck out as being an abuse of the legal process as the issue had been resolved in the criminal proceedings. The judge dismissed the police application and allowed the action of the six men against the police to proceed. However, this decision was overturned by the Court of Appeal. The three Appeal Court judges were unanimous in their decision. Giving judgment, the presiding judge stated the following:

> 'Just consider the course of events if this action is allowed to proceed to trial . . . If the six men fail, it will mean that much time and money will have been expended by many people for no good purpose. If the six men win, it will mean that the police were guilty of perjury, that they were guilty of violence and threats, that the confessions were involuntary and were improperly admitted in evidence and that the convictions were erroneous. That would mean the Home Secretary would either have to recommend they be pardoned or he would have to remit the case to the Court of Appeal. This is such an appalling vista that every sensible person in the land would say: It cannot be right that these actions should go any further.'

The House of Lords upheld the decision of the Court of Appeal in November 1981.

New Evidence

In October 1985, however, new evidence emerged concerning the reliability of the forensic evidence and was the subject of a television programme 'World in Action'. Two forensic scientists had examined the tests carried out in 1974 by forensic scientist Dr Skuse, and they challenged the validity of these tests.

On 19 November 1986 Thomas Clarke, an ex-police officer, also came forward to support the convicted men's allegations of ill-treatment in Queen's Road police station.

The Home Secretary, in light of the new evidence, decided to refer the case to the Court of Appeal.

Appeal Hearing

At the appeal the appellants contended that, in light of fresh evidence concerning their treatment while in police custody and the forensic tests, the original convictions were unsafe and unsatisfactory. They requested the Court of Appeal to quash the convictions and order a re-trial. The Court dismissed the request for a re-trial as an unreal suggestion as it was 13 years after the event. The Court said that 'if there is any doubt in our minds as to whether the conviction is safe or satisfactory the appeals must be allowed and the convictions quashed.'

The following new evidence was presented to the Court of Appeal to support the appellants' claims that their confessions had been obtained through coercion:

1 Mr William Bailey, a cleaner/supervisor at Morecambe police station, stated that he saw two of the appellants unsteady on their feet as they were being led out of the police station to a police vehicle on 22 November 1974, and that he found blood on the walls of a cell on 25 November.

2 Mrs Joyce Lynas, a police cadet at the time, gave evidence in two stages. The first time she said there was an atmosphere of intimidation that prevailed in the station, that she saw the prisoners being manhandled and sworn at while they were being escorted around the station; that she heard abuse and shouting during interrogations; that she saw one man limping, heard screams and saw armed officers in the cell area; and that the prisoners were deliberately kept awake during the night. The second time she described an incident in the interrogation room where she witnessed one appellant being kneed in the groin. She attributed her initial reluctance to speak about the assault to intimidation by a police officer reminding her that 'we all have families' and to a threatening telephone call of someone saying 'don't forget you have got children' which she received after being contacted by one of the appellants' solicitors.

3 Mr Thomas Clarke, a former police officer, stated that he saw the appellants being made to stand up and sit down during the night; that a dog was set to bark at the appellants during the night; and that guns were poked through the hatches of cell doors during the night. He also stated that the men seemed frightened and that their faces were red and puffy.

4 Mr Brian Sharp and Mr Peter Bourne were prison officers on duty at the reception of Winson Green prison at the time of the appellants' arrival there after four days in police custody. Mr Sharp testified that he had noticed marks of an old bruising on the chest of one of the prisoners, John Walker. Mr Bourne testified that on the appellants' arrival the police officers accompanying them curtailed the normal handing-over procedure avoiding the recording of the prisoners' physical condition.

5 Mr Paul Berry and Mr Kenny Garrington are police officers who saw the prisoners at Queen's Road police station in Birmingham while the prisoners were there. Mr Berry stated that one appellant had a puffed and swollen eye and swollen lips. Mr Garrington stated that he saw the men standing to attention with an 'expressionless glare' on their faces.

6 A schedule listing the times during which the men were interrogated while in police custody was handwritten by Detective Superintendent Reade, the police officer in charge of the investigation. This schedule

was put forward to substantiate allegations that the police testimony at the trial was fabricated and the appellants' version of events was correct. This schedule contained entries of a suspicious character, alterations of the times of the interviews, deletion of a detailed entry of an interview with Patrick Hill at a time which corresponded more with Patrick Hill's version of events, and there was no satisfactory explanation given for its purpose.

7 Mr Clarke testified that the duty officers had been given specific instruction not to interfere with the charge sheet where the conditions of detention were usually recorded.

The extent to which the new evidence concerning the forensic tests casts doubt on their findings is of significance primarily insofar as this evidence, if it had been available at the time of the trial, would have influenced the manner in which allegations of ill-treatment were assessed by judge and jury. The two seriously challenged findings of the forensic evidence, produced by specialist Frank Skuse on the spot in Morecambe police station, were at that time stated to have been conclusive. This in the first instance might reasonably be assumed to have been an indication for the police officers investigating the crime that the suspects they had arrested were indeed the men responsible. It may have spurred police efforts to find corroborative evidence of the men's guilt in obtaining out-of-court statements by any methods they thought fit. Similarly, in the trial stage, the importance of the scientific evidence presented clearly weighed heavily on the manner in which the out-of-court testimonies were assessed. In this regard, the evidence at the appeal hearing concerning the scientific tests, while not proving conclusively that the evidence in its entirety must be rejected out of hand, adds significantly to the doubt as to its fallibility. This element was not present in the original trial.

If account is taken as well of evidence offered at the six men's trial in 1975 and at the trial in 1976 of officers from Winson Green Prison on charges of assault, there exists now a considerable body of evidence that they were physically ill-treated while in police custody.

The Court of Appeal delivered its judgment on 28 January 1988. The Court did not consider that the new evidence cast sufficient doubt on the original convictions so as to render the verdict of the jury 'unsafe or unsatisfactory', and thus upheld the convictions. In connection with the evidence about how the confessions had been obtained, the Court dismissed the testimony of all fresh witnesses as either dishonest or irrelevant. For example, regarding Mrs Joyce Lynas' evidence the Court stated that the remark 'Don't forget, we all have families' was a poor reason for lying. According to the Court there was nothing in this remark which constituted a threat. 'All one can say of her evidence is that on one or other of the occasions she gave evidence before this court she committed perjury.' The Court said that she demonstrated herself to be a witness who was 'not worthy of belief'. With respect to Mr Thomas Clarke the Court said that he was 'a most unconvincing witness. He was also an embittered man. On September 25, 1977, he was charged with stealing a £5 note from a prisoner in his custody. He pleaded not guilty. He was tried by a jury, gave evidence, was disbelieved and sentenced to three months' imprisonment. On the following day he was dismissed by the police force. . . As he gave evidence before us, it became clear increasingly that his motive was not, as he asserted, to see that these appellants should escape the sort of injustice which he had suffered but, at first at least, to make money and secondly to blacken the reputation of the West Midlands Police Force'. The Court concluded that 'the longer the hearing has gone on the more convinced this Court has become that the verdict of the jury was correct. We have no doubt that these convictions were both safe and satisfactory. The appeals are dismissed'.

Under English law it is for the prosecution to prove beyond reasonable doubt the the confessions alleged to have been obtained by physical ill-treatment were not so obtained. It appears clear to Amnesty International that this has not been proved.

Rather, the judgment of the Court of Appeal seems to rest on an assessment that the six prisoners failed to prove beyond reasonable doubt, or on a standard close to that, that they were ill-treated. In its judgment the Court of Appeal consistently refused to give the prisoners the benefit of the doubt on any important point. It is striking overall that the Court of Appeal did not specifically deal with the cumulative effect of the testimony supporting the prisoners' allegations. It is also striking that, even though according to the Court the prisoners' convictions rested on their confessions, the testimony of every fresh witness in support of the submission that the confessions were involuntary, was dismissed as being either dishonest or mistaken or irrelevant.

Amnesty International believes that the most grave doubt remains regarding official denials that these prisoners were ill-treated while in police custody, and hence regarding the safeness of allowing the confession evidence against them to stand.

Amnesty International believes that the case should not be closed, and that the allegations of ill-treatment must be subject to further review.

(August 1988)

The shocking lessons of the Guildford Four case should not be lost on international opinion or on the British authorities. How much longer must other innocent people languish in prison because of the British government's refusal to face the 'Appalling Vista' of their innocence?

The case of the Birmingham Six must now be immediately re-opened with a view to their urgent release. Only then can innocent men reclaim their lives and British justice reclaim its international credibility.

Petra Kelly, MEP

In light of the long-standing doubts about the 'confessions' and guilt of the six men convicted of the Birmingham Pub bombings; and because now of the disbandment by the Chief Constable of the West Midlands of his Serious Crimes Squad and his suspension or transference of officers connected with that squad; there would seem to me to be a *prima facie* case for the re-examination of the guilt of those who were convicted. The fact that the Appeal rejected in 1988 pre-dated the decision of the Chief Constable regarding his own Force, gives added reason for the re-examination of the issue now. I urge that the re-examination be undertaken without delay.

†Derek Worlock
Archbishop of Liverpool
February 14, 1990

RECOMMENDED FURTHER READING

DEREK DUNNE
The Birmingham Six. Published by the Birmingham Six Committee. This book in addition to the English version is also available in Irish, German, French and Spanish.

CHRIS MULLEN
Error of Judgement. Published by Poolbeg Press.

BOB WOFFINDEN
Miscarriages of Justice. Published by Coronet Books, Hodder and Stoughton.

NOTES ON CONTRIBUTORS

KADER ASMAL: Senior Lecturer in Law, Trinity College Dublin. President Irish Council for Civil Liberties and member of the Constitutional and Legal Committee, African National Congress.

SASCHA ANDERSON: Poet. Born 1953 Weimar GDR. Imprisoned for two years for 'Demagogy against the State'. Has lived in West Berlin since 1984. Founder of GALREV Publishing Co. 1990. Publications include *Die Tage sind gezählt,* poetry (1983); *Totenreklame,* Eine Reise (with Ralf Kerbach, 1983); and *Waldmaschine* (with Ralf Kerbach, Cornelia Schleime and Michael Wildenhain, 1985)

NANNI BALESTRINI: Born Milan 1935. Poet and novelist. Is the author of several volumes of poetry including most recently *Blackout* and *Ipocalisse.* His novels include *Tristano* (1964), *Vogliamo tutto* (1971) and *La violenza illustrata* (1976), member of the influential avant-garde 'Gruppo 63' along with Umberto Eco and Eduardo Sanguineti.

ROBERT BALLAGH: Artist, born Dublin 1943. Studied architecture, worked as a professional musician, commenced painting in 1967. Has exhibited extensively in Ireland and abroad. Recent major exhibitions in Warsaw, Moscow and Sofia. His graphic designs include stamps, book covers, posters and the like. In the theatre he has designed several award-winning productions. Member of Aosdána.

MARY BENSON: Born Pretoria, South Africa. Poet, writer, novelist and playwright. Her published writing includes a biography of Nelson Mandela published by Penguin Books and *South Africa: The Struggle for Birthright.*

TERENCE BROWN: Writer. Associate Professor of English and Fellow of Trinity College Dublin. His published works include *Northern Voices: Poets from Ulster, The Whole Protestant Community* and *Ireland: A Social and Cultural History 1922-1985.*

JÖRG BURKHARD: Writer. Lives in Heidelberg.

ANTHONY W. CLARE MD.: Born Dublin. Graduated from University College Dublin in Medicine in 1966. Appointed Professor of Psychological Medicine at St Bartholomew's Hospital London in 1983. Returned to Dublin 1989 as Medical Director of St Patrick's Hospital and Clinical Professor of Psychiatry at Trinity College Dublin. Writer, broadcaster and reviewer. Has regular radio interview series on BBC4 – 'In the Psychiatrist's Chair'.

SEAMUS DEANE: Poet and writer, born Derry 1940. Professor of Modern English and American Literature at University College Dublin. His *Selected Poems* was published by Gallery Press in 1988. His most recent critical works are *A Short History of Irish Literature* (1986) and *The French Enlightenment and Revolution in England 1789-1832* (1988). He is a Director of Field Day.

GERTRUDE DEGENHARDT: Born in New York in 1940. Was brought up in Berlin-West. Since 1966 has worked as an independent painter and graphic artist. In 1968 received the award of the Graphic Art Biennial in Cracow, Poland, in 1976, the award of the Graphic Art Biennial in Fredrikstad, Norway. Exhibitions at home and abroad. Lives and works in Mainz.

PETER de ROSA: Professor of Metaphysics and Ethics Westminster Seminary six years; Dean of Theology Corpus Christi six years; BBC Radio producer and writer. Wrote his own TV series. Author of best selling *Vicars of Christ*. Now lives in Wicklow.

PAUL DURCAN: Poet. Born Dublin 1944. Studied archaeology and medieval history at University College Cork. In 1974 won the Patrick Kavanagh Award and received creative writing bursaries from the Arts Council – An Chomhairle Ealaíon, Ireland, in 1976 and 1980. Has given readings of his poems throughout the world. Is a member of Aosdána. His latest published works are: *Jesus and Angela,* Blackstaff Press, Belfast 1988; *Daddy, Daddy,* Blackstaff Press, Belfast 1990.

TERENCE EAGLETON: Born Salford England 1943. Educated in local schools and Cambridge University where he became Fellow in English in 1969. Was Fellow and Tutor Wadham College, Oxford. Now teaches at Linacre College, Oxford. His many published works include *Marxism and Literary Criticism* (1976) and *Literary Theory: An Introduction* published by Verso 1983. His new play *Saint Oscar* was published by Faber and Faber early in 1990.

BRIAN FRIEL: Playwright. Born 1929 in Omagh, Co. Tyrone. 1963 Macauley Fellowship. Is a member of the Irish Academy of Letters. Co-founder of the Field Day Theatre Company in 1980. Irish American Cultural Institute Literary Award 1981. His published works include *Selected Plays* (1984) and *Dancing at Lughnasa* (1990), published by Faber and Faber.

PATRICK GALVIN: Born in Cork, poet and dramatist. Member of Aosdána. Plays include *The Last Burning; We do it for Love,* and *The Devil's own People*. Poetry includes *Heart of Grace; Christ in London,* and *The Wood Burner.* His first prose work *Song for a Poor Boy* was published by Raven Arts Press in November 1990.

CHRISTIAN GEISSLER: Born 1928 in Hamburg. Co-founder of the magazine *Kürbiskern* in 1965. Lecturer at the German Academy for Film and Television 1972-74. Numerous radio and television dramas, novels. Most recent publication: *Kamalatta* (1988).

LORD GIFFORD Q.C.: The distinguished lawyer who represented the Birmingham Six.

DAVOREN HANNA: Born 1975 in Dublin where he lives and works. Cannot talk because of cerebral palsy. Has been writing since age eight. Recipient of four awards for his work. Excerpts from his first book of poetry *Not Common Speech* have already been translated into German. The story of his life was told in the RTE television documentary 'Poised for Flight'.

MICHAEL HARTNETT: Poet in Irish and English. Most recent work includes *An Phurgóid: Foignhe Chrainn* (Coiscéim 1984). His *Collected Poems* published by Raven Arts/Carcanet (1984). He is also a notable translator and his *Poems in Translation* was published by Raven Arts/Carcanet in 1986. Member of Aosdána.

SEAMUS HEANEY: Born in Co. Derry 1939. Has published several volumes of poetry and criticisms. Most recently has done *A Version of Sophocles' Philoctetes* which Field Day Productions produced in 1990. Teaches one term a year at Harvard.

DESMOND HOGAN: His latest publication is *Lebanon Lodge* (Faber and Faber 1988).

PEARSE HUTCHINSON: Born of Irish parents in Glasgow 1927. Learned Munster Irish in school and Castilian in University College Dublin. His collections include *Faoistin Bhacach; Watching the Morning Grow* and *The Frost is all Over.* With Melita Cataldi published Italian versions of Old Irish poetry: *Antica Lirica Irlandese* (1982). Is a member of Aosdána.

ELFRIEDE JELINEK: Born 1946 in Mürzzuschlag, Austria. Studied Theatrical Science, Art and Music. Numerous radio-plays and novels, of which *Lust* (1989) and *Wolken. Heim* (1990) are the most recent.

JENNIFER JOHNSTON: Fiction writer and dramatist. Born in Dublin. Has lived in London, now lives in Derry. Has published eight novels including *The Captains and the Kings* and *How Many Miles to Babylon?*

KLAUS JÜNSCHKE: Born 1947. Joined the Red Army Faction (RAF) at the age of 24. Arrested and sentenced in 1972. After 14 years of solitary confinement and two years in a standard prison released on Bloomsday 1988. Broke links with the RAF during imprisonment. The story *Into the Free Part of Diez* was first published in his book *Spätlese* (Frankfurt, Main: Verlag Neue Kritik, 1988).

RICHARD KEARNEY: From Cork, Ph.D. Studied at University College Dublin, McGill University Montreal, and the University of Paris. Associate Professor and Lecturer in Philosophy in University College Dublin. Co-editor of *The Crane Bag: Journal of Irish Studies.* Author and editor of several books on philosophy and literature, including *La Poètique du Possible* (Beauchesne 1984), *The Irish Mind: Exploring Intellectual Traditions*, (Wolfhound Press 1985) and more recently *The Wake of Imagination* (Hutchinson 1988).

ROBERT KEE: Writer, journalist, broadcaster and historian. Published works include his three-volume, *History of Irish Nationalism; Ireland a History*, the book of the BBC/RTE Television series and *The World We Fought For.*

THOMAS KENEALLY: Born 1935. Lives in Sydney. Has published some eighteen novels. Two were short-listed for the Booker McConnell Prize. His *Schindler's Ark* (1982) won the award. His most recent publication is *Journey Towards Asmara* (1989).

LUDOVIC KENNEDY: Writer and broadcaster. Is the author of several books on miscarriages of justice, in particular, *10 Rillington Place* (posthumous free pardon for Timothy Evans), *A Presumption of Innocence* (free pardon for Patrick Meehan) and *Wicked Beyond Belief* (immediate release from prison for David Cooper and Michael McMahon). His autobiography *On My Way to the Club* (1989) was published by Collins.

BRUCE KENT: CND activist and President International Peace Bureau.

MARIE THÉRÈSE KERSCHBAUMER: Born Garches near Paris, lives in Vienna. First publication 1964. *Neun Canti auf die irdische Liebe, Für mich hat Lesen etwas mit Fließen zu tun, Eine Frau ein Traum. Kein Requiem* (radio play) all 1989.

THOMAS KINSELLA: Poet and translator. Born in Dublin in 1928. His most recent publications are *Poems from Centre City* and *Personal Places* published by the Dedalus Press in 1990 and *Blood and Family*, a collection of earlier Peppercanister pamphlets, published by the Oxford University Press in 1988. Other works from his extensive range are his translation of the Irish prose epic *Táin Bó Cuailgne* (1969) and his verse translations for *An Duanaire 1600-1900: Poems of the Dispossessed* both published by the Dolmen Press.

LOUIS LE BROCQUY: Irish painter. Born Dublin 1916. Is married to the artist Anne Madden. Since 1976, large retrospective exhibitions of his work have been held in museums in Dublin, Belfast, Paris, Antibes, Charleroi, Granada, New York State, Adelaide, Melbourne and Brisbane.
Throughout 1991 a further retrospective exhibition of his paintings is to take place at the Museums of Modern Art of Kamakura, Osaka and Hiroshima.

FRANCO LOI: Born Genoa 1930. Has lived in Milan since 1937. After careers in advertising and public relations is now a full time writer. Published work includes short stories, plays and several volumes of poetry – also in Milanese dialect. Among his most recent collections of poems are *L'angel – l'angelo* (1981), *Bach* (1986) and *Liber – Libro* (1988).

ANNE MADDEN LE BROCQUY: Irish painter. Married to the artist Louis le Brocquy. Major exhibitions of her work have taken place in Dublin, Belfast, London, New York, Paris, Barcelona and Fondation Maeght St Paul, France.

NELL McCAFFERTY: Born Derry City 1944. Graduated from Queen's University Belfast with BA degree. Now works in Dublin as a freelance journalist, author, playwright and television and radio commentator. Her most recent published work includes *Peggy Deery – A Derry Family at War* (1988) and *A Woman to Blame: The Kerry Babies Case* (1985).

HUGH MAXTON: His volume of translations, *Between; Selected Poems of Agnes Nemes Nagy,* is jointly published by Corvina Press of Budapest and Dedalus Press of Dublin; his new and selected poems appear from Dedalus Press in 1991.

EDNA O'BRIEN: Born 1930 in Tuamgraney, Co. Clare. Educated at the Convent of Mercy at Loughrea, and the Pharmaceutical College in Dublin. Novelist and short story writer. Screenplay *X, Y and Zee,* starring Elizabeth Taylor in 1972. *Yorkshire Post* Novel Award 1971. Lives in London with her two sons.

JULIA O'FAOLAIN: Born 1932 in Dublin. Educated at University College, Dublin and in Rome and Paris. Worked as teacher and translator. Her book *No Country for Young Men* was shortlisted for the Booker McConnell Prize 1980. Lives in London and Los Angeles.

NUALA O'FAOLAIN: Is a columnist with *The Irish Times.*

LIAM Ó MUIRTHILE: Poet, writer, journalist. Born in Cork. Now lives with his family in Dún Laoghaire.

SEÁN Ó TUAMA: Poet, critic, dramatist. Professor of Modern Irish Literature at University College Cork, and visiting Professor at Harvard, Oxford, Toronto and Catholic University of Washington. Most of his published work is in the Irish language.

TOM PAULIN: Poet, writer dramatist. Lectures in English at University of Nottingham. Edited the Faber Book of Political Poetry. His published books of poetry include *A State of Justice; The Strange Museum; The Book of Juniper* and the *Liberty Tree.* Prose works include essays on Irish and English literature published under the title of *Ireland and the English Crisis.*

BERT PAPENFUSS-GOREK: Poet. Born 1956 in Reuterstadt Stavenhagen GDR. Recent publications: *aton-notate* (1984), *harte zarte hertsn* (1984), *Tiské* (1990), *SoJa* (1990).

GABRIEL ROSENSTOCK: Chairman Poetry Ireland. Trustee Irish Children's Book Trust. Assistant Editor *An Gúm.* Author of some 30 books in Irish.

JÜRGEN SCHNEIDER: Born 1952 in Wiesbaden. Educated at Frankfurt University. Has been living in Dublin as translator and publicist since 1989.

RALF SOTSCHECK: Born 1954 in Berlin, educated at Freie Universität Berlin. Journalist and publicist. Has been working as Irish correspondent for *Die Tageszeitung,* Berlin, since 1985. Lives in Dublin.

FRANCIS STUART: Novelist, born 1902 in Australia. His best known novels include *The Pillar of Cloud* (1948), *Redemption* (1949), *Black List, Section H* (1971), *Memorial* (1973). His latest published work is: *A Compendium of Lovers,* Raven Arts Press Dublin (1990).

A. J. P. TAYLOR: Late historian, writer, journalist, lecturer in history at Manchester University until his retirement. Had published some 28 works of history or biography including his autobiography *A Personal History.*

WILLIAM TREVOR: Born 1928 in Mitchelstown, Co. Cork. Has written many novels and collections of short stories as well as plays for television, stage and radio. Recipient of numerous literary awards.

KATHARINA WILCZEK: Born 1946 in Künsdorf, Thuringia. Arts education in Wuppertal, Kassel and Academy of Arts Düsseldorf under Professor Joseph Beuys and Professor Sackenheim. Co-founded the gallery, The Green Door, in Wuppertal, 1977. Has been working as an independent artist since 1977.

VOLKER WILCZEK: Born 1947 in Göttingen. Educated at Kassel State Theatre, Academy of Arts Kassel, Academy of Arts Düsseldorf under Professor Joseph Beuys and Professor Sackenheim. Co-founder of the gallery, The Green Door, in Wuppertal, 1977. Exhibitions, Multimedia Shows, Installations and Film Productions in Germany and abroad.

BOB WOFFINDEN: Born in 1948. Took a political degree at Sheffield University. From 1973 to 1978 was Associate Editor of *New Musical Express.* Since 1978 has worked as freelance journalist contributing to newspapers and magazines such as the *New Statesman* and *The Listener*. His book *Miscarriages of Justice* was published by Coronet Books 1989.

DONALD WOODS: South African journalist banned by government from writing, public speaking or free association with his countrymen for twelve years for publishing facts about the death in police custody of Steve Biko. Ban removed on February 2, 1990, as part of a general amnesty for political organisations and dissidents in that country. The story of his experiences was told in Sir Richard Attenborough's film *Cry Freedom.*

MACDARA WOODS: Poet. Born in Dublin in 1942. Founder editor of literary magazine *Cyphers*. Married to the poet Eiléan Ní Chuilleanáin. His recent publications include *Stopping the Lights in Ranelagh,* (1987) and *Miz Moon* 1988.